S0-DSZ-917

Metropolitan Crime Patterns

Metropolitan Crime Patterns

Edited by
Robert M. Figlio,
Simon Hakim,
and George F. Rengert

CRIMINAL JUSTICE PRESS
a division of
Willow Tree Press, Inc.
Monsey, New York
1986

Copyright © 1986 by
Willow Tree Press, Inc.

Library of Congress Cataloging in Publication Data

Metropolitan crime patterns.

Includes bibiliographies and index.
1. Crime and criminals—United States—Addresses,
essays, lectures. 2. Metropolitan areas—United
States—Addresses, essays, lectures. I. Figlio,
Robert M. II. Hakim, Simon. III. Rengert, George F.
HV6177.M47   1986   364'.973   85-51936
ISBN 0-9606960-1-6 (Clothbound)
       0-9606960-3-2 (Paperbound)

Table of Contents

About the Editors

Robert M. Figlio is Associate Director for Research, Center for Studies in Criminology and Criminal Law, University of Pennsylvania, Philadelphia, and Associate Professor in Social Systems Sciences, the Wharton School, at the same institution.

Simon Hakim is Associate Professor of Economics at Temple University, Philadelphia, Pennsylvania, and Visiting Professor at Haverford College, Haverford, Pennsylvania.

George F. Rengert is Associate Professor of Criminal Justice at Temple University, Philadelphia, Pennsylvania.

About the Contributors

Roy Bahl is Professor of Economics at the Maxwell School of Citizenship and Public Affairs, Syracuse University.

Patricia L. Brantingham is Associate Professor of Criminology at Simon Fraser University. She is currently on leave in order to serve as Director of Programme Evaluation in the Department of Justice, Canada.

Paul J. Brantingham is Professor of Criminology at Simon Fraser University. He is currently on leave in order to serve as Director of Evaluation in the Public Service Commission of Canada.

Diane Butcher is a graduate student in the Department of Criminology at Simon Fraser University.

C. Michael Costanzo is Research Associate of Geography at the University of California, Santa Barbara, and Senior Economic Geographer, Applied Systems, Santa Barbara.

Marcus Felson is Associate Professor at the University of Southern California Department of Sociology, and Senior Research Associate for the Social Science Research Institute at the same institution.

Nathan Gale is a postgraduate researcher in the Department of Geography at the University of California, Santa Barbara.

William C. Halperin is a postgraduate researcher in the Department of Geography at the University of California, Santa Barbara.

C. Ronald Huff is Director of the Program for the Study of Crime & Delinquency, Ohio State University, Columbus, Ohio, and Associate Professor of Public Administration at the same institution.

Ralph Lenz is Associate Professor in the Department of Geography, Wittenberg University, Springfield, Ohio.

Greg Lewis is Assistant Professor of Political Science at the University of Georgia.

Bruce L. Peterson is a graduate student in the Department of Political Science at the University of Chicago.

Alicia Rand is Research Associate, Response Analysis Corporation, Princeton, New Jersey.

Robert J. Sampson is Assistant Professor in the Department of Sociology at the University of Illinois, Urbana-Champaign, and a member of the Graduate Faculty of Sociology and Graduate College Statistics Department.

Lyle W. Shannon is Director of the Iowa Urban Community Research Center at the University of Iowa, Iowa City.

John M. Stahura is Associate Professor of Sociology at Purdue University.

D. Garth Taylor is Associate Professor of Political Science at the University of Illinois, Chicago.

Richard P. Taub is Professor of Social Sciences and Director of the Program for Urban Neighborhoods, University of Chicago.

Introduction

Though crime is a natural component of every society,[1] communities within societies differ in their degree of criminality. This difference defines the spatial ecology of crime.

The spatial ecology of crime was recognized by early sociological theorists, who argued that urban areas were more prone to crime than the rural countryside. Perhaps the most influential of these theorists was Louis Wirth, who observed that life in cities creates anomie at the societal level and alienation at the individual level.[2] Similarly, Tonnies, Simmel, and Maine viewed urban living as essentially amoral and normless.[3]

This scholarly perspective mirrored an essentially negative attitude toward urban areas in the United States, as exemplified by Thomas Jefferson's warnings against the dangers inherent in urban living: "When we get piled up upon one another in large cities, as in Europe, we shall become corrupt as in Europe, and go to eating one another as they do there."[4] Thus, crime came to be viewed as an urban problem.

Urban ecology studies soon taught us that all urban areas could not be painted with the same broad brush of amoral lifestyles and crime. Beginning with the early work of Burgess,[5] and culminating in factorial ecology studies,[6] we learned that urban areas are very diverse, containing expensive neighborhoods with relatively low crime rates as well as crime-ridden ghetto areas. It was not until quite recently that suburbs also were recognized as diverse both in physical infrastructure and in social and criminal conditions.[7]

The ecological approach to crime is not new, but it has evolved since the earlier studies by the Chicago School of urban ecologists in the 1920s, exemplified in the work of Park.[8] Park viewed communities as functionally specialized areas within an industrial economy. The patterning of communities was determined by competition, and changes were determined by invasion and social succession. The ecological spatial patterns of cities were further exemplified by Burgess's concentric circles[9] and Hoyt's sectors.[10] In crime research, this approach was represented in Shaw's work on delinquency areas in Chicago.[11]

Ecological research began to wane in the 1930s and the 1940s in response to well-founded criticisms, including its total exclusion of cultural and motivational factors in explaining land use patterns; the failure of its general structural concepts, such as concentric circles and natural areas, to hold up under comparative examination; and, most importantly from our perspective, its excessive reliance on competition as the basis of human organization.[12] Because of this mounting criticism, human ecologists began to abandon their broad theoretical and empirical studies of community structure. The last major criminological work of this type was Shaw and McKay's *Juvenile Delinquency and Urban Areas*.[13]

With the decline of the ecological approach, many researchers shifted their attention to objective descriptions of spatial patterns. They abandoned general theoretical and empirical studies of community structure, and began to map and describe social data to discover spatial correlations and differences. This approach came to be known as areal differentiation. The result was a vast inventory of social data collected for various subareas of cities, but the data were difficult to generalize into meaningful explanatory concepts or theories of individual and social behavior. Schmid's study of crime in Washington State was of this nature.[14]

A significant aspect of the ecological approach to this point was its commitment to the stability of the ecological substructure of the city. Shaw and McKay, for example, viewed the city's delinquency areas as ecologically specialized habitation niches for low income migrants into the city. These niches would be used by a succession of immigrant groups from different ethnic backgrounds at different time periods. As the social and economic situation of groups improved, they would move into the mainstream of American life, leaving space for the new immigrant groups. Therefore, crime control efforts were to be concentrated in the few urban areas seen as a breeding ground for the city's criminal population.

The 1950s marked the end of the era of relative stability in urban ecological patterns. The trend toward increasing decentralization, associated with the shift from fixed rail to highway transportation, led to a rapid development of suburban areas, which decisively altered the character of the invasion-succession process conceptualized by earlier urban ecologists. In response to the suburbanization of the middle class and its replacement by low income minorities, researchers now began identifying areas likely to undergo change from low to high crime rates and isolating factors associated with this change. This led to a revival of the ecological approach.

The revival started in 1950 when Amos Hawley published *Human Ecology*,[15] a work emphasizing functional interdependencies. Rather than determining how areas differ from each other, Hawley sought to identify how areas are interrelated and interconnected, and how populations move through these areas as they adapt to the urban environment. He viewed urban communities as interconnected areas in which the character of one community helps determine the character of its neighbors in space and time.

Two important lines of research have resulted from this revival in ecological research. The first examines the relation of changing urban land use to the social character of surrounding communities. For example, Kobrin and Schuerman demonstrated that changes in land use lead to changes in an area's population, which can then lead to an increase in crime.[16] This line of research is extended by studies presented in Part 1 of this volume.

A second and related research thrust is in-depth analysis of the impact of crime on neighborhood viability. Recent fear of crime research is in this vein, as are studies of the relationship between crime and residential mobility. For example, Katzman found that while crime is not an important cause of why people leave an area, it is an important determinant of the new area people will choose if they decide to move for other reasons.[17] Skogen and Maxfield came to the same conclusion.[18] Important extensions of this theory are found in Part 3 of this volume.

Study of space and time relationships has also been extended to the level of the individual in recent research, with applications to victims and offenders. Thus, a seminal time study by Cohen and Felson demonstrated the interaction between home guardianship and the routine activities of individuals.[19] Rengert and Waselchick extended this approach to the lives of criminals, demonstrating that an individual's choice of activities such as work and recreation affects his or her ability to engage in criminal activity.[20]

Recent ecological research has also analyzed the spatial mobility of criminals as they choose among urban environments for offenses. This research has existed in a rather crude form from the time of A.M. Guerry,[21] but only recently has it helped predict changes in crime patterns based on changes in the spatial mobility of criminals. In previous ecological studies, the community of the criminal was assumed to be the community of the victim. With greater spatial mobility of criminals, this assumption loses much of its validity. Important empirical and conceptual development of this type of research is presented in Part 2 of this volume.

ORGANIZATION OF THIS VOLUME

This volume is the first to examine crime from a metropolitan perspective, including the spread of crime to the suburbs and the spatial movement of criminals. The text is divided into four sections. The first contains ecological analyses of crime patterns in metropolitan regions. The second section extends the relatively new concentration on criminal spatial movement patterns by examining not only the environments of offenders and offenses, but also the spatial movement associated with the search for a crime site. The third section enriches recent research on fear of crime by describing the effects of crime and fear of crime on the viability of communities. The final section discusses the formal public response to crime in the form of policing expenditures.

Part 1 includes three studies that frame crime within a metropolitan context. Sampson, using United States National Crime Survey (NCS) data, examines the nationwide relationships among personal victimization, age of victim, extent of urbanization, neighborhood poverty, racial composition, and neighborhood structural density. He finds that the extent of urbanism, structural density (a function of the number of apartment houses and other multi-family dwellings), and poverty, are significant positive predictors of both violent and property crime. Structural density is positively related to higher rates of victimization both in urbanized and in less populated areas. This is probably because high density dwelling units inhibit surveillance and increase anonymity. In urban areas, poverty acts jointly with structural density to elevate the rates of theft and violence.

Shannon, in his path-analytic studies of ecological change over time in Racine, Wisconsin, reports that the inner city's declining population, poor and vacated housing, and changing population composition, are all related to the "hardening" of its high crime environment. In addition to describing the "hardened" areas where crime has persisted for some time, Shannon documents the recent diffusion in metropolitan crime patterns beyond the inner city.

Stahura and Huff find a persistence in suburban crime patterns in the United States over three time periods—1960, 1970, and 1980. However, "transitional" areas, formerly associated with inner cities, have diffused into suburban fringe areas. Therefore, the traditionally observed inverse linear relationship between crime and distance from the central city no longer applies to many American cities. As a result, crime in the suburbs must be considered alongside inner city crime as a metropolitan problem requiring metropolitan-wide solutions.

Part 2 of this volume examines the spatial movement of criminals. Using a sophisticated procedure to measure spatial autocorrelation, Costanzo, Halperin, and Gale find that criminals who live near each other travel in similar directions to commit the same type of crime. Delineating such "corridors of crime" would represent a potentially significant advance in crime prediction.

Lenz plots robbery patterns using the method of Thiessen Polygons for the city of Milwaukee, Wisconsin, during the years 1960 and 1970. He finds that the clustering of robberies has declined over this time, implying a greater diffusion throughout the metropolitan area. Of particular interest is his discovery that although criminals' residences have dispersed into outlying areas to some extent, the diffusion of robberies far exceeds the diffusion of criminal residences. Thus, criminals have become more mobile.

Rand, using data from the Philadelphia cohort studies, suggests that propinquity among offenders' and victims' residences, and the place of the criminal event, may also be functions of crime type. Crimes involving contact with a victim's person and property tend to concentrate near his or her home, while thefts without contact diffuse to those areas where appropriate opportunities exist, perhaps along predictable pathways and at some distance from the offender's residence.

Felson was one of the first to use potential models derived from social physics to predict criminal spatial movement and crime potential at any place in the metropolitan area. Using census and police data, he demonstrates that in a highly mobile city (Los Angeles), the relative safety of an area depends not only on the characteristics of the local neighborhood, but also on the characteristics of surrounding neighborhoods and the relative mobility of criminals.

Part 3 of this anthology offers two selections relating neighborhood viability to the fear of crime. The aggregate data collected by the NCS on the extent of fear of crime tend to mask neighborhood variation. Thus, Brantingham, Brantingham, and Butcher attempt to replicate the findings of the NCS using a similar sampling and research design in a "gentrifying" neighborhood of Vancouver, Canada. Contrary to the aggregated United States findings, the Canadian respondents perceive crime to be a greater problem closer to home rather than farther away. Yet, in spite of the perception of high local criminal activity, individuals do not feel particularly vulnerable to attack, report taking few security precautions, and have little interest in community crime programs.

In another attempt to reduce the level of aggregation, Taylor, Taub, and Peterson, using recently developed measurement models, analyze the responses from a telephone survey in eight Chicago neighborhoods. They find that individuals who attempt defensive actions against criminal victimizations are slightly more afraid of crime and are no less likely than their neighbors to be victimized. On the other hand, group participation in community crime prevention reduces crime rates as well as criminal victimization. In addition, neighborhood residents do not fear high crime levels as much as they fear aging and decaying housing stock and changing population characteristics that are also possible causes of criminal activity. Thus, individuals react more to physical and social characteristics of neighborhoods than to abstract perceptions of the threat of criminal violation.

Part 4 of this volume addresses the issue of metropolitan-wide cooperation, using the example of policing. Bahl and Lewis examine the differences in police expenditures between the city and suburbs. It is instructive to divide the policing function into capital and labor intensive elements. Police patrol is labor intensive, and once an acceptable level of patrol is reached, little utility remains in spending public funds to increase the size of the force. Therefore, decisions about the level of patrol are best left to the discretion of the local community. Other aspects of policing are capital intensive, and therefore enjoy economies of scale that make regional cooperation advantageous. For example, crime laboratories, data storage and analysis facilities and, in some cases, dispatching centers, are best funded on a regional scale.

CONCLUSION

The papers presented in this collection demonstrate that, in our increasingly mobile society, crime has become a metropolitan problem rather than just an inner city problem. With the aid of new, more sophisticated ecological analyses, we now have better tools with which to analyze metropolitan crime patterns and, in turn, manage our crime control resources more effectively. In view of the diffusion of crime and increased mobility of criminals, the effort to optimize use of public resources can no longer be a local one; community cooperation at the metropolitan level is essential.

The Editors

Notes

1. See Emile Durkheim, "Crime as a Normal Phenomenon," in Sir Leon Radzinowicz and Marvin Wolfgang, eds, *Crime and Justice*, vol. 1 (N.Y.: Basic Books, 1977), 657-661.

2. Brian J.L. Berry, *Comparative Urbanization* (N.Y.: St. Martin's Press, 1981), 14-15.

3. Ibid., 9-14.

4. Norman D. Levine, *Human Ecology* (North Scituate, Mass.: Duxbury Press, 1975), 306.

5. Ernest Burgess, "The Growth of the City: An Introduction to a Research Project," in Robert Park, Ernest Burgess, and R.D. McKenzie, eds., *The City* (Chicago: University of Chicago Press, 1925), 47-62.

6. See, for example, Brian J.L. Berry and P. Rees, "The Factorial Ecology of Calcutta,"*American Journal of Sociology* 74 (March 1969):445-491.

7. Peter Muller, *Contemporary Suburban America* (Englewood Cliffs, N.J.: Prentice-Hall, 1981).

8. Robert Park, "The City: Suggestions for the Investigation of Human Behavior in the Urban Environment," *American Journal of Sociology* 20 (1915):577-612.

9. Burgess, "Growth of the City."

10. Homer Hoyt, "The Structure of American Cities in the Post-War Era," *American Journal of Sociology* 48 (1943):475-492.

11. Clifford Shaw, *Delinquency Areas* (Chicago: University of Chicago Press, 1929).

12. Brian J.L. Berry and John D. Kasarda, *Contemporary Urban Ecology* (N.Y.: Macmillan, 1977), 6.

13. Clifford Shaw and H. McKay, *Juvenile Delinquency and Urban Areas* (Chicago: University of Chicago Press, 1942).

14. Calvin Schmid, "Urban Crime Areas, Part 1," *American Sociological Review* 25 (1960a):527-543; and "Urban Crime Areas, Part 2," *American Sociological Review* 25 (1960b):65-678.

15. Amos Hawley, *Human Ecology: A Theory of Community Structure* (N.Y.: Ronald Press, 1950).

16. Solomon Kobrin and Leo Schuerman, "Crime and Urban Ecological Processes: Implications for Public Policy," paper presented to the American Society of Criminology, Denver, Colorado, 1983.

17. Martin Katzman, "The Contribution of Crime to Urban Decline," *Urban Studies* 17 (1980):277-286.

18. W.G. Skogan and M.G. Maxfield, *Coping With Crime* (Beverly Hills: Sage, 1981).

19. L.E. Cohen and Marcus Felson, "Social Change and Crime Rate Trends: A Routine Activity Approach," *American Sociological Review* 44 (1979):588-608.

20. George Rengert and John Wasilchick, *Suburban Burglary: A Time and A Place For Everything* (Springfield, Ill.: Charles Thomas, 1985).

21. A.M. Guerry, *Essai Sur la Statistique Morale de la France* (Paris: Chez Corchard, 1831).

Part 1

Crime Trends Across the Metropolis

The Effects of Urbanization and Neighborhood Characteristics on Criminal Victimization

Robert J. Sampson

Although urbanization has long been an accepted correlate of crime, surprisingly little is known about patterns of victimization across the urban-suburban-rural dimension. In particular, little information is available about the structural determinants of victimization in suburban and rural areas, and the interaction between urbanization and neighborhood characteristics. To address these issues, the present study uses National Crime Survey victimization data from 1973–1978 to examine the effects of neighborhood characteristics and extent of urbanization on rates of theft and violent personal victimization. The results underscore the importance of urbanization and the physical environment in predicting victimization risk. Regardless of age, racial composition, and poverty, both the extent of urbanization and housing density had significant positive effects on victimization. Several important interactions were also uncovered: Poverty tends to increase victimization risk only in urban areas, while density exerts an increased effect on victimization in suburban and rural areas. Overall, the results confirm the need for researchers to take into account both neighborhood factors and the urban-rural dimension in explaining victimization.

The higher level of crime in U.S. cities compared to suburban or rural areas has long been an accepted fact in criminology. Regardless of the data source used, crime statistics consistently show that urban crime rates are substantially greater than non-urban crime rates.[1] Moreover, population size has been shown to be an important predictor of crime rates across U.S. cities.[2] The apparent strong impact of urbanism on crime has led to an interesting development in the ecological study of crime: almost every ecological study of crime to date has been conducted within central cities. From the early pioneering works of Shaw and McKay[3] to the most recent studies, criminologists have directed their attention to variations in crime rates within cities[4] or variations in city crime rates across a national sample of cities.[5]

Both recent crime trends and theoretical developments suggest that the limitation of areal studies of crime to cities is unwarranted. First, crime trends indicate that crime is rising at a faster rate in suburban and rural areas than in large cities. For example, the percentage increase in violent crime from 1973–1981 for Standard Metropolitan Statistical Areas (SMSAs) was 37 percent, compared to a 50 percent increase in violent crime in suburbs.[6] Even more surprising, the percentage increase in property crime was 51 percent in rural areas, compared to a 37 percent increase in SMSAs.[7] Particularly noteworthy is the fact that rural crime rates today are roughly equal to urban crime rates of 1967. Clearly, the phenomenon of serious crime in the United States is not limited to the confines of our major cities.[8] Indeed, the reality of criminal victimization is becoming commonplace in areas once considered idyllic settings.[9] Thus, although the absolute level of crime is still higher in cities than in surrounding areas, projections from recent trends suggest that rate differences are quickly converging.[10]

Despite the importance of viewing crime within the entire metropolitan-wide spectrum in which it occurs, surprisingly little is known about the patterns of criminal victimization across the urban-suburban-rural dimension. In particular, little information is available about the structural determinants of crime in suburban and rural areas, and the interaction between urbanization and neighborhood characteristics. This is an important limitation of criminological research, for there is no a priori reason for assuming that the same factors that predict crime rates in cities also explain suburban and rural crime patterns. To address these issues the present study uses National Crime Survey (NCS) victimization data from 1973 to 1978 to examine the effects of neighborhood characteristics and extent of urbanization on rates of both theft and violent personal criminal victimization. Two important areas are emphasized: (1) the independent effect of urbanism and neighborhood characteristics on personal victimization, and (2) the interaction effects of neighborhood characteristics and urbanization.

RESEARCH FRAMEWORK

Classic theoretical explanations for the effect of urbanism on crime are usually derived from Wirth.[11] Wirth argued that interpersonal ties, social cohesion, and the normative consensus of the population were weakened by the size, density, and heterogeneity of cities. In essence, Wirth[12] posited that social disorganization caused by urbanism led to a breakdown in social control mechanisms, which in turn led to high rates of crime and deviance. However, an alternative explanation holds that urban-rural differences in crime rates are due to the differential composition of the population across the urban-rural dimension rather than to the ecological characteristics of size and density. This position, referred to as compositional theory,[13] asserts that composition variables such as race, age, life-cycle stage, and economic status account for the relationship between urbanization and crime.[14] Thus, the main thesis of the compositional school is that urbanization has no *independent* effect on crime.

As Laub[15] has noted, compositional theorists have focused principally on race in accounting for the correlate of urbanization.[16] A well-established finding of criminological research is that blacks have higher offending rates than whites for serious personal crimes such as robbery, murder, and assault.[17] Furthermore, blacks tend to reside in large cities rather than suburban and rural areas. Thus, compositional theorists argue that there is a confounding of urbanism and race, where urban crime rates are higher largely because of the disproportionate black population in cities. According to this perspective, persons in urban areas have a high risk of victimization because of their proximity to black offenders, not because of the criminogenic effects of living in heterogeneous, high density environments. While most city-based ecological research has introduced percent black as a control, this approach is inadequate since there is in effect no variation in urbanization, i.e., rates are analyzed across urban centers. This study analyzes the independent effects of urbanization and racial composition on rates of criminal victimization.[18] Compositional theory is supported to the extent that the effect of urbanization is attenuated or eliminated once percent black is controlled. However, it is also possible that urbanization and racial composition interact to explain victimization patterns. Therefore, in the analysis that follows special attention is given to the extent to which urbanization modifies the impact of race on crime.

Another important area of inquiry concerns poverty. A phenomenal amount of contemporary ecological research has been devoted to studying the effect of poverty and inequality on urban crime rates.[19] Indeed, much of the recent supporting evidence for relative deprivation theory has come from ecological research using cities and SMSAs as units of analysis.[20] Again, however, this body of research is by definition confined to cities. Yet, poverty is quite pervasive in rural areas of the country, and even in some suburban areas. Since much of the theoretical apparatus in criminology is tied to the concept of poverty, it seems necessary to examine its effects in non-urban contexts. To the extent that the poverty thesis is correct, then poverty should exert an independent effect on patterns of victimization in urban, suburban, and rural areas.

There is some evidence to believe, however, that urbanization modifies the impact of poverty. A consistent finding of studies of ecological structure is that residential differentiation in terms of social class is more pervasive in urban areas than in suburban and rural areas.[21] Rural areas tend to be more homogeneous and cohesive in nature, and lack the degree of economic and cultural differentiation found in highly urbanized areas. Moreover, some have suggested that in non-urban areas class differentiation may not have developed sufficiently for it to result in distinctive patterns of behavior and culture.[22] These observations led Sampson and Castellano[23] to hypothesize that the effect of poverty on crime would be attenuated in rural areas. This hypothesis is addressed further by examining the interaction effects of urbanization and poverty on crime, controlling for other neighborhood characteristics. The results have important implications for both theoretical development and social policy, since in the past both have operated on the untested assumption that the criminogenic effects of poverty are ubiquitous.

Many theories of crime at both the individual and community level speak to factors that affect motivation and propensities to offend, e.g., blocked opportunity, inequality. Recently, however, Hindelang and Cohen and their colleagues[24] have formalized a theory that explicitly focuses on the *opportunity* factors that influence crime independent of motivational factors. In other words, there is assumed to be a virtually infinite supply of motivated offenders. Theoretical attention centers on how variations in criminal opportunities are related to the risk of victimization. The opportunity model of Cohen, Kluegel, and Land is relevant to the research efforts by Sampson[25] and Greenberg[26] in the case of neighborhood structural density. Briefly, the perspective suggests that structural density, i.e., a high proportion of multiple dwelling-unit structures, is positively related to the density and accessibility of criminal targets, particularly for theft crimes such as robbery and burglary. Furthermore, structural density inhibits effective means of surveillance and guardianship both through sheer physical barriers[27] and by increasing anonymity. As Roncek[28] and Newman[29] note, as the number of households sharing common living space increases, residents are less able to recognize neighbors, be concerned for them, or engage in guardianship activities.[30] Thus, by offering increased criminal opportunities in a context of limited guardianship and defensible space capacity, structural density is hypothesized to directly increase the risk of victimization, regardless of factors presumed to affect offender motivation, e.g., poverty. Sampson's research partially supported this proposition by indicating that structural density is positively related to victimization.[31] In addition, Greenberg found that low structural density, i.e., areas with a high proportion of single-family homes, was associated with lower levels of fear and perceived neighborhood disorder, independent of both individual-level characteristics and other neighborhood characteristics.[32]

Recently, Jackson has suggested that the relationship between opportunity structure and crime is modified by extent of urbanization.[33] Specifically, Jackson argues that because of their lower levels of cohesion, greater levels of anonymity, and less effective informal neighborhood surveillance systems, larger concentrations of population are more vulnerable to crime than are smaller concentrations of people. Jackson tested her thesis by examining the ecological predictors of crime patterns in a sample of large (> 50,000) and small (25,000–50,000) cities. She concludes from the empirical results that opportunity factors are in fact more criminogenic in larger cities, thus supporting her main contention.[34] While representing an important analytical insight, Jackson's study is limited by the restriction of her sample to cities. To address this limitation, this study examines the independent effects of neighborhood structural density across the urban-rural dimension. According to Jackson's interpretation of the Cohen and Felson model, and by extension the opportunity model of Cohen et al., we should expect structural density to have a significant impact on crime in urban areas, a weaker one in suburban areas, and a weak to insignificant effect in rural areas. On the other hand, to the extent that the Cohen model is generally valid, the effect of density should be positive and significant regardless of extent of urbanization.

DATA AND METHOD

The data base for the present study is the National Crime Survey (NCS) national household sample. Victimization data are collected independent of the selection mechanisms of the criminal justice system and thus provide a rich data base in which to explore the effects of ecological characteristics on crime. This is an important advantage since by far the vast majority of prior ecological studies have used officially recorded Uniform Crime Reports (UCR) to generate estimates of crime rates.[35] The data were collected by the United States Bureau of Census, in cooperation with the Bureau of Justice Statistics of the U.S. Department of Justice. The NCS is a continuous panel survey in which nationally representative samples of households and persons are interviewed twice per year, at six month intervals.[36] Crimes are classified according to definitions used in the UCR.[37] This study is concerned with personal crimes of theft (larceny and robbery) and violence (rape, aggravated assault, and simple assault). The annual interview sample has approximately 60,000 households containing about 136,000 individuals. The data used in this study are from the survey years 1973 to 1978, representing approximately 800,000 interviews with household respondents.

Each household record in the NCS sample contains information on the socio-demographic, economic, and physical characteristics of the neighborhood in which the household was sampled. The neighborhood characteristics selected and their measures are as follows: *poverty* (percent of families with less than $5000 family income); *racial composition* (percent black); and *structural density* (percent units in structures of five or more units). The data set used in this study was formed by combining households with similar values of these neighborhood characteristics according to 1970 census statistics. To preserve confidentiality, neighborhoods defined by the Census Bureau are not identifiable census tracts, but are aggregated enumeration districts or block groups with a population minimum of 4,000. A study of these neighborhoods has indicated that the aggregation procedure utilized by the Census Bureau resulted in neighborhoods being relatively compact, contiguous, and homogeneous areas approximately the size of a census tract.[38] To construct reliable rates each neighborhood characteristic was trichotomized into categories of low, medium, and high.[39] The NCS national sample was used to estimate both the population base 12 years of age and older (persons under 12 are not eligible to be interviewed) and the number of victimizations that occurred each year to persons residing in each category or combination of categories of neighborhood characteristics.

In the NCS data, Office of Management and Budget areal categories are utilized to measure extent of urbanization.[40] SMSAs are defined as a county or group of contiguous counties that contain at least one city of 50,000 persons, or "twin cities" with a combined population of at least 50,000. Also, other contiguous counties are included in the SMSA if they are socially and economically integrated within the central city.[41] In the present study urban areas are defined as the core central city (or twin cities) within the SMSA. Suburban areas are defined as the balance of the SMSA, which includes those metropolitan areas within an SMSA but outside central cities. Finally, rural areas are non-metropolitan areas not located within an SMSA.[42]

Analysis of variance models are used to examine the effects of ecological characteristics on victimization. Analysis of variance is well suited to the structure of the NCS data analyzed in this study, which consist of interval-level measurements of the dependent variable and grouped categories (low, medium, and high) of the independent variables. Based on previous examination of NCS data, victimization rates are assumed to be a multiplicative function of independent variables and random error, i.e., linear in the log scale.[43] The additive effects assumption of ANOVA models is met by taking logarithms of the rates, and then performing the additive analysis of variance on the logarithms of the rates. Multiplicative parameters were obtained by taking antilogarithms of the effects.

Cell population sizes are often used as cell weights when each analysis of variance factor is observed rather than determined by the investigator.[44] In our case, neighborhood characteristics reflect the prior grouping of the population, and thus each category is not equally important. To address the unbalanced nature of the NCS data, a model employing cell weights is used in testing hypotheses and estimating effect parameters. The U.S. population base at each combination of levels of the ANOVA factor cross-clarification is defined as the weight.

PLACE OF CRIME

The census data analyzed in this study refer to characteristics of the victim's neighborhood, and not the place where crimes necessarily occurred. Unfortunately, the NCS instrument does not allow the precise identification of where crimes occurred.[45] However, a review of the literature indicates that the majority of personal crimes, e.g., rape, robbery, assault, are "ecologically bound"—that is, crimes occur near the residences of victims.[46] The evidence thus suggests that a large proportion of serious personal crimes does take place near the victim's residence. Even for those victimizations that take place outside the neighborhood boundaries defined by the Census Bureau, it seems reasonable to assume that a large percentage occurred in adjacent neighborhoods. Given the residential segregation patterns dominant in American communities,[47] adjacent neighborhoods are very similar with respect to the neighborhood characteristics studied here, e.g., racial composition, poverty, density. There is much less of a problem with misclassification of victimization incidents in regard to the extent of urbanization data since approximately 93 percent of victims are victimized within their city of residence.[48]

Perhaps most important, however, the lifestyle/opportunity theory of victimization[49] predicts that *proximity* to offenders and criminogenic areas is a major determinant of the probability of victimization. Thus, it is not necessary to assume that all victimizations occur in the victim's neighborhood to study the effect of neighborhood characteristics. Simply living in a certain type of environment increases risk factors that affect probabilistic exposure, even if actual victimizations may occur outside specific neighborhood boundaries defined by the Census Bureau, e.g., residents victimized while travelling from their neighborhood to work, shopping, and school.[50]

FINDINGS

The analysis proceeds in two stages. In the first stage the independent effects of urbanization and the neighborhood characteristics of poverty, racial composition, and structural density are separately assessed when age of victim is introduced into the model (see Tables 1–3). Of all individual-level predictors of victimization, age is one of the most powerful.[51] Perhaps surprisingly, race and income of victim are not strong predictors of victimization in multivariate analysis.[52] Since age is related to selected ecological characteristics, e.g., young people tend to reside in suburban areas, it is important to initially control its possible confounding effects.[53] Once the effects of urbanization and neighborhood characteristics are ascertained independent of the effects of age of victim, stage two examines the multivariate effects of poverty, racial composition, structural density, and urbanization (see Table 4).

Neighborhood Poverty

Panel A of Table 1 presents ANOVA statistics for the three-way cross-classification of personal victimization by age of victim, extent of urbanization, and neighborhood poverty, for theft and violent crimes separately.[54] First, note that age of victim, poverty, and urbanization are all significant at the .001 level for both theft and violent crimes. The interaction of poverty and urbanization is significant only for violent crimes.

Table 1

Weighted Analysis of Variance of Personal Criminal Victimization,[a]
by Age of Victim, Extent of Urbanization, Neighborhood Poverty,
and Type of Crime,[b] NCS National Data, 1973–1978 Aggregate

A. ANOVA Statistics		Theft			Violent		
Source of variation	*Degrees of freedom*	*Mean square*	*F*	*P*	*Mean square*	*F*	*P*
Main effects:							
1. Age	2	.211	23.21	.00	.608	220.48	.00
2. Urbanization	2	.615	67.45	.00	.135	49.08	.00
3. Poverty	2	.043	4.73	.02	.027	9.99	.00
Interaction:							
23	4	.015	1.65	.21	.008	3.15	.04
Residual	16						

B. Parameter Estimates[c]	Theft		Violent	
	($\bar{x}$ = 834)		($\bar{x}$ = 2,460)	
Variable + Category	*Effect*	*R^2*	*Effect*	*R^2*
Age of victim:				
12–17	1.42		1.86	
18–20	1.70	21.7	2.42	75.0
21 or older	.86		.76	
Extent of urbanization:				
Urban	1.87		1.34	
Suburban	.99	63.2	.97	16.7
Rural	.49		.71	
Poverty:				
Low	1.14		1.13	
Medium	1.03	4.4	1.00	3.4
High	.81		.84	

[a]Estimated rates of victimization were transformed to logarithmic (base 10) scale.
[b]Theft crimes include robbery and larceny. Violent crimes include rape, aggravated assault, and simple assault.
[c]Multiplicative parameters obtained by taking antilogarithms of the effects.

Although statistical significance is of course essential in determining relationships, it is of interest to examine the pattern and magnitude of effect estimates to assess substantive importance of variables. Hence, Panel B of Table 1 presents effect parameter estimates for age, poverty, and urbanization, and also the percent of variance explained by each factor. Using the multiplicative model, one can estimate predicted rates for levels of the independent variables. For example, the overall level of *theft* victimization (per 100,000 persons) is 834. The effect of living in an urban area is to raise this rate by a factor of 1.87, yielding a predicted rate of 1,560 (834×1.87). Conversely, rural areas have a predicted rate of 409 (834×.49). Thus, the predicted theft rate in urban areas is almost four times greater (3.8) than the rate in rural areas, independent of the effect of age and poverty.[55] Note that this ratio is equivalent to simply taking the ratio of effect parameters (1.87/.49=3.8). The pattern of effects can thus be easily shown by taking ratios. In addition, Panel B also displays R^2 estimates, in this case revealing that extent of urbanization alone accounts for 63 percent of the explained variance in personal theft victimization.

Applying these methods to the other explanatory factors, it can be seen that poverty has very little effect on either theft or violent victimization, explaining 4 and 3 percent of the variance, respectively. Moreover, note that the pattern of parameter estimates for poverty is counter to traditional theoretical expectations. For both theft and violent crimes, predicted victimization rates are higher in the *low* category of poverty than the high category. Consequently, the results suggest that persons living in higher income neighborhoods suffer a greater risk of victimization than those residing in low income areas, all else being equal. However, the data do suggest a tendency for poverty to interact with urbanization. Although not statistically significant, poverty tends to be positively related to theft victimization in urban areas (data not shown in tabular form). This same interaction pattern is repeated for violent victimization, but there the interaction is significant at the .05 level.

As expected on the basis of prior research, age of victim has a strong effect on the risk of personal victimization, particularly for crimes of violence. While age explains 22 percent of the variance in theft victimization, it explains over three times that (75%) in violent victimization. Thus, the results in Table 1 are fairly clear: The ecological characteristics of urbanization and poverty have a negligible impact on rates of violent victimization. This type of crime is most influenced by the individual-level predictor of age. On the other hand, urbanization has a strong effect on theft victimization, and poverty a weak and inconsistent one. While victimization patterns in urban areas lend some support to poverty theorists, the main effect of poverty is negative and small.

Neighborhood Racial Composition

Table 2 presents the three-way cross-classification of personal victimization by age, urbanization, and neighborhood racial composition. The

Table 2

Weighted Analysis of Variance of Personal Criminal Victimization,[a]
by Age of Victim, Extent of Urbanization, Neighborhood Racial Composition,
and Type of Crime,[b] NCS National Data, 1973–1978 Aggregate

A. ANOVA Statistics

Source of variation	Degrees of freedom	Theft Mean square	F	P	Violent Mean square	F	P
Main effects:							
1. Age	2	.284	36.40	.00	.606	193.87	.00
2. Urbanization	2	.746	95.63	.00	.125	39.91	.00
3. Percent black	2	.229	29.40	.00	.044	14.25	.00
Interaction:							
23	4	.002	.27	.89	.017	5.52	.01
Residual	16	.0078			.0031		

B. Parameter Estimates[c]

Variable + Category	Theft ($\bar{x} = 777$) Effect	R^2	Violent ($\bar{x} = 2,404$) Effect	R^2
Age of victim:				
12–17	1.39		1.84	
18–20	2.06	21.4	2.68	72.6
21 or older	.85		.78	
Extent of urbanization:				
Urban	1.89		1.21	
Suburban	1.10	56.2	1.12	14.9
Rural	.49		.72	
Percent black:				
Low	.73		.87	
Medium	1.03	17.3	1.02	5.3
High	1.55		1.21	

[a]Estimated rates of victimization were transformed to logarithmic (base 10) scale.
[b]Theft crimes include robbery and larceny. Violent crimes include rape, aggravated assault, and simple assault.
[c]Multiplicative parameters obtained by taking antilogarithms of the effects.

ANOVA statistics in Panel A reveal that all three explanatory factors have a significant main effect on rates of both theft and violent victimization. The interaction effect of urbanization and percent black is significant for violent but not for theft victimization. The parameter estimates in Panel B show that urbanization once again has the strongest effect on theft victimization, explaining 56 percent of the variance. Independent of the effect of age and percent black, urban theft rates are some 3.5 times greater than theft rates in rural areas. Urbanization has a moderate effect on violent crime, explaining about 15 percent of the variance.

Percent black also has a direct effect on both theft and violent crime, albeit a much smaller one than urbanism. Racial composition accounts for 17 percent of the variance in theft victimization and only 5 percent for violent victimization. However, the *direction* of effects for percent black is in accordance with theoretical predictions: Rates of both theft and violent victimization are disproportionately high for persons residing in neighborhoods with a high percentage of black population. Examination of the interaction effect of urbanization and racial composition for violent crime did not reveal any pattern that appears to be substantively important. The interaction arises because percent black has an attenuated effect in rural areas.[56] The results of Table 2 support both the ecological and compositional arguments reviewed earlier, although clearly the former garners more support in the empirical data, at least for theft victimization. Regardless of the individual characteristic of age and the racial composition of the neighborhood, urbanism has a strong direct effect on theft victimization. However, percent black also has a direct effect, thus supporting some of the claims of the compositional theorists. Nevertheless, the magnitude of effects is much larger for urbanization. For example, the ratio of high/low effect parameters for extent of urbanization is 3.8, compared to approximately 2 for percent black. For violent crimes the compositional argument fares much better, as an individual level characteristic—age of victim—explains almost all the variance. These results underscore the considerable type of crime differences that exist when the effects of ecological characteristics are studied.

Neighborhood Structural Density

Table 3 presents the three-way analysis of variance of age, extent of urbanization, and neighborhood structural density. Panel A significance tests show a significant effect of all three factors for both crime types. Interestingly, the interaction of urbanization and structural density is significant for both theft and violent victimizations. Panel B parameter estimates indicate that structural density has a strong positive effect on theft victimization. The predicted theft rate for residents of neighborhoods with a high proportion of multiple dwelling-unit structures is over three times greater than the theft rate of residents living

Table 3

Weighted Analysis of Variance of Personal Criminal Victimization,[a]
by Age of Victim, Extent of Urbanization, Neighborhood Structural Density
and Type of Crime,[b] NCS National Data, 1973–1978 Aggregate

A. ANOVA Statistics

Source of variation	Degrees of freedom	Theft			Violent		
		Mean square	F	P	Mean square	F	P
Main effects:							
1. Age	2	.238	40.30	.00	.607	133.28	.00
2. Urbanization	2	.614	103.84	.00	.105	23.11	.00
3. Struc. density	2	.454	76.85	.00	.091	19.90	.00
Interaction:							
23	4	.017	2.90	.05	.014	3.14	.04
Residual	16						

B. Parameter Estimates[c]

Variable + Category	Theft ($\bar{x} = 756$)		Violent ($\bar{x} = 2,326$)	
	Effect	R^2	Effect	R^2
Age of victim:				
12–17	1.42		1.96	
18–20	1.86	17.2	2.54	69.9
21 or older	.89		.81	
Extent of urbanization:				
Urban	2.02		1.30	
Suburban	1.04	44.2	1.06	12.1
Rural	.49		.73	
Structural density:				
Low	.58		.75	
Medium	.86	32.7	.98	10.4
High	1.82		1.26	

[a]Estimated rates of victimization were transformed to logarithmic (base 10) scale.
[b]Theft crimes include robbery and larceny. Violent crimes include rape, aggravated assault, and simple assault.
[c]Multiplicative parameters obtained by taking antilogarithms of the effects.

in neighborhoods characterized by low structural density, independent of the effect of urbanization and age. Still, urbanism does have the strongest effect on theft crimes, while age has the strongest effect on violent crime. These results follow the patterns noted above for poverty and racial composition.

The pattern of interaction effects in Table 3 is of interest, particularly since density and urbanization interact to predict theft victimization. Recall that Jackson[57] argued that opportunity structures of crime should have the strongest effect on crime in large cities, where social cohesion and neighborhood surveillance systems are thought to be weaker than in smaller cities and rural areas. The interaction parameter estimates for the model in Table 3 indicate just the opposite. Structural density tends to have a greater effect in *rural* areas than in suburban areas or SMSA central cities. This interaction pattern occurs for both theft and violent victimizations.[58] The results thus do not support Jackson's general contentions, although her basic argument may be useful in accounting for the results. As she argues, levels of social cohesion, levels of anonymity, and neighborhood surveillance are weaker in urban areas. Yet precisely for this reason urban areas may have already reached a "saturation" point in terms of attenuated social controls. That is, since urban areas are characterized by a generally high level of structural density, the variation in density *within* cities may account for little additional variation in criminality.

Rural areas and suburban areas, on the other hand, have been throughout history dominated by a single-family home and low structural density housing pattern, perhaps increasing the salience of the criminogenic effects of the high building density that does exist. As argued earlier, a residential environment of apartment buildings and other high density buildings offers considerable criminal opportunities in a context characterized by a reduced capacity for surveillance and guardianship.[59] The empirical results are consistent with the notion that the criminogenic effects of structural density are greater in areas dominated by an overall low level of high density apartments and complexes. One counter-argument might be that multiple dwelling-unit structures in suburban and rural areas are newer than those in older suburban areas. Since there may be more criminal opportunities in high density wealthy neighborhoods than in high density poorer neighborhoods, income level may be a confounding factor producing the interaction effect. In other words, residents of high building density suburban and rural areas may suffer a higher risk of victimization than urban counterparts simply because they reside in higher income, newer developments that attract more criminals, not because the reduction in surveillance and guardianship caused by structural density is any more salient in non-urban than urban environments. To address this counter-argument, it is necessary to assess the simultaneous effects of urbanization, structural density, and neighborhood economic status, having already demonstrated the importance of these ecological characteristics vis-à-vis age of victim.[60]

Racial Composition, Poverty, and Structural Density

Table 4 presents the four-way factor cross-classification of theft and violent victimization by extent of urbanization, percent black, poverty, and structural density. Focusing first on theft victimization, one notes that poverty does not have a significant main effect. In contrast, the main effects of urbanization, percent black, and structural density are all significant at the .01 level, as are the interaction effects of poverty and urbanization and poverty and density. The parameter estimates in Panel B of Table 4 indicate that the strongest predictors of theft are the ecological characteristics of urbanization and structural density. In fact, density and urbanism both explain about 30 percent of the variance. The predicted theft rates in urban areas and high density neighborhoods are more than four times greater than theft rates in rural and low density areas. Percent black also has a significant main effect, but it explains less than 10 percent of the variance in theft victimization. Thus, the compositional argument is shown once again to be insufficient to predict theft victimization patterns. Regardless of neighborhood racial composition, residents suffer a much greater risk of theft victimization in high density, urban neighborhoods than residents of low density suburban and rural areas. This is a major finding considering that race is one of the strongest predictors of involvement in criminal offending.[61]

The interaction effect of urbanization and poverty is of considerable interest given the theoretical arguments developed above. Although poverty has no main effect, it interacts with urbanization to predict theft victimization rates. The interaction arises because poverty is positively related to theft in urban areas. Specifically, the interaction of high poverty, urban areas raises theft rates by a factor of 1.22, compared to .71 for low poverty, urban areas (data not shown in tabular form). By contrast, poverty is either unrelated or negatively related to theft in suburban and rural areas.

The interaction of poverty and structural density arises from the increased effect of structural density in poor neighborhoods. Apparently, the criminogenic effect of multiple dwelling-unit structures is more salient in areas characterized by a high proportion of poor residents. This may be because residents of higher income neighborhoods

Table 4

Weighted Analysis of Variance of Personal Criminal Victimization,[a]
by Extent of Urbanization, Percent Black, Poverty, Structural Density,
and Type of Crime,[b] NCS National Data, 1973–1978 Aggregate

A. ANOVA Statistics

Source of variation	Degrees of freedom	Theft Mean square	F	P	Violent Mean square	F	P
Main effects:							
1. Urbanization	2	1.753	75.28	.00	.278	26.99	.00
2. Percent black	2	.557	23.95	.00	.032	3.15	.05
3. Poverty	2	.055	2.36	.10	.045	4.36	.02
4. Structural density	2	1.755	75.38	.00	.480	46.62	.00
Interaction:							
12	4	.015	.65	.63	.005	.50	.74
13	4	.118	5.08	.01	.045	4.38	.01
14	4	.047	2.06	.10	.047	4.60	.00
23	4	.050	2.17	.09	.129	1.26	.30
24	4	.024	1.05	.39	.006	.62	.65
34	4	.287	12.32	.00	.055	5.33	.01
Residual	48	.023			.010		

B. Parameter Estimates[c]

Variable + Category	Theft ($\bar{x}=724$) Effect	R^2	Violent ($\bar{x}=2,395$) Effect	R^2
Extent of urbanization:				
Urban	2.16		1.32	
Suburban	1.09	30.4	1.08	19.5
Rural	.44		.71	
Percent black:				
Low	.77		.92	
Medium	1.07	9.7	1.11	2.2
High	1.84		1.01	
Poverty:				
Low	1.08		1.03	
Medium	1.06	.1	1.07	3.1
High	.84		.86	
Structural density:				
Low	.47		.63	
Medium	.89	30.4	1.01	33.7
High	1.99		1.33	

[a] Estimated rates of victimization were transformed to logarithmic (base 10) scale.
[b] Theft crimes include robbery and larceny. Violent crimes include rape, aggravated assault, and simple assault.
[c] Multiplicative parameters obtained by taking antilogarithms of the effects.

18

have more protective and buffering devices against crime such as alarms and block patrols, thus attenuating somewhat the deleterious effects of high density housing. In any event, the stability and meaning of this interaction is deserving of future research attention. In terms of other interaction effects, note that the interaction of density and urbanization in predicting theft victimization is only marginally significant ($p=.10$) here. The consistency of the interaction observed earlier in Table 3 is thus questionable.

Poverty and Violence

Turning to the analysis of violent crime, a pattern can be discerned that is quite similar to theft crime patterns. Again extent of urbanization and structural density have the strongest effects, together accounting for over one half of the explained variance in rates of violent victimization. Interestingly, structural density has a greater effect on violent victimization than urbanization, explaining 34 percent of the variance compared to 20 percent for urbanization. The noticeable difference between patterns of theft and violent victimization is that poverty has a significant main effect only on the latter. However, the strength of the poverty effect is miniscule. Indeed, poverty and percent black *combined* explain only five percent of the variance in violent crime. Moreover, predicted poverty rates are highest in the medium category of poverty, not the low. The weak and inconsistent effects of poverty and percent black are particularly noteworthy given the recent scholarly attention devoted to the importance of racial composition and poverty as structural determinants of criminality.[62]

The only manner in which poverty conforms to traditional theoretical expectations in predicting violent crime is in its interaction with extent of urbanization. As with theft crimes, detailed analysis of the interaction parameter estimates (not shown) indicated that poverty is positively related to rates of violent victimization only in SMSA central cities. This consistency across crime types of the interaction between urbanization and poverty is potentially quite important, suggesting that the economic predictors of crime vary across the urban-rural dimension. In a related vein, structural density also interacts with urbanization ($p < .01$) in predicting violent victimization. However, in this case the interaction arises from the increased effect of density in suburban and rural areas. This interaction supports the observations and arguments developed in reference to the density-urbanization interaction noted in Table 3. Finally, one notes that poverty and density also interact to predict rates of violent victimization, with lower than expected rates found in high density, low poverty areas. In sum, the results of the multivariate analysis of variance summarized in Table 4 highlight the importance of urbanization and structural density as predictors of both theft and violent victimization, and the differential effect of poverty and density in relation to extent of urbanization.

SUMMARY

Despite rises in suburban and rural crime, the present study reaffirms the importance of urbanism in predicting crime. Regardless of age, racial composition, poverty, and density, residents of central cities suffer a risk of theft and violent victimization considerably higher than their suburban and rural counterparts. While future crime rates in suburban and rural areas may approach or reach those of our nation's urban centers, the data suggest that for the time being at least, a relatively high victimization risk is one of the prices to be paid for living in cities.

The present study also underscores the importance of the physical environment in predicting victimization. Neighborhood structural density was a significant positive predictor of victimization rates regardless of other explanatory factors. In fact, structural density explained almost as much variance in theft victimization as urbanism, and had a stronger effect on violent crime. The results support the opportunity model of victimization, which suggests that structural density inhibits effective means of surveillance and guardianship both through physical barriers and by increasing anonymity.[63] Residents of areas with high building density are less able to recognize strangers and to engage in guardianship activities for neighbors.[64] Consequently, high density neighborhoods facilitate the convergence in time and space of motivated offenders with plentiful victims and low guardianship potential. In short, the independent effects of the ecological factors of urbanization and structural density do not support the overall argument of compositional theorists, who hold that ecological characteristics have no autonomous effect on behavior once relevant population composition characteristics are taken into account.

Another important finding is the presence of significant interactions of poverty and structural density with urbanization in predicting victimization. In particular, poverty has no main effect on theft victimization, but a significant interaction effect with urbanization. This interaction arises from the positive effect of poverty on theft in urban areas. The same interaction is significant in predicting rates of violent crime as well. There was also a tendency for structural density to interact with urbanization. Although in all cases structural density had a significant main effect on both theft and violent crimes, this effect appeared to be greater in suburban and rural areas than in urban centers. As noted above, this may indicate that non-central cities are more conducive to the criminogenic effects of high density housing structures. Indeed, the greater rise in rural and suburban crime than urban crime in recent years may be due, in part, to the tremendous housing development now under way in the nation's suburbs and "ex-urban" territories.[65] That is, the increase in apartments, condominiums, and other multiple dwelling-unit structures in the outskirts of metropolitan areas, combined with the lack of construction activity in inner city housing markets, may have helped trigger the recent phenomenon of suburban and rural crime. If this hypothesis is correct, it suggests that offenders from central cities will travel increasing distances into outlying suburbs and rural areas where criminal opportunities are perceived to be greater.

This study suggests that criminologists interested in ecological patterns of crime should not limit themselves to urban crime. While the results presented here are preliminary and call for replication, they nonetheless suggest that certain neighborhood characteristics interact with extent of urbanization to predict victimization. Thus, although some factors may be useful in accounting for crime in urban areas, e.g., poverty, other characteristics, e.g., structural density, may be paramount in explaining victimization patterns in suburban and rural areas. The need to recognize urban-rural differences in areal crime research will probably become even more important in the future. As crime continues to increase in suburban and rural areas, we are likely to see an increased demand there for police services, community crime prevention programs, and theoretical explanations. However, to the extent that criminal justice programs and theoretical responses are based on the underlying assumption that the structural determinants of crime in suburban and rural areas are the same as those in central cities, then such policies and theoretical models may be misguided.

Notes

1. See e.g., Keith Harries, *Crime and Environment* (Springfield: Charles Thomas, 1980); John J. Gibbs, *Crimes Against Persons in Urban, Suburban, and Rural Areas: A Comparative Analysis of Victimization Rates* (Washington, D.C.: U.S. Government Printing Office, 1979).

2. See Bruce Mayhew and Roger Levinger, "Size and the Density of Interaction in Human Aggregates," *American Journal of Sociology* 82 (1976):86–110, and Harries, *Crime and Environment.*

3. Clifford Shaw and Henry McKay, *Juvenile Delinquency in Urban Areas* (Chicago: University of Chicago Press, 1942).

4. For reviews of intra-urban delinquency research, see John Baldwin, "Ecological and Areal Studies in Great Britain and the United States," in *Crime and Justice: An Annual Review of Research* (Chicago: University of Chicago Press, 1979); Ruth Kornhauser, *Social Sources of Delinquency* (Chicago: University of Chicago Press, 1978); and Chris Dunn, "Crime Area Research," in *Crime: A Spatial Perspective* (eds.) Daniel Georges-Abeyie and Keith Harries (New York: Columbia University Press, 1980) pp. 5-25.

5. For reviews of city-level crime studies, see Harries, *Crime and Environment*; James Byrne, "Ecological Correlates of Property Crime in the United States: A Macroenvironmental Analysis," Ph.D. dissertation (Newark: Rutgers University, 1983).

6. U.S. Department of Justice, Department of Justice Statistics, *Report to the Nation on Crime and Justice: The Data* (Washington, D.C.: U.S. Government Printing Office, 1983) p. 13.

7. Ibid. For more comparisons of urban, suburban, and rural crime rates and trends, see John H. Laub and Michael J. Hindelang, *Juvenile Criminal Behavior in Urban, Suburban, and Rural Areas* (Washington, D.C.: U.S. Government Printing Office, 1980); Gibbs, *Crimes Against Persons*.

8. See also Claude Fischer, "The Spread of Violent Crime from City to Countryside: 1955-1975," *Rural Sociology* 45 (1980):417-431.

9. See John Herbers, "Growth in Rural Regions Brings Rapid Crime Rise," *The New York Times*, November 4, 1979:26.

10. In fact, evidence suggests that crime rates in central cities are beginning to decrease, while suburban and rural crime continues to rise. See John Herbers, "Decline in Crime Rate is Reported: May Aid Renewal of Central Cities," *New York Times*, June 5, 1978: 1, 36.

11. Louis Wirth, "Urbanism as a Way of Life," *American Journal of Sociology* 44 (1938):1-24.

12. See the overview of the Wirthian model in Claude Fischer, "Toward a Subcultural Theory of Urbanism," *American Journal of Sociology* 80 (1975):1319-1341.

13. The primary adherent of compositional theory is Herbert Gans, *The Urban Villagers* (New York: Free Press, 1962). Compositional theory has also been referred to as the *non-ecological* position, since it assigns no independent causal status to ecological variables. For more details, see James Byrne, "Cities, Citizens, and Crime: The Ecological/Non-Ecological Debate Reconsidered," in *The Social Ecology of Crime*, (eds.) James M. Byrne and Robert J. Sampson (New York: Spring-Verlag, 1985).

14. For an explicit review of the connections between compositional theory and crime and deviance, see Fischer, "Toward a Subcultural Theory"; John H. Laub, "Urbanism, Race, and Crime," *Journal of Research in Crime and Delinquency* 20 (1983):183-198; Byrne, "Cities, Citizens, and Crime."

15. Laub, "Urbanism, Race, and Crime."

16. See also Robert A. Gordon, "Prevalence: The Rare Datum in Delinquency Measurement and Its Implications for the Theory of Delinquency," in *The Juvenile Justice System*, (ed.) Malcolm Klein (Beverly Hills: Sage, 1976) pp. 201-284.

17. See Michael J. Hindelang, "Race and Involvement in Common-Law Personal Crimes," *American Sociological Review* 43 (1978):93-109.

18. See Laub, "Urbanism, Race, and Crime," for an examination of compositional theory through an analysis of race-specific offending rates in urban and rural areas.

19. See the review in John Braithwaite, "The Myth of Social Class and Crime Reconsidered," *American Sociological Review* 46 (1981):36-57; Judith Blau and Peter Blau, "The Cost of Inequality: Metropolitan Structure and Violent Crime," *American Sociological Review* 47 (1982):114-129.

20. Relative deprivation theory asserts that the sense of injustice and hostility engendered by inequality and poverty is the primary determinant of criminal violence. See Blau and Blau, "The Cost of Inequality."

21. See D. Timms, *The Urban Mosaic: Towards a Theory of Residential Differentiation* (Cambridge: Cambridge University Press, 1971).

22. S. Box and J. Ford, "The Facts Don't Fit: On the Relationship Between Social Class and Criminal Behavior," *The Sociological Review* 19 (1971):31-52.

23. Robert J. Sampson and Thomas C. Castellano, "Economic Inequality and Personal Victimization: An Areal Perspective," *British Journal of Criminology* 22 (1982):363-385.

24. Michael J. Hindelang, Michael Gottfredson, and James Garofalo, *Victims of Personal Crime: An Empirical Foundation for a Theory of Personal Victimization* (Cambridge: Ballinger, 1978); Lawrence Cohen and Marcus Felson, "Social Change and Crime Rate Trends: A Routine Activities Approach," *American Sociological Review* 44 (1979):588-607; Lawrence Cohen, James Kluegel, and Kenneth Land, "Social Inequality and Predatory Criminal Victimization: An Exposition and Test of a Formal Theory," *American Sociological Review* 46 (1981):505-524.

25. Robert J. Sampson, "Structural Density and Criminal Victimization," *Criminology* 21 (1983):276-293.

26. Stephanie Greenberg, "Fear and Its Relationship to Crime, Neighborhood Deterioration, and Informal Social Control," in Byrne and Sampson, *The Social Ecology of Crime.*

27. See Oscar Newman, *Defensible Space* (New York: Collier, 1972).

28. Dennis Roncek, "Dangerous Places: Crime and Residential Environment," *Social Forces* 60 (1981):74-96.

29. Newman, *Defensible Space.*

30. See also Greenberg, "Fear and Its Relationship to Crime."

31. Sampson, "Structural Density and Criminal Victimization."

32. See Greenberg, "Fear and Its Relationship to Crime."

33. Pamela I. Jackson, "Opportunity and Crime: A Function of City Size," *Sociology and Social Research* 68 (1984):172-193.

34. It should be noted that Jackson's empirical test concerned the effects of the household activity ratio (see Cohen and Felson, "Social Change and Crime Rate Trends") on crime in large and small cities. However, her theoretical argument was sufficiently general, and applied to myriad aspects of the criminal opportunity and routine activities framework.

35. For an overview of the limitations of official data, see Wesley Skogan, "Measurement Problems in Official and Survey Crime Rates," *Journal of Criminal Justice* 3 (1975):17-32; and Robert O'Brien, "Metropolitan Structure and Violent Crime: Which Measure of Crime?," *American Sociological Review* 48 (1983):434-437. Some ecological research has been conducted with the city sample of the NCS surveys (O'Brien, ibid.), but NCS city data are by definition limited to urban centers, and thus cannot address the questions posed in this paper.

36. For additional details of the NCS design and collection procedures, see James Garofalo and Michael J. Hindelang, *An Introduction to the National Crime Survey* (Washington, D.C.: U.S. Government Printing Office, 1977).

37. See W. Webster, *Crime in the United States, 1977* (Washington, D.C.: U.S. Government Printing Office, 1977).

38. See U.S. Bureau of Census, *Public Use Samples of Basic Records from the 1970 Census: Description and Technical Documentation: Technical Report 1* (Office of Budget Management, undated).

39. See Robert J. Sampson, Thomas C. Castellano, and John H. Laub, *Juvenile Criminal Behavior and Its Relationship to Neighborhood Characteristics* (Washington, D.C.: U.S. Government Printing Office, 1981), for a discussion on how cutting points were determined. Because neighborhood characteristics were derived from the 1970 Census, all housing units constructed since then (about 9 percent of the sample) do not have neighborhood characteristic identifiers, and are thus excluded from analysis.

40. Statistical Policy Division, Office of Management and Budget, *Standard Metropolitan Statistical Areas* (Washington, D.C.: U.S. Government Printing Office, 1975).

41. U.S. Bureau of Census, *1970 Census of Population: Supplementary Report*, Series PC S1-7 (Washington, D.C.: U.S. Government Printing Office, 1972).

42. For a complete discussion of the definitions and criticisms surrounding the SMSA concept, see Laub and Hindelang, *Juvenile Criminal Behavior*.

43. See James F. Nelson, "Similarities and Differences in the Relationship of Personal Victimization to Demographic Variables in 26 American Cities," Mimeograph (Albany, New York: Criminal Justice Research Center, 1978).

44. See M. Davidson and J. Toporek, "General Univariate and Multivariate Analysis of Variance and Covariance, Including Repeated Measures," in *BMDP Statistical Software* (ed.) W. Dixon (Berkeley: University of California Press, 1983) p. 393.

45. For example, the NCS place-of-crime-occurrence category, "on street, park, field," representing about 45% of all personal victimizations, does not specify the neighborhood of occurrence. One may be victimized in the street in one's own neighborhood or in the street outside of one's neighborhood.

46. For a review of this literature, see G. Pyle et al., *The Spatial Dynamics of Crime* (Chicago: University of Chicago Department of Geography, 1974); Robert J. Sampson, "The Neighborhood Context of Criminal Victimization," Ph.D. dissertation (Albany, New York: State University of New York, 1983). See also the articles in Simon Hakim and George Rengert, *Crime Spillover* (Beverly Hills: Sage, 1981).

47. See A. Sorensen and K. Taeuber, "Indexes of Residential Segregation for 109 Cities in the U.S., 1940-1970," *Sociological Focus* 8 (1975):125-142.

48. See John H. Laub, "Criminal Behavior and the Urban-Rural Dimension," Ph.D. dissertation (Albany, New York: State University of New York, 1980, pp. 57-58).

49. See Hindelang, Gottfredson, and Garofalo, *Victims of Personal Crime*; Cohen, Kluegel, and Land, "Social Inequality and Predatory Criminal Victimization."

50. Recent examination of NCS data supports these observations. Sampson et. al., *Juvenile Criminal Behavior*, compared rates of victimization for a subset of victimizations that occurred at or near the victim's home (e.g., in own dwelling, in garage or other building on property) with total rates of victimization. As expected, the patterns for "at or near home" rates were reflective of total rates for five neighborhood characteristics. In fact, Sampson ("Structural Density and Criminal Victimization") showed that the "at or near home" patterns for structural density were virtually identical to total patterns, controlling for extent of urbanization. Given the demonstrated strong congruence between "at or near home" and total rates, it was concluded that although some victimizations undoubtedly take place in settings extraneous to the victim's neighborhood, such events do not offset overall *patterns* of relationships. Therefore, in the present study rates of victimization were constructed from total personal victimizations. It is not possible to examine "at or near home" rates because when several neighborhood characteristics are examined simultaneously there are not enough cases to produce reliable rates.

51. See Hindelang, Gottfredson, and Garofalo, *Victims of Personal Crime*.

52. See Cohen, Kluegel, and Land, "Social Inequality and Predatory Criminal Victimization"; Sampson, "The Neighborhood Context of Criminal Victimization."

53. Sex is also an important predictor of victimization risk, but unlike age, it is virtually unrelated to the ecological characteristics studied here.

54. The error term was measured by assuming the third-order interaction (age by poverty by urbanization) was insignificant, and incorporating the resulting sum of squares into the residual sum of squares. This procedure is followed throughout analysis. Also, the interaction of age with urbanization and neighborhood characteristics is not of substantive interest in the present study. Therefore in Tables 1 to 3 all interactions involving age are pooled into the residual sum of squares. Preliminary analysis indicated that the interactions involving age were, as expected, small and for the most part insignificant. See G. Iversen and H. Norpoth, *Analysis of Variance* (Beverly Hills: Sage, 1976) pp. 69–70, for a detailed discussion of the measurement of random error in designs with one observation per cell.

55. The actual value of the overall level of victimization is not of theoretical interest to the present study nor are the actual values of the predicted rates. The overall level is simply a standard against which neighborhood effects react to either increase or decrease the predicted rate. The central research question is how neighborhood characteristics affect victimization rates. This question is most easily answered by examining ratios of effect parameters.

56. This interaction should be viewed with caution. It appears only for violent crimes, where there are measurement problems with race. Hindelang, "Race and Involvement," has shown that NCS measurement bias tends to be greatest for personal crimes of violence reported by black interviewees. Therefore, there are a priori grounds for viewing with suspicion an interaction that appears only for violent crimes and is associated with percent black.

57. Jackson, "Opportunity and Crime."

58. This particular interaction also holds for residential robberies that occur in the victim's home or on surrounding property. See Sampson, "Structural Density and Criminal Victimization."

59. Compare Newman, *Defensible Space*, and Roncek, "Dangerous Places."

60. More detailed analysis than is possible here also revealed that poverty, racial composition, and density predict victimization independent of sex, race, income, and marital status of victim. See Gibbs, *Crimes Against Persons*; Laub and Hindelang, "Juvenile Criminal Behavior"; Sampson, "The Neighborhood Context of Criminal Victimization."

61. See Hindelang, "Race and Involvement."

62. See the discussions in James M. Byrne and Robert J. Sampson, "Key Issues in the Social Ecology of Crime," in Byrne and Sampson, *The Social Ecology of Crime*; Braithwaite, "The Myth of Social Class"; Steven Messner, "Poverty, Inequality and the Urban Homicide Rate," *Criminology* 20 (1982):103–114.

63. See Cohen, Kluegel, and Land, "Social Inequality and Predatory Criminal Victimization"; Sampson, "Structural Density."

64. See Newman, *Defensible Space*; Greenberg, "Fear and Its Relationship to Crime."

65. See Herbers, "Growth in Rural Regions"; Bureau of Justice Statistics, *Report to the Nation.*

Ecological Evidence of the Hardening of the Inner City*

Lyle W. Shannon

Path analysis, an adaptation of multiple regression analysis, is used to describe the changing relationship of juvenile delinquency and adult crime to the ecological structure of Racine, Wisconsin from the 1950s to the 1970s. It is concluded that the process of urban growth and development generates an expansion of delinquency and adult crime in old as well as new areas, and that a disproportionate share of the residents engage in this behavior as an alternate way of responding to changes in the social or economic structure of the community. Examples of this phenomenon include the stabilization of high offense rates in the inner city—or the "hardening" of the inner city—and the increasingly higher rates in interstitial areas.

Delinquency and crime are products of the complex social life of a community. Different types of delinquency and crime are generated in dif-

*The research for this paper was conducted with the support of the National Institute of Justice, Grant Number 79-NI-AX-0081. An earlier version based on a similar analytic approach was included in the author's final report to NIJ, *The Relationship of Juvenile Delinquency and Adult Crime to the Changing Ecological Structure of the City*, October 1981. Dr. James P. Curry, at the time Assistant Research Scientist for the Center, conducted the analysis for the earlier version. Judith McKim, Senior Research Assistant, and Lawrence Haffner, Programmer of the Iowa Urban Community Research Center, assisted in this analysis. Points of view or opinions in this document are those of the author and do not necessarily represent the official position or policies of the U.S. Department of Justice.

ferent social milieus and are as normal to their setting as are other more highly valued behaviors in the larger society. This paper describes the changing relationship of juvenile delinquency and adult crime to the ecological structure of the city.

The analyses that follow were guided by the working hypothesis that social areas with the physical, institutional, and demographic characteristics that have long marked them as areas productive of high rates of delinquency and crime will continue to produce high rates of delinquency and crime as long as they and their residents are unchanged. Furthermore, as areas of deteriorated and overcrowded housing, abandoned buildings, commercial-industrial establishments, numerous taverns, and a population neither integrated into the economy nor into the broader social organization of the community continue to expand or, as new areas develop with comparable characteristics, delinquency and crime will expand as well.

At the same time, this combination of physical, institutional, and demographic characteristics and high rates of delinquency and crime generates population movement. The problem is thus exacerbated, and physical deterioration, institutional change, and the breakdown of social controls expand into new areas; social areas with a tradition of crime, areas in which group values make delinquent and criminal behavior seem the most viable alternative, become even more widespread.[1]

In the analysis to be presented, zero-order correlations are examined to demonstrate the changing relationship of ecological variables to different types of offenses. This precedes the more complex multivariate analyses, thus giving the reader an opportunity to see how relationships change when the interrelationship of ecological variables is taken into consideration. The analysis is also conducted with several offense measures, rates and number of offenses, to be sure that the conclusions are not an artifact of any specific measure. The final analysis leads to the conclusion that prior offense rates are the most powerful determinant of present offense rates.

THE CHANGING CITY

In order to understand the changing spatial patterns of delinquency and crime, their continuities and discontinuities, we must understand how the organization of society and its related ecological structure, although changing in some respects, has sufficient stability to result in the "hardening" of the inner city. The term "hardening" is used to refer to the perpetuation of high in-area and by-residence delinquency and crime, whether represented by number of events in an area or by rates based on the number of persons residing in the area.

At the same time that the inner city has been hardening, has become an area of stable high delinquency and crime rates, other areas (interstitial and transitional) that once had lower rates of delinquency and crime become settings in which higher rates are generated and perpetuated. The latter may have undergone population change or acquired commercial and recreational facilities that invite illegal behavior. Thus, while rates for previous years are the best predictor of future rates because of the hardening phenomenon, they are not perfect predictors—new areas with high rates develop as the conditions that generate high rates appear in the cycle of change.

In the context of this research, the ecological organization of the community refers to the economic base of the community, the types of employment available, the race/ethnic composition of the population, and the distribution of each group within the various sectors of the economy. Changes in ecological organization are indicated by such changes as the proportion of the population employed in various sectors of the economy, the unemployment rate, the race/ethnic composition of the population, changes in land use, and changes in the distribution of the population by place of residence. The ecological structure of Racine, Wisconsin, has been identified for the years 1950, 1960, and 1970 (and to a limited extent for 1980) from block data aggregated into statistical units or subareas: census tracts, police grid areas, natural areas, and neighborhoods. In this analysis neighborhoods are utilized as spatial units.

Measures of delinquency and crime were taken from official police data for the years 1949 through 1979 for the entire city, but it is the three combined cohorts of persons (born in 1942, 1949, and 1955) on whom more detailed data have been obtained. These cohorts are disaggregated to neighborhoods that are utilized for the ecological analyses described in this paper. Although it might seem that there are some problems involved when birth cohorts are combined to produce crime rates for 10-year periods, we found that these rates were comparable to offense rates for the city as a whole during the same periods of time.

Variations in delinquency and crime (as measured by total offense rates for the city or by combined cohorts) between 1949 and 1969 did not coincide with fluctuations in Racine's economy or fit into a patterned lag behind its economic trends. One would expect offenses against property to parallel economic indicators, but neither property offenses in general nor theft alone followed unemployment rates or other measures of the economy's ability to provide jobs. Therefore, there is no support for a simple economic explanation of the rise and fall of property crime rates. Racine experienced rapid growth during the 1950s and early 1960s. This growth was accompanied by increasing individual spatial mobility, as evidenced by automobile registrations and traffic counts, both of which had increased disproportionately to the city's population growth.

The more that the growth and development and the accompanying changes in the social organization of the community are considered, the easier it is to see how delinquency and crime become part of a pattern of change. This change involves decline and deterioration in the inner city and interstitial areas, an outgrowth of expanding residential development and population movement to peripheral areas, as well as commercial and recreational development on the periphery of the city.

THE ECOLOGICAL MODEL

Although many researchers in the past have questioned the viability of aggregate-level research, it has more recently been pointed out that the ecological fallacy is one instance of a family of cross-level observations including the "individualistic fallacy," i.e., inferring the behavior of aggregates from observations of individuals.[2] In addition, a number of statistical treatments have clarified the direction and nature of biases in parameter estimates under different conditions of aggregation.[3] It is our position that aggregate-level analysis has a valid and useful place in the investigation of the relationship between ecology and crime, even though individual variation may be found within the areas of any spatial system.

While the occurrence of crime in an area may have certain consequences for the ecological development of that area, our emphasis is on neighborhood effects, including prior delinquency and crime in the neighborhoods, or delinquency and crime at any given time. More complete explanations of these relationships must ultimately refer to the behavior of the individuals who reside in each area and who may differ in respects that are not captured by the ecological or prior criminal history of the neighborhood.

THE DATA AND VARIABLES

Neighborhood boundaries were delineated to produce 65 relatively homogeneous ecological units, taking into account physical barriers, such as the river, railroads, and major thoroughfares (see Map 1). The results of various analyses led to the conclusion that neighborhoods are more sensitive to changes in the social organization of the community and present a more precise picture of changing patterns of delin-

MAP 1

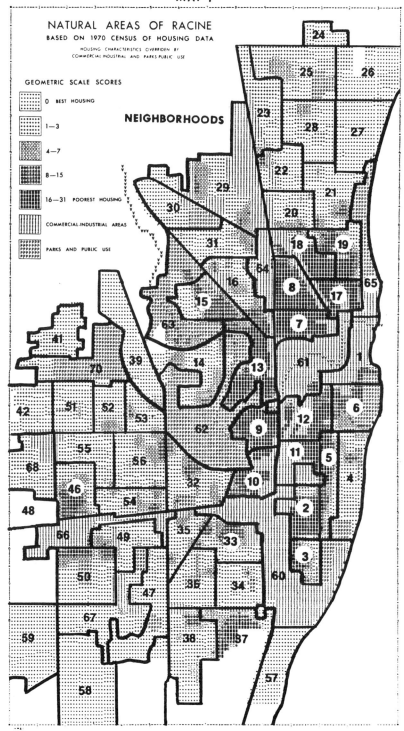

NATURAL AREAS OF RACINE

BASED ON 1970 CENSUS OF HOUSING DATA

HOUSING CHARACTERISTICS OVERRIDEN BY
COMMERCIAL INDUSTRIAL AND PARKS PUBLIC USE

GEOMETRIC SCALE SCORES

0   BEST HOUSING

1—3

4—7

8—15

16—31   POOREST HOUSING

COMMERCIAL-INDUSTRIAL AREAS

PARKS AND PUBLIC USE

NEIGHBORHOODS

quency and crime than do larger spatial units such as census tracts, police grid areas, or natural areas.

Five indicators of neighborhood characteristics are employed in the present analysis: the housing quality factor score, percent black, the land use canonical score, target density, and residential vacancies. ("Target density" refers to the mean number of taverns and liquor stores, grocery and convenience stores, and gasoline stations which serve as targets for crime and in some cases play a part in the generation of delinquency and crime.)

Also included in this analysis are indicators of the three major dimensions of ecological differentiation which have been consistently identified in research on urban areas in the United States: social rank, racial segregation, and family status.[4] An indicator of transiency, a concept that has received some empirical support in previous ecological research, has also been included.[5] The ecological variables and indicators of delinquency and crime are briefly described in Table 1.

While it is possible that the delinquency and crime rates of other Racine cohorts differ, these three cohorts (6,127 persons spanning 30 years of recorded police contacts) exhibit significant similarities in careers and causal processes to suggest that they are not atypical of other cohorts that might have been selected.[6] In fact, combined cohort offense rates paralleled official rates for the entire community. To facilitate time-period analyses and to determine that the cohorts were distributed over the years in a manner roughly proportional to the distribution of Racine's population within each spatial system, the place of residence for each cohort member was coded into a convenient set of periods, 1950 through 1959, 1960 through 1969, and 1970 up to 1976.[7] This indicated the extent to which members of the cohorts moved about the community.[8]

The statistical method employed is path analysis, an adaptation of multiple regression analysis to those cases where the independent variables are proposed to have causal effects on the dependent variables. The path coefficients (ranging between zero and one) represent the proportioned standard deviation unit change in the dependent variable associated with one standard deviation unit change in the dependent variable.

THE MAPPING APPROACH
AS A PRELIMINARY REPRESENTATION OF RELATIONSHIPS

While some people readily grasp the nature of relationships between variables from the statistical analyses, others find maps quite helpful

Table 1

Description of Variables Used
in the Neighborhood-Level Path Analysis*

Variable	Description
Housing Score	Mean housing quality factor score per block. This score is a summary measure of the block's housing quality as measured by dollar value of owner-occupied residences, average rent, percent overcrowded, percent lacking plumbing, and percent renter-occupied.
Percent Black	Mean percent of occupied dwelling units occupied by blacks per block.
Land Use	Mean canonical land use score per block. This score is a summary measure of the neighborhood's characteristics in terms of residential vs. manufacturing land use. A high score indicates a high level of residential land use.
Targets	Mean number of targets per block. This variable is computed as the sum of the number of taverns, grocery and liquor stores, restaurants, and gas stations per block.
Residential Vacancies	Mean percent of residential vacancies per block. Computed as the ratio of occupied units to total units times 100.
Total Contacts	Cohort police contact rate per 100 persons for all types of police contacts.
Non-traffic	Cohort police contact per 100 persons for all types of non-traffic contacts.
Persons	Cohort police contact rate per 100 persons for homicides, felonious sex offenses, assaults, and robberies.
Property	Cohort police contact rate per 100 persons for burglaries, thefts, auto thefts, fraud, and property destruction.
Public Disorder	Cohort police contact rate per 100 persons for disorderly conduct, vagrancy, misdemeanor, sex offenses, weapons offenses, gambling, and obscenity.
Status Offenses	Cohort police contact rate per 100 persons for incorrigibility and truancy.
Moving Vehicle	Cohort police contact rate per 100 persons for moving traffic violations

*The ecological variables are based on block-level data which were aggregated to the neighborhood level. The crime rates are based on individual police contacts which were aggregated according to the neighborhood in which they occurred. The 1950 contacts occurred during the years 1948–59, the 1960 contacts during the years 1960–69, and the 1970 contacts during the years 1970–76. The rates per 100 persons were computed by dividing the number of contacts occurring in a neighborhood by the prior census year population and multiplying by 100.

in showing the nature of spatial relationships. Maps 2 and 3, for example, contrast the distribution of police contacts during the 1970s by place of contact and place of residence, while Maps 3 and 4 indicate that concentration by place of residence is even greater when seriousness of police contact is considered. The changing spatial distribution of police contacts by cohort neighborhood of socialization is shown by Maps 5, 6, and 7. The data clearly indicate that a disproportionate number of the alleged offenses that resulted in police contacts involved residents of the inner city, and that this has increased from cohort to cohort at the same time that population has declined in the area.

While these maps dramatize the concentration of contacts in areas where they are expected to be, they do not tell us the extent to which specific ecological variables are related to the distribution of police contacts by neighborhoods.

THE ECOLOGY OF THE NEIGHBORHOOD AND CRIME

Zero-Order Relationships

In order to provide a better grasp of the data used in the path analysis, brief mention is made of the zero-order correlations of the neighborhood ecological characteristics. That some of these correlations systematically change from 1950 to 1970 forewarns us that the effects of neighborhood characteristics on delinquency and crime are likely to vary between 1950 and 1970. For example, percent residential vacancy had a positive relationship (.192) to housing scores in 1950, but was negative (−.409) in 1960 and even more negative (−.676) in 1970 when the proportion of vacancies greatly increased in the poorest housing areas. Likewise, percent of the occupied dwelling units occupied by blacks had a negative correlation (−.092) with residential vacancy in 1950, but by 1970 those neighborhoods with higher proportions of blacks also had high residential vacancies (.710). The number of targets had a low negative correlation (−.167) with residential vacancy in 1950, but this had increased to a positive correlation (.480) by 1970.

The intercorrelations of various offense rates and number of offenses by neighborhoods also differed from time period to time period for some offenses, notably between the 1950s and 1960s for offenses against the person and status offenses. Otherwise, there was considerable stability between age periods for most offense category spatial patterns. It should be noted that whether rates or sheer number of offenses are considered, a similar pattern of correlations was usually ob-

MAP 2

CONTACTS PER 100 PERSONS BY NEIGHBORHOOD–1970'S

BY NEIGHBORHOOD OF CONTACT

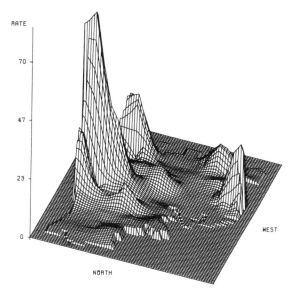

RATE BASED ON COHORT MEMBERS IN NEIGHBORHOOD

MAP 3

MEAN NUMBER OF CONTACTS BY NEIGHBORHOOD–1970'S

BY NEIGHBORHOOD OF RESIDENCE

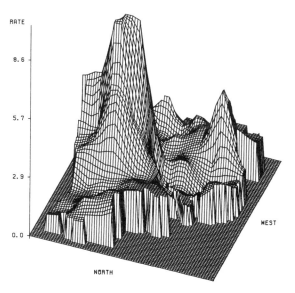

BASED ON COHORT MEMBERS IN NEIGHBORHOOD

MAP 4

MEAN SERIOUSNESS SCORES BY NEIGHBORHOOD--1970'S

BY NEIGHBORHOOD OF RESIDENCE

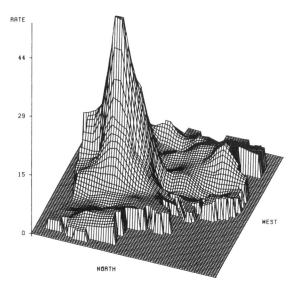

BASED ON COHORT MEMBERS IN NEIGHBORHOOD

MAP 5

MEAN NUMBER OF CAREER CONTACTS: 1942 COHORT

BY NEIGHBORHOOD OF JUVENILE RESIDENCE

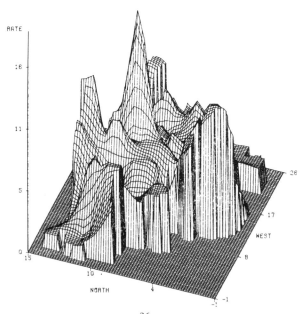

MAP 6

MEAN NUMBER OF CAREER CONTACTS: 1949 COHORT
BY NEIGHBORHOOD OF JUVENILE RESIDENCE

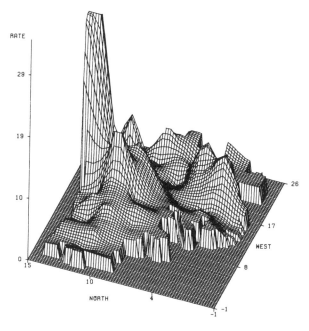

MAP 7

MEAN NUMBER OF CAREER CONTACTS: 1955 COHORT
BY NEIGHBORHOOD OF JUVENILE RESIDENCE

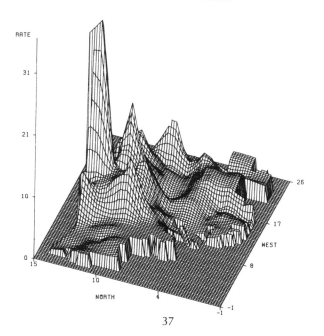

tained. Since we have been concerned about differences in results based on differences in methods by which rates are computed, considerable attention is devoted to this problem.[9]

Table 2 illustrates that housing quality scores have their most consistent relationship with all offense category rates during the 1960 time period. Percent black changed from low correlations with most offense categories in the 1950s to modest positive correlations in the 1960s. By contrast, non-residential land use was inconsistently correlated with offense types in the 1950s, but consistently correlated with all offense types in the 1960s and 1970s. The pattern for targets was even different—there was relatively little correlation during the 1950s, but most offense rates were substantially correlated with targets in the 1960s followed by a decline during the 1970s. Perhaps the most unexpected correlations were those for residential vacancies, which were very low and negative in the 1950s, modest or relatively high and positive in the 1960s for all offense categories, but low again, although still positive, in the 1970s.

Number of offenses presented a somewhat different pattern of correlations with ecological variables than did offense rates. The fact remained, however, that the sheer number of offenses was greatest in the inner city and transitional areas. Differences in the correlations obtained with rates versus numbers require that the analyses which follow must be conducted with each as the dependent variable.

The Path Analysis

Reference has been made to both stability and change over three time periods in the characteristics of neighborhoods—their ecological structure, offense rates, and numbers of offenses. Even with population movement toward the periphery of the city, neighborhood stability in offense rates has been maintained. Evidence of increasing stability was apparent when correlations were based on number of offenses, most correlations between 1960 and 1970 offenses being greater than their 1950–1960 counterparts. We shall later see how this relates to our position that the inner city is "hardening" at the same time that new areas with high offense rates and sheer numbers of offenses are developing.

The 1950s

The path analysis results for the effects of the 1950 ecological variables on the 1950 offense rates are presented in Table 3. Although standard

Table 2
Correlations of Offenses and Neighborhood Characteristics*

	Rates					Number of Offenses				
	Housing Score	Percent Black	Land Use	Targets	Percent Residential Vacant	Housing Score	Percent Black	Land Use	Targets	Percent Residential Vacant
1950s										
Total Contacts	-.503	.108	-.513	.114	-.108	-.448	.202	-.047	.651	-.165
Non-Traffic	-.510	.084	-.520	.049	-.098	-.460	.200	-.040	.638	-.166
Person	.029	-.107	.088	.080	-.027	.019	-.105	.082	.096	-.028
Property	-.471	.079	-.475	.209	-.059	-.398	.099	.053	.681	-.111
Public Disorder	-.369	.094	-.637	.032	-.094	-.303	.159	-.110	.368	-.146
Status Offenses	-.402	-.005	-.208	-.127	-.050	-.494	.229	-.052	.388	-.122
Traffic	-.334	.150	-.344	.274	-.107	-.325	.173	-.057	.558	-.127
1960s										
Total Contacts	-.472	.256	-.480	.573	.555	-.752	.335	-.074	.833	.462
Non-Traffic	-.483	.238	-.518	.544	.526	-.749	.337	-.032	.788	.413
Person	-.434	.351	-.552	.387	.625	-.552	.319	-.037	.436	.330
Property	-.422	.225	-.485	.529	.568	-.624	.270	-.101	.730	.477
Public Disorder	-.451	.174	-.456	.532	.409	-.732	.319	-.010	.788	.344
Status Offenses	-.524	.290	-.646	.419	.461	-.606	.284	.027	.576	.218
Traffic	-.428	.271	-.338	.591	.573	-.634	.280	-.155	.798	.498
1970s										
Total Contacts	-.400	.230	-.576	.219	.159	-.693	.458	-.134	.422	.544
Non-Traffic	-.418	.214	-.513	.274	.186	-.675	.462	-.097	.433	.550
Person	-.409	.298	-.414	.156	.152	-.591	.484	-.045	.258	.478
Property	-.224	.129	-.446	.309	.004	-.365	.233	-.133	.507	.234
Public Disorder	-.437	.254	-.495	.251	.213	-.680	.525	-.111	.384	.614
Status Offenses	-.514	-.256	-.491	.267	.212	-.559	.375	.024	.197	.398
Traffic	-.334	.242	-.649	.116	.104	-.671	.397	-.228	.349	.465

*Offenses per 100 population and number of offenses

tests of significance are reported, it is recognized that such tests are not entirely appropriate for these data since the cohorts constitute populations rather than probability samples.

The housing quality factor score has a significant effect on three delinquency rates during the 1950s, those for total contacts, non-traffic offenses, and juvenile status offenses. The sign of the coefficients (−.412, −.492, and −.742) indicates that the higher the housing quality, the lower the offense rate. There was only one significant effect on number of offenses, that being negative for status offenses. This finding is noteworthy since individual-level analyses in recent years have shown rather consistently that the less serious offenses such as status offenses are not related to the individual's social class,[10] although serious offenses, whether they be based on official or self-report data, are so related.

Four of the path coefficients between percent black and offense rates were statistically significant, those for total offense, non-traffic offenses, property offenses, and public disorder offenses. The higher the percent black, the lower the crime rate. Since this finding is not consistent with other research,[11] there are two points to consider. First, an examination of the zero-order correlations shows that this is due to the intercorrelations among the independent variables. For example, the zero-order correlation of percent black with all offense rates is low, whereas it is −.488 with the housing quality factor score. In substantive terms, this means that although there was virtually no zero-order relationship between neighborhood racial composition and delinquency during the 1950s, when neighborhood socioeconomic status and other variables are held constant, neighborhoods with a high concentration of blacks tend to have lower delinquency rates. It is possible that this result reflects the process of neighborhood cohesion since, during the 1950s, blacks represented a small proportion of the total population in Racine and tended to be concentrated in a few areas. It must also be noted that there were no significant path coefficients between percent black and number of offenses, and that, with one exception, these were also negative. This was the opposite or the zero-order correlations which were in all instances except one positive. Here again, holding neighborhood socioeconomic status constant presented a different picture of the relationship of percent black to number of offenses.

The land use canonical score is related to five indicators of delinquency: rates for total contacts, non-traffic contacts, property, public disorder, and traffic offenses. The signs of all these coefficients are negative, which means that the higher the level of residential land use in a neighborhood, the lower the delinquency rate. Since our land use

Table 3

Path Analysis Results for 1950 Cohort Crime Rates and Numbers

Independent Variables[1]	Total Contacts	Non-Traffic	Person	Property	Public Disorder	Status Offenses	Traffic
			Dependent Variables				
				Offense Rates			
Housing Score	−.412*	−.492*	.032	−.320	−.122	−.742*	−.047
Percent Black	−.282*	−.298*	−.139	−.324*	−.277*	−.196	−.147
Land Use	−.498*	−.469*	.013	−.510*	−.760*	.045	−.444*
Targets	.014	−.085	.141	.181	.085	−.439*	.310
Residential Vacancies	−.178	−.163	−.019	−.125	−.272*	.013	−.171
R^2[2]	.386*	.418*	−.090	.341*	.478*	.265*	.158*
				Number of Offenses			
Housing Score	−.136	−.180	.033	−.145	−.073	−.474*	.010
Percent Black	−.127	−.128	.147	−.222	−.064	−.013	−.094
Land Use	−.108	−.081	.001	−.022	−.163	.115	−.162
Targets	.623*	.586*	.161	.688*	.346*	.144	.597*
Residential Vacancies	−.073	−.066	−.021	.005	−.120	.021	−.079
R^2[2]	.392*	.377*	−.086	.442*	.074	.190*	.251*

[1] The ecological variables were measured in 1950.
[2] R^2 adjusted for degrees of freedom.
*Statistically significant at the .05 level or beyond.

score is also a proxy for family status, these data suggest that neighborhoods with a high proportion of residences experienced a lower delinquency rate. Another interpretation is that residential areas serve as "guardians" against the intrusion of delinquency and crime.[12] This would explain the negative relationship between land use and property offenses which we might expect to be positive if residential dwellings were major targets for offenses such as burglary and if the land use score simply measured the availability of targets. These coefficients were consistent with the zero-order correlations. On the other hand, land use did not produce a single significant path coefficient (most had the same signs as for rates) with number of contacts. In other words, there was less relationship between residential land use and number of offenses than between residential land use and rates.

The finding that the mean number of targets in a neighborhood is significantly related to status offense rates may be surprising. However, consider that the 1950 rates are based only on juvenile offenses, which are more likely to be committed in neighborhoods of residence and which include such targets as convenience stores and gasoline stations, as mentioned earlier and detailed in Table 1. We shall see whether analysis of offense rates with a large adult component sheds a different light on this issue. On the other hand, targets and number of offenses produced five significant positive coefficients consistent with the zero-order correlations, all of which were also positive. Therefore, regardless of the relationships obtained with a rate based on population, targets did generate significantly large numbers of offenses, with the exceptions of offenses against the person and status offenses.

Finally, we find that residential vacancies are, with the exception of public disorder offenses, unrelated to the 1950 offense rates and number of offenses. This is essentially as they were at the zero-order level. Thus, residential vacancies (an indicator of transiency), net of land use and housing quality, may not have much effect on juvenile offense rates—or on number of offenses.

The independent variables together accounted for significant proportions of the variance in total offense rates, and non-traffic, property, public disorder, and traffic offenses. Still, only 38 percent of the variance for total offenses was accounted for by these ecological variables. With the exceptions of property and traffic offenses, the independent variables accounted for essentially the same or a lesser amount of the variance in the number of offenses.

To summarize, analysis of the 1950 contact rates shows that the most important effects are associated with land use, followed by housing quality and percent black. The higher the level of residential land use in a neighborhood, the lower the offense rate. The higher the proportion of dwelling units occupied by blacks, and the higher the quality of the housing, the lower the offense rates. Number of offenses was best accounted for by the presence of targets.

The 1960s

Table 4 presents results of the analysis of the effects of the 1960 ecological variables on the 1960 offense rates. Both juveniles and adults are represented since persons from the three cohorts range in age from 6 through 27. The pattern of relationships in Table 4 is quite different

Table 4

Path Analysis Results for 1960 Cohort Crime Rates and Numbers

Independent Variables[1]	Total Contacts	Non-Traffic	Person	Property	Public Disorder	Status Offenses	Traffic
				Dependent Variables			
	Offense Rates						
Housing Score	−.053	−.117	−.127	−.016	−.112	−.291	.064
Percent Black	−.147	−.196	−.052	−.171	−.221	−.195	−.055
Land Use	−.300*	−.376*	−.217*	−.308*	−.397*	−.566*	−.152
Targets	.419*	.370*	.095	.385*	.425*	.156	.481*
Residential Vacancies	.248	.190	.396*	.296*	.052	.034	.332*
R^2[2]	.457*	.455*	.419*	.436*	.382*	.495*	.439*
	Number of Offenses						
Housing Score	−.507*	−.576*	−.581*	−.375*	−.538*	−.543*	.266*
Percent Black	−.074	−.057	.016	−.107	−.039	.009	−.096
Land Use	.360*	.408*	.380*	.293*	.372*	.349*	.198
Targets	.452*	.376*	−.023	.410*	.434*	.232	.553*
Residential Vacancies	.305*	.280*	.315*	.367*	.173	.095	.313*
R^2[2]	.831*	.791*	.344*	.613*	.756*	.443*	.678*

[1] The ecological variables were measured in 1960.
[2] R^2 adjusted for degrees of freedom.
*Statistically significant at the .05 level or beyond.

from those found in Table 3. It must be remembered, of course, that seven neighborhoods which now had a sufficient population to produce a valid rate were added to the analysis in 1960. In 1950 only juvenile offenses were measured.

Rather than discussing these differences at length, let it simply be said that the ecological variables now account for an even greater proportion of the variance in neighborhood delinquency and crime rates. The R^2's indicate that 46 percent of all offenses are accounted for by these variables. When number of offenses is considered, even larger amounts of the variance (83% of total contacts) are accounted for.

In a second analysis, the 1950 offense rate was added to the analytical scheme as an independent variable for all neighborhoods that had rates in both 1950 and 1960. The effects of the 1950 offense rates on the 1960 rates were sufficient to equal or exceed the effect of ecological variables on the total offense rate, non-traffic offenses, offenses against property, and traffic offenses, i.e., the prior offense rate had significant effects that were greater than any of the ecological variables for these offenses. In fact, only target density remained as having consistently significant effects on offense rates. It is important to emphasize that these effects are found when the intervening ecological characteristics are held constant, and therefore they represent the direct effect of the prior offense rate. Finally, the explanatory power of the equations with 1950 rates included (except for offenses against persons) was considerably higher than those shown in Table 4—74 percent of the variance for total offenses now being accounted for, and ranging to a high of 85 percent for traffic offenses. Little or no improvement in accounting for number of offenses was made by inclusion of the 1950 rates in the equation (with the exception of traffic offenses). As a matter of fact, significant effects remained for all ecological variables except percent black for total contacts.

To summarize, since the effects of 1950 rates are net of the 1960 ecological variables, this indicates that a tradition of delinquency and crime has been developing in certain neighborhoods. Furthermore, since few important effects of neighborhood socioeconomic status, racial composition, land use, or residential vacancies remain when other factors—such as previous offense rate and targets—are held constant, the "hardening" concept becomes even more attractive as an explanation of continuities in delinquency and crime rates. In terms of sheer numbers of offenses, however, all neighborhood characteristics except percent black continue to have important effects on the distribution of delinquency and crime.

The 1970s

Table 5 presents the results of the path analysis of the 1970 offense rates; another 11 peripheral neighborhoods had been added to the analysis as a consequence of city growth. One of the differences from the previous results is the stronger influence of the housing quality score on the offense rates; the higher the quality of the housing in a neighborhood, the lower the offense rate. For both rates and number of offenses the path coefficients are now quite consistent with the zero-order correlations.

Table 5

Path Analysis Results for 1970 Cohort Crime Rates and Numbers

Independent Variables[1]	Total Contacts	Non-Traffic	Person	Property	Public Disorder	Status Offenses	Traffic
Offense Rates							
Housing Score	−.339*	−.361*	−.435*	−.198	−.378*	−.532*	−.278*
Percent Black	.058	−.003	.261	.095	.053	.051	.150
Land Use	−.494*	−.426*	−.277*	−.418*	−.389*	−.353*	−.584*
Targets	.151	.206	.053	.376*	.155	.161	.053
Residential							
Vacancies	−.298	−.253	−.416*	−.474*	−.244*	−.342*	−.350*
R^2[2]	.370*	.326*	.257*	.303*	.304*	.382*	.437*
Number of Offenses							
Housing Score	−.614*	−.582*	−.546*	−.301*	−.520*	−.621*	−.641*
Percent Black	.105	.116	.298*	.064	.165	.202	.065
Land Use	.128	.163	.220*	−.016	.159	.275*	.010
Targets	.143	.155	−.032	.479*	.055	−.065	.097
Residential							
Vacancies	.015	.038	−.037	−.248	.155	−.071	−.059
R^2[2]	.484*	.477*	.383*	.253*	.500*	.337*	.415*

[1] The ecological variables were measured in 1970.
[2] R^2 adjusted for degrees of freedom.
*Statistically significant at the .05 level or beyond.

There are still no significant relationships between percent black and offense rates, although number of offenses against the person is now positively associated with percent black. It is important to note that the sole significant relationship of percent black is to number of offenses against persons in the 1970s.[13] The commonly accepted view of a relationship between race and crime may, at the neighborhood level, be one that reflects evolving patterns of racial segregation and concentration as well as the dynamics of intergroup relations.

Although Table 5 reveals that significant amounts of the 1970 neighborhood offense rate variation were accounted for by the ecological variables, they did not account for as much of the variation as had been accounted for in 1960. Similarly, the ecological variables accounted for less of the variation in number of offenses for all types of offenses except those against persons than previously.

Again, there was a significant level of stability in the various offense rates; neighborhoods with a high level of a given type of crime during the 1960s tended to have a high level of that type of crime during the 1970s. The increase in stability was especially apparent for offenses against persons, which showed no evidence of stability from the 1950 to 1960 decade but did between 1960 and 1970. The rate for 1960 offenses against persons accounted for 59 percent of the variance in 1970 neighborhoods.

The addition of the 1960s offense rates increased the amount of the variance that was accounted for to 85 percent for total offense rates *and* number of offenses. In every case the effect of prior time period rate overshadowed the ecological variables even more than when the 1950s rates were added to the equation that accounted for the 1960s rates. This also became the case for addition of the 1960s rates to the equation for number of offenses in neighborhoods for the 1970s. Only for property offenses did the ecological variables continue to have significant effects.

To summarize, it is clear that neighborhood socioeconomic status, as measured by the quality of housing, emerges as an important influence on the delinquency and crime rate during the 1970s. Neighborhood racial composition is related only to number of offenses against persons. A high level of residential land use is associated with low offense rates, but also with a high number of offenses against persons and status offenses. A high target density is associated only with offenses against property. Residential vacancies show anomalous relationships with most offenses, but these may be explained by changes in the location of high vacancy areas which have not been consistent with changes in offense patterns. Finally, from 1960 to 1970, there is evidence of considerable stability in the delinquency and crime rate and net of ecological characteristics (as there was at the zero-order level). The explained variances for rates with prior rates included are even higher than for the 1960s with the 1950s included. The total explained variances for number of offenses are also about as high or higher than for the 1960s.

The next logical step was to conduct the same analysis but to include both offense rates for the 1950s and 1960s at the same time in order to ascertain the cumulative effect of these rates on the 1970s rates. This is followed by inclusion of both rates and the ecological characteristics of neighborhoods to determine the extent to which all could account for variance in the 1970s rates. This analysis included, of course, only those 47 neighborhoods for which offense rates had been ascertained for three time periods.

Rates for the 1950s and the 1960s accounted for 81 percent of the total contact rates, 88 percent of the non-traffic rates, 83 percent of the public disorder rates, but declined to only 41 percent for traffic offenses. These figures lend further evidence to the considerable continuity in the pattern of high and low offense rates in those neighborhoods of the city that have been in existence over the years. When the ecological variables were added, 92 percent of all offenses were accounted for, as were 93 percent of the non-traffic offenses, 90 percent of the traffic offenses, 88 percent of the public disorder offenses, 87 percent of the property offenses, 69 percent of the offenses against persons, and 58 percent of the status offense rates. The ecological variables that remained considerably significant were land use and residential vacancies.

It is clear from these results that there is no single dimension of neighborhood ecology that acts as a consistent, powerful predictor of delinquency and crime rates or number of offenses over time. Nonetheless, most of the relationships which do appear are more or less consistent with previous ecological analyses. For example, the importance of neighborhood housing quality in its influence on 1970 crime rates is consistent with a class interpretation of ecological crime differences. However, this did not appear in both earlier decades and is consistent with more recent findings at the individual level, which suggests a problematic class differential over time.[14]

The Possibility of Alternate Explanations

We have utilized three time periods and have examined rates and number of offenses for these periods with prior rates (1950 and 1960) included as independent variables and excluded, and have found differences in significant effects on rates and number of offenses with some continuity as well as discontinuities. This suggests that there are variables the effects of which change with changes in the social organization and ecology of the city. There are, however, several other plausible explanations for these findings. The first is that the apparent instability in causal effects is due to methodological problems. For example, it is possible that measurement error has caused our estimates of the path coefficients to fluctuate from period to period.

Another possibility is that multicollinearity among the independent variables causes some fluctuation in the estimates. We have previously discussed the correlation between the housing quality factor score and percent black in this context. During the 1950 period this correlation was −.488. It was −.584 during the 1960 period and −.531 during the 1970 period. Thus, while there is some variation in the source of multicollinearity, it would not account for the apparent reversal of the relationship between percent black and offenses against persons from the 1960 to the 1970 period.

From a more substantive point of view, the data reflect changes in the relationship between ecological structure and crime over time.[15] In addition, as we have argued elsewhere, there appears to be a "hardening" of the ecological structure over time, more specifically a hardening of the inner city. This is especially apparent where inner city areas experience a loss of population and residential land use, and where patterns of racial segregation have become entrenched.[16] We have previously stated that the meaning of residential vacancies in a "hardened" ecological context is different from that in more fluid, developing areas. Residential vacancies are possible in any area where residential units exist, but taking residential vacancies as a measure of transiency and postulating an invariant relationship between transiency and crime over time are not consistent with our data.

Because of our concern about the possibility that measurement error for rates could influence the findings, we decided to compare rates derived in three different ways (rates based on the census population of each neighborhood at the start of each time period; rates based on the mid-decade census population; and rates based on the number of persons from each cohort who resided in the neighborhood during each decade). Would the findings be consistent for total police contacts when the findings from each of these rates were compared?

The results are presented in Table 6. With one exception, for each time period there are significant path coefficients for the 1950s and 1960s for land use and target density regardless of the delinquency rate utilized. Land use became less important as a significant determinant and targets became more important. Percent black and housing scores decline in importance when the basis for calculating the rates is mid-decade or cohort population. Turning to the 1970 data, land use again becomes the most significant determinant, and housing score replaces target density as a significant ecological variable. One must note, however, that the pattern of coefficients does vary somewhat depending on the rate utilized even though there is considerable consistency in which variables produced statistically signficant coefficients.

When the 1950 offense rates were included in the 1960 analysis, they overshadowed the ecological variables regardless of the offense rate utilized; in fact, there was relatively little more of the variance accounted for by the ecological variables (targets remained the only vari-

Table 6

Path Analysis Results for 1950, 1960, and 1970 Cohort**

	Residential Vacancies	Land Use	Targets	Percent Black	Housing Score			Ecology R²		
	Independent Variable Path Coefficients[1]								Explained Variance[2]	
1950 Rates										
Start	.030	−.572*	.102	−.260	−.281			.337*		
Mid-decade	.014	−.673*	.317*	−.215	−.182			.496*		
Cohort	.030	−.487*	.444*	−.192	−.087			.295*		
1960 Rates										
Start	.248	−.300*	.419*	−.147	−.053			.457*		
Mid-decade	.259	−.292*	.403*	−.074	−.033			.470*		
Cohort	.249	−.075	.607*	−.247	.045			.412*		
1970 Rates										
Start	−.297	−.494*	.151	.058	−.339*			.370*		
Mid-decade	−.257	−.473*	.140	.023	−.340*			.338*		
Cohort	−.074	−.323*	.246*	−.182	−.322*			.227*		
						1950 Rate			1950 Off. Rate R²	1950 Rate + Ecology R²
1960 Rates										
Start	.121	−.177	.416*	−.101	−.008	.550*			.499*	.738*
Mid-decade	.188*	−.008*	.286*	.018	.076	.694*			.756*	.842*
Cohort	−.011	.023	.266*	−.105	.060	.853*			.879*	.920*
						1960 Rate			1960 Off. Rate R²	1960 Rate + Ecology R²
1970 Rates										
Start	−.162	−.189*	−.058	.170*	−.083	.816*			.802*	.850*
Mid-decade	−.061	−.147*	−.052	.098	−.022	.891*			.900*	.923*
Cohort	−.100	−.254*	.047*	.083	−.036	.879			.852*	.925*
						1950 Rate	1960 Rate		50–60 Off. Rate R²	50–60 Rate + Ecology R²
1970 Rates										
Start	−.225*	−.306*	−.098	.139*	−.115	−.004	.809*		.814*	.923*
Mid-decade	−.063*	−.237*	−.080	.074	−.111*	.015	.855*		.906*	.962*
Cohort	−.087	−.269*	.044	.035	−.044	.307*	.582*		.895*	.963*

[1]The independent ecological variables were measured in 1950, 1960, and 1970.

[2]All R² adjusted for degrees of freedom.

*Statistically significant at the .05 level or beyond.

**Total offense rates based on neighborhood population at start of 10-year period, at mid-decade, and on number of cohort members residing in neighborhood.

able with significant effects) than was accounted for by prior offense rate.

When first the 1960 and then the 1950 and 1960 offense rates were included in the 1970 analysis, land use continued as the only ecological variable with significant effects regardless of rate utilized. Although there were some irregular significant differences in the effects of the ecological variables, the high percentage of the variance accounted for by prior rates was quite consistent regardless of rate utilized with few exceptions. That 85 to 95 percent of the variance was accounted for in all cases for the 1970s when prior rates and ecology had been introduced, gave added strength to the position that continuities in neighborhood rates, however calculated, led to similar conclusions.

Summary of the Path Analyses

A multivariate analysis has been presented of the interrelationships among various indicators of delinquency, crime, and ecology at the neighborhood level of analysis. These analyses are important because they show the influences of the independent "causal" variables net of other variables in the model over an extended period of time. The analyses also operationalize some of the major theoretical concepts employed in various ecological studies of juvenile delinquency and crime. In addition, the total offense rate was decomposed into various components to ascertain whether or not there were systematic differences in the way the various dimensions of ecology related to different types of delinquency and crime at the aggregate level.

Although the effects of ecology on delinquency and crime were generally consistent with previous theory and research, the patterns found differed from period to period. Thus, we found that a high level of residential land use was associated with a low offense rate during each decade, but there were less consistent effects for housing quality on delinquency rates during the 1950s, practically none on delinquency and crime during the 1960s, followed by the emergence of more consistent effects during the 1970s. Significant effects of targets were greatest during the 1960s, while residential vacancies had effects in both the 1960s and 1970s. In sum, there were changes in the relationships among ecological structure, delinquency and crime during the period(s) that the city had been experiencing the transition from a generally low delinquency and crime rate to a high delinquency and crime rate.

We have reported elsewhere that analysis of the effects of crime on the subsequent ecological characteristics of the neighborhoods where the crime occurred shows that any such effects are scattered and weak at best.[17] It is evident that the relatively simple kinds of ecological effects many persons have come to accept as sure consequences of spatial continuities in delinquency and crime are much more complex. Oversimplification leads to conclusions that may point to oversimplified solutions to the problems of delinquency and crime. Although the effects of high offense rates on the ecology of the community may be quite modest, this is not to say the individuals who must live and work in high crime areas do not perceive and react to that crime.[18]

THE AREAS WHICH HAVE HARDENED

It is clear that there has been a hardening of the inner city at the same time that delinquency and crime rates have been increasing in peripheral and outlying areas. In the course of examining a multitude of tables and maps it became obvious that there were 12 inner city and interstitial or transitional neighborhoods (11 were inner city) whose residents were becoming increasingly differentiated from those in other areas, and that there had also been an increasing focus on youthful offenders in these neighborhoods. Without exception, these neighborhoods also had the high in-neighborhood offense rate which was utilized as the dependent variable in the analyses. They are the neighborhoods numbered 1, 2, 6, 7, 8, 9, 10, 11, 12, 13, 17, and 18 on Map 1. Only the latter is considered interstitial or in transition. Note that all had a preponderance of poor housing, but that some were also predominantly commercial-industrial areas with relatively little housing. All had declining populations from 1950 to 1980. Residential vacancies ranged from 4 percent to 14 percent and were generally higher than in other neighborhoods by 1970. All except one had numerous taverns, and all except two had relatively high target densities. The percent of the population that was black in 1970 ranged from less than 2 percent to 80 percent, although all but three of these neighborhoods had more than 10 percent black population.

Three other inner city and eight interstitial or transitional areas were included in the 16 other neighborhoods which either had relatively high in-neighborhood police contact rates or relatively high police contact rates by their residents. These areas were spatially located adjacent to the inner city or were peripheral neighborhoods in which commercial-industrial development was taking place and which now included establishments such as taverns, that could well be the locus of delinquent and criminal behavior. None, however, had the multitude of ecological characteristics differentiating the 12 neighborhoods with high in-neighborhood and by-residents police contact rates from other neighborhoods in the community. The very highest police contact rates continue over the years in the inner city, although higher rates have more recently been developing in interstitial and outlying transitional areas.

SUMMARY

Areas of delinquency and crime are being solidified and there are other areas in the process of transition to high delinquency and crime. But we cannot conclude that if an ecological indicator seems to account for much of the variance in delinquency and crime, it is a specific causal variable. It may well be that it is simply one of many indicators of the real antecedents of delinquency and crime.

That target density has sometimes accounted for significant amounts of the variance in property offense rates and number of property offenses tells us that a large segment of the offenses in some neighborhoods is probably target-related, directly or indirectly. It does not tell us that a policeman at the door of every store is the answer. Similarly, that residential vacancy is high and becomes higher in these areas does not tell us that eliminating residential vacancies will have an impact on delinquency and crime rates. It is what these vacancies represent that is most important. In some areas they represent an attitude, and in others a change in the present population, that make delinquent and criminal behavior more normal forms of behavior in an increasingly larger residential area.

Notes

1. See Solomon Kobrin, "The Conflict of Values in Delinquency Areas," *American Sociological Review* 16 (1951):653–661.

2. William S. Robinson, "Ecological Correlations and the Behavior of Individuals," *American Sociological Review* 15 (1950):351–357; Erwin K. Scheuch, "Social Context and Individual Behavior," in Mattei Dogan and Stein Rokkan, eds., *Quantitative Ecological Analysis in the Social Sciences* (Cambridge, MA: M.I.T. Press, 1969), 135–155.

3. Leigh Burstein, "Assessing Differences Between Grouped and Individual-level Regression Coefficients," *Sociological Methods and Research* 7 (1978):5–28; and Michael T. Hannon and Leigh Burstein, "Estimation from Grouped Observations," *American Sociological Review* 39 (1974):374–392.

4. Brian J.L. Berry and John D. Kasarda, "The Social Areas of the City: From Classical to Factorial Ecology," *Contemporary Urban Ecology* (New York: Macmillan, 1977), 108–157.

5. Roland J. Chilton, "Continuity in Delinquency Area Research: A Comparison of Studies for Baltimore, Detroit, and Indianapolis," *American Sociological Review* 29 (1964):71–83.

6. The first cohort, born in 1942, consists of 1,352 persons, the second, born in 1949, consists of 2,099, and the third, born in 1955, consists of 2,676. The married names of females in each cohort were obtained from the records of the County Health Department. Their names have been followed through the Records Division of the Racine Police Department in order to ascertain the total number and nature of police contacts of each person in each cohort.

7. The address at which the offender lived at time of contacts and addresses where contacts occurred were coded for each contact so that addresses of offender and place of contact could be computer-related to or mapped with controls for any other variable.

8. The extent of the mobility problem is revealed by the fact that even after collapsing census tracts into six groups of similar tracts, 52.1% of the 1942 cohort had moved to a different SES level tract between 1950 and 1960 and 38.5% of the 1949 cohort had done so. When police grid areas were collapsed in six similar levels the figures were 53.5% for the 1942 cohort and 35.8% for the 1949 cohort. Slightly larger figures were obtained when the natural areas and neighborhoods were collapsed into seven levels.

9. Rates have been compared in a variety of ways: (1) the number of offenses in a neighborhood was divided by the census population of the neighborhood at the begin-

ning of the period; (2) the number of offenses was divided by the census population at mid-period; (3) the number of offenses was divided by the number of cohort members residing in the neighborhood during the 10-year period. During the 1950s the two rates based on census populations had a Pearsonian coefficient or correlation of .852. The beginning census population correlated with the cohort population based rates .771 and the mid-period rate correlated with the cohort population based rates .895. For the 1960s the correlations were .988, .921, and .907. For the 1970s the correlations were .994, .907, and .926.

10. Delbert S. Elliott and Suzanne S. Ageton, "Reconciling Race and Class Differences in Self-reported and Official Estimates of Delinquency," *American Sociological Review* 45 (1980):95–110; John W.C. Johnstone, "Social Class, Social Areas and Delinquency," *Sociology and Social Research* 63 (1978):49–72.

11. Michael J. Hindelang, "Race and Involvement in Common Law Personal Crimes," *American Sociological Review* 43 (1978):93–109.

12. Lawrence E. Cohen and Marcus Felson, "Social Change and Crime Rate Trends: A Routine Activity Approach," *American Sociological Review* 44 (1979):588–608.

13. Research designed to answer questions at the individual level may or may not produce different findings from research designed to answer questions with aggregated ecological data. When Blau and Blau recently investigated violent crime with 1970 data for the largest 125 American metropolitan areas they found that socioeconomic inequality between races, as well as economic inequality in general, increases rates of violent crimes. When economic inequalities are controlled, the proportion of blacks in a metropolitan area has little influence on the rate of violent crime. Judith R. Blau and Peter M. Blau, "The Cost of Inequality: Metropolitan Structure and Violent Crime," *American Sociological Review* 47 (1982):114–129. See also, A.D. Watts and T.M. Watts, "Minorities and Urban Crime: Are They the Cause or Victims?" *Urban Affairs Quarterly* 16 (1981):423–436; D.W. Roncek, "Dangerous Places: Crime and Residential Environment," *Social Forces* 60 (1981):74–96.

14. Charles R. Tittle, Wayne J. Villemez, and Douglas A. Smith, "The Myth of Social Class and Criminality: An Empirical Assessment of the Empirical Evidence," *American Sociological Review* 43 (1978):643–656.

15. As suggested by Leo Schuerman and Solomon Kobrin in "Ecological Processes in the Creation of Delinquency Areas," paper presented to the Seventy-Sixth Annual Meeting of the American Sociological Association, Toronto, August 28, 1981.

16. Darden, for example, has shown that racial segregation remained at a high level in Pittsburgh from 1930 to 1970. Although considerable change in residential segregation by census tracts took place between 1930 and 1970, racial change occurred only in tracts that were less than one percent segregated at the outset. Joe T. Darden, *Afro-Americans in Pittsburgh: The Residential Segregation of a People* (Lexington, MA: D.C. Heath, 1973). While some blocks and neighborhoods in Racine without black residents in 1950 had them by 1960 and even more by 1970, most inner city blocks that were black remained black and some became even more so if they continued to be residential blocks. Reference is, of course, to more than residential segregation when speaking of the "hardening" of the inner city and refers to its physical characteristics and its offense rates as well.

17. Lyle W. Shannon, *The Relationship of Juvenile Delinquency and Adult Crime to the Changing Ecological Structure of the City*, Final Report to the National Institute of Justice, Grant #79-NI-AX-0081, October 1981.

18. Wesley G. Skogan and M.G. Maxfield, *Coping with Crime: Individual and Neighborhood Reactions* (Beverly Hills: Sage, 1981).

Crime in Suburbia, 1960–1980

John M. Stahura
and C. Ronald Huff

Societal concern with crime has been directed primarily toward central city crime, with relatively little attention to crime in the suburbs. In an earlier study, we found that the traditionally observed inverse linear relationship between crime rates and distance from the central city may no longer be valid, due to the diffusion of "transitional" areas into the suburban fringe. This paper extends our research on a cohort of 247 American suburbs by analyzing the spatial distribution of suburban violent and property crime rates, their ecological determinants, and their persistence. Both suburban crime rates and their determinants exhibit substantial stability over three time points (1960, 1970, and 1980), reflecting the persistence of suburban populations and their characteristics. A theoretical explanation of this phenomenon is offered and policy implications are discussed.

Studies of the metropolitan distribution of crime and delinquency have generally concluded that crime tends to be concentrated in the central cities of metropolitan areas and that as one moves further into the metropolitan fringe, rates of crime decrease.[1] However, this inverse linear relationship between areal crime rates and distance from the central city, though common, never has characterized all metropolitan areas in the United States,[2] nor has it satisfactorily fit the distribution of metropolitan crime in other nations.[3]

The inverse relationship between crime rates and distance from the central city is commonly explained via the Burgess zonal model of urban ecology,[4] which posits that central cities have the highest rates of crime because they have the highest concentrations of social and physical conditions commonly associated with crime. In an earlier paper, we offered the alternative explanation that crime tends to occur at disproportionately high rates in areas where traditional social norms operate ineffectivoly due to changes in population size or changes in the employment/residential balance.[5] We further concluded that the inverse relationship between crime rates and distance from the central city may no longer be valid, since "transitional" areas, formerly a part of the central city, have diffused into the suburban fringe.

In our 1979 study we demonstrated that the inverse linear gradient relating crime to distance from the central city no longer adequately described the distribution of crime in American metropolitan fringes.[6] We found that the innermost metropolitan fringe zone had the lowest crime rate of several contiguous distance zones, with the remaining distance zones exhibiting the expected inverse gradient pattern.

TRACKING SUBURBAN CRIME: THE THIRD DECADE

The purpose of this research is to examine trends in suburban violent and property crime rates between 1960 and 1980. This research extends our earlier studies of suburban crime rates, which explored a number of important issues, such as: (1) spatial distribution of crime rates by distance zone;[7] (2) the ecological determinants of crime rates;[8] and (3) the persistence of crime rates.[9] The present study builds upon our earlier research and extends our analysis by analyzing 1980 data for a cohort of 247 American suburbs that have been in existence since 1960 and for which all relevant data are available. In the following three sections, we examine the spatial distribution of suburban violent and property crime rates, their ecological determinants, and their persistence. These sections address different theoretical issues and employ somewhat different methodologies; however, all three analyses utilize the same sample cohort of 247 suburbs.

The units of analysis, then, are 247 American suburbs for which Uniform Crime Reports (UCR) data and other relevant data were available for 1960, 1970, and 1980.[10] A suburb is defined as an incorporated place with a population of at least 10,000 located within the bounds of a standard metropolitan statistical area (SMSA) but outside of its central city. The 1960 UCR reported crime data only for places larger than 25,000; this limited the number of suburbs that could be included in our longitudinal study.[11] In 1960, there were in the United States 247 suburbs with populations exceeding 25,000 for which crime data were reported.

SPATIAL DISTRIBUTION OF SUBURBAN CRIME

Table 1 presents violent and property crime rates by distance zone for the 247 sample suburbs in 1960, 1970, and 1980. Data for Los Angeles and Chicago suburbs are presented separately. Metropolitan fringe distance zones are defined by successive ten mile increments (0–10 miles, 10–20 miles, 20–30 miles, and 30–40 miles). Suburban distance from the central city is operationally defined as the number of miles from the center of the central business district to the approximate geographical center of the suburb. It should be noted that the ecological meaning of distance has changed in recent decades due to new developments in transportation systems. However, utilizing the same ten mile zone operationalizations for 1960, 1970, and 1980 facilitates the longitudinal analysis of crime rate gradients. Operational definitions of all study variables appear as footnotes to Table 2.

Table 1

Suburban Violent and Property Crime Rates*

| | All Suburbs | | | | | | |
| | Property Crime | | | Violent Crime | | | N |
Distance	*1960*	*1970*	*1980*	*1960*	*1970*	*1980*	
0–10	1809	3046	5607	69	294	479	113
10–20	2212	3345	5768	84	311	497	91
20–30	2384	3167	6918	98	297	626	27
30+	2472	3261	6412	80	304	603	16
	Los Angeles						
Distance							
0–10	3185	2483	6317	139	264	1072	4
10–20	4483	5149	6473	195	657	843	14
20–30	3439	3299	7496	125	227	661	7
30+	2873	3759	6952	91	276	729	9
	Chicago						
Distance							
0–10	1378	1380	4088	172	168	234	3
10–20	1644	2468	4997	92	302	319	10
20–30	1577	1312	6875	25	34	673	3
30+	1459	2432	5943	98	385	455	4

*Per 100,000 by distance zone, in miles, for all suburbs, Los Angeles, and Chicago suburbs, 1960–1980.

As indicated by the aggregate data in Table 1, several interesting changes have occurred in suburban crime gradients since 1960. In 1960, there was essentially a direct relationship between crime rates and distance from the central city; that is, crime rates increased as distance from the central city increased. By 1970 the pattern we previously observed had emerged for both property and violent crime rates;[12] the 10–20 mile distance zone had the highest crime rates, with the innermost zone (0–10 miles) having the lowest crime rates. By 1980 a shift had occurred, with the 20–30 mile zone exhibiting the highest property and violent crime rates and the two inner zones having considerably lower crime rates. Furthermore, the area with the highest crime rates continued to decentralize further into the fringe, apparently at a rate of about 10 miles per decade.

In considering these findings, we stress that our study does not take into account crime rates for new suburbs added since 1960, nor do we consider suburbs with populations under 25,000. We would assume that both new suburbs and smaller suburbs would have substantially lower crime rates than do the older and larger suburbs represented in Table 1. The impact of including newer and smaller suburbs is therefore unknown. However, in an earlier study we demonstrated that the inclusion of newer and smaller suburbs did not radically alter the stated fringe crime gradients, but did cause some reduction in the average crime rates.[13]

Table 1 also demonstrates that crime rates have been increasing rather dramatically in all distance zones. The increases in crime appear to be largest in the outer distance zones, especially the 20–30 mile zone, where property and violent crime increased by 118 percent and by 111 percent, respectively, between 1970 and 1980. In general, the crime rate increases for each distance zone between 1970 and 1980 surpass the increases between 1960 and 1970. This pattern appears to agree with data contained in a report recently released by the Bureau of Justice Statistics; that report indicates that aggregate suburban crime in the United States grew dramatically during the period 1973–1981 (violent crime rose by 50%, property crime by 36%).[14]

Table 1 also reflects crime data for Chicago and Los Angeles suburbs by distance zone for 1960–1980. The gradients for Chicago and Los Angeles are generally similar, with certain exceptions. The violent crime gradient for suburban Los Angeles represents a departure from the general gradient pattern, inasmuch as the innermost zones reflect the highest violent crime rates. In fact, violent crime in the 0–10 mile zone grew by 306 percent between 1970 and 1980. The meaning of this variation is unclear, but given the small number of suburbs per zone included in our study, it is amazing that there is not more fluctuation in the gradient pattern. Overall, the gradient patterns for Chicago and Los Angeles mirror the aggregate suburban patterns, with the greatest inter-urban differences being in the rates of crime, rather than its spatial distribution. Suburban Chicago has lower than average crime rates, while crime in the Los Angeles suburbs tends to be above average. Again, the small number of suburbs in the Chicago and Los Angeles distance zones necessitates caution in interpreting the results, but the individual metropolitan findings tend to support the findings for the aggregated sample.

ECOLOGICAL DETERMINANTS OF SUBURBAN CRIME

During the 1970s a number of studies identified significant predictors of areal crime rates.[15] Building on these studies, we specified a causal model of suburban crime rates in which these predictors of crime were causally ordered.[16] We now turn to a comparison of the significant determinants of crime rates between 1960 and 1980 for our sample cohort of 247 suburbs. Since our intent is to compare determinants across time, multiple equation causal models are not specified. Instead, single equation multiple regression models are specified for each time point for which previously identified ecological determinants of crime rates are regressed on both property and violent crime rates.

We hypothesize that both violent and property crime rates are related to a number of population and environmental characteristics that have been shown to be significant predictors of crime in previous studies. Specifically, census region, population density, suburban age, industrial/commercial concentration, percent black population, and percent high income population have all been shown to be related to property and violent crime rates. Each of these predictor variables warrants further discussion.

Regional differences in suburbanization patterns of various population groups[17] and employment activities,[18] as well as regional differences in other suburban characteristics such as age and size of suburb,[19] have been demonstrated. In a prior study we also found that region was positively related to both suburban violent and property crime rates (southern and western suburbs had higher crime rates).[20] As a result, southern and western suburbs are hypothesized to be related to both violent and property crime rates.

A number of studies have also demonstrated the relationship between population density and crime rates.[21] It is argued that density can affect crime rates in several ways. For example, high density conditions may result in social pathology due to greater levels of stress and anxiety produced in such environments, and high density conditions also permit residents to have greater access to information about what opportunities (both legitimate and illegitimate) are available. We hypothesize, then, that density is positively related to both property and violent crime rates.

Suburban age is used as an indicator of the degree of physical deterioration of an area, including housing, services, streets, and other facilities. This deterioration can lead to lower levels of security due to inferior services and unresponsive government. It also means fewer legitimate outlets through which individuals can vent their frustrations in socially acceptable ways. Thus, suburban age is hypothesized to affect positively suburban crime rates.

The degree of commercial/industrial concentration (employment specialization) is also hypothesized to be related to suburban crime. The "E/R ratio," which reflects the degree to which a suburb may be characterized as an "employing" or a "residential" suburb, has been used in a number of studies as an indicator of suburban functional role.[22] The E/R ratio is calculated by dividing the number of local jobs in manufacturing, retail and wholesale trade, and service industries by the number of local residents employed in the same industries. A high E/R ratio indicates a substantial concentration of employment in a suburb and also a net influx of commuters who work there. Commuters who are not residents tend to inflate an area's crime rate by increasing the number of potential victims and offenders in that area. Since official crime rates are based on resident (*de jure*) populations, areas with larger daytime (*de facto*) populations are likely to have artificially high crime rates. The E/R ratio can therefore be positively related to suburban crime rates.

Measures of income and black population composition have often been shown to be significant predictors of crime when using official crime statistics.[23] In this study income is measured as that proportion of the population that is considered "high income" ($10,000 or more in 1960; $15,000 or more in 1970; and $20,000 or more in 1980). We hypothesize that in high income suburbs, residents are less likely to have an economic motivation for crime; therefore, there should be a negative relationship between income and crime rates. We also know that blacks are victimized disproportionately and, as a result, areas with large black populations are likely to have higher crime rates.[24]

Table 2 presents the results of a multiple regression analysis of suburban violent and property crime rates for 1960, 1970, and 1980. The analysis at each time point is for the same sample of 247 suburbs.

Table 2

Correlates of Suburban Violent and
Property Crime Rates, 1960–1980;
Standardized (Beta) and Unstandardized (B)
Regression Coefficients and Multiple R's (n = 247)

Violent Crime Rates[a]

	1960		1970		1980	
	Beta	B	Beta	B	Beta	B
Region[c]	.25*	45.580*	.11*	73.229*	.26*	289.689*
Density[d]	.14*	.003	.08	.005	.16*	.018*
Age[e]	−.07	− 2.830	−.08	−11.629	−.09	−21.079
E/R Ratio[f]	.22*	.409*	.18*	1.246*	.20*	2.210*
% Black[g]	.42*	5.235*	.57*	17.944*	.50*	25.143*
Income[h]	−.04	− 2.554	−.11*	−29.372*	−.15*	−62.358*
Intercept	–	14.756	–	137.148	–	306.528
R^2	.38	–	.45	–	.50	–

Property Crime Rates[b]

	1960		1970		1980	
	Beta	B	Beta	B	Beta	B
Region	.58*	1520.634*	.41*	1203.498*	.29*	1737.830*
Density	.14*	.035*	.05	.014	−.03	− .019
Age	−.06	− .645	.03	23.756	−.04	−49.456
E/R Ratio	.19*	5.209*	.15*	4.811*	.21*	12.546*
% Black	.03	6.179	.38*	54.342*	.27*	71.574*
Income	.05	49.392	.02	25.968	−.01	−23.599
Intercept	–	1355.712	–	1515.942	–	4432.100
R^2	.43	–	.35	–	.22	–

*Statistically significant at the .05 level.

[a] Suburban violent crime rates per 100,000 population in 1960, 1970, 1980. Violent crime is defined as the number of rapes, homicides, assaults, and robberies.

[b] Suburban property crime rates per 100,000 population. Property crime is defined as the number of larcenies, thefts, auto thefts, and burglaries per 100,000. Arson was not included so that 1980 would be comparable to 1960 and 1970.

[c] Region is coded 1 = South and West; 0 = Northeast and North Central.

[d] Density is population per square mile in 1960, 1970, and 1980.

[e] Age is the number of decades that a suburb has had a population of 10,000 or more.

[f] E/R ratio is the employment/residence ratio. E/R ratio for 1958 is taken from the Municipal Yearbook and is calculated for 1967 and 1977 using the Censuses of Business and Manufacturers and the 1970 and 1980 Censuses of Population.

[g] % Black is percent black in 1960, 1970, and 1980.

[h] Income is the percent earning over $10,000 in 1960; $15,000 in 1970; and $20,000 in 1980.

61

Both standardized (beta) and unstandardized (B) coefficients are reported for several reasons. Within-equation comparisons should be based on standardized coefficients, while across-equation comparisons should be based on unstandardized coefficients. We shall consider the question of *overall* differences among 1960, 1970, and 1980 determinants of crime in a later section.

With respect to violent crime rates, a number of significant effects emerged from our analysis. Region, employment specialization, and percent black population were found to be statistically significant predictors at each time point, while density and income were significant in two of the three equations. With the exception of suburban age, all of the effects are in the hypothesized directions and are consistent across the three time points. Since violent crime rates have increased considerably over the time period, the interpretation of B-values across time becomes somewhat difficult. However, analyzing the relative increases in B-values may be of use in assessing the relative importance of determinants. For example, the impact of employment specialization (E/R ratio) has remained significant, but has not substantially increased in explanatory importance in analyzing violent crime (1960: B-value=.409; 1970: 1.246; and 1980: 2.210). The effect of income, however, appears to have increased (from −2.554 in 1960 to −62.358 in 1980) and has become statistically significant. Region has had a significant effect throughout the period, but between 1970 and 1980, its relative effect increased. The effects of percent black population, density, and suburban age, on the other hand, have not increased disproportionately. Overall, the general pattern is one of relative stability of crime determinants.

To determine whether these factors were significantly different across time points, an additional analysis was conducted. An aggregate sample was created that included each of the suburbs at each time point (n=247 × 3=741), and a time variable was created. Another regression analysis was carried out in which the time variable was included as a predictor of violent crime to test for a main effect of time. In addition, first-order interactions between time and the determinants of violent crime were included in the equation. We found that time had no main effect, nor was there evidence of any first-order interaction effects. If there were significant interactions, we would expect to find significant changes in the determinants of violent crime across time. While this analysis does not rule out the possibility that other factors may have become important in the explanation of violent crime rates during the 20 year interval, it does show that there has been little change in the determinants of crime utilized in this study.

The determinants of property crime rates are also presented in Table 2. For each year, statistically significant effects of region and employment specialization (E/R ratio) were observed, in addition to the effects of percent black population (1970 and 1980) and the effect of density (1960). Again, the effects were remarkably consistent across time, both in sign (direction of influence) and in statistical significance. The only variable that exhibited a disproportionately large change in its unstandardized coefficients was percent black population between 1960 and 1970 (from 6.179 to 54.342); this variable also assumed statistical significance. The income variable had no significant effect on property crime in any of the three equations. Finally, we tested for significance of difference between equations. Again, we found no direct effect of time and no evidence of interaction between time and any of the determinants of property crime.

PERSISTENCE OF SUBURBAN CRIME RATES

In an earlier study, we demonstrated the longitudinal persistence of suburban violent crime rates between 1960 and 1970.[25] However, the persistence of suburban property crime rates has not been addressed in the literature, nor has an analysis of crime rate persistence between 1970 and 1980 been undertaken. We next consider these questions, utilizing our sample cohort of 247 suburbs. In addition, we attempt to replicate our earlier analyses of the determinants of change in suburban crime rates.[26]

The persistence/change in suburban property and violent crime rates between 1960 and 1980 is analyzed by specifying several lagged, endogenous-variable models in which current levels of crime are related, in multiple regression equations, to earlier levels of crime. Specifically, we hypothesize that 1970 and 1980 violent and property crime rates are positively related to 1960 and 1970 crime rates, respectively. This yields the four equations reported in Table 3. The rationale for the above hypotheses follow (1) from our earlier findings that violent crime rates are highly persistent,[27] and (2) from the literature on suburban persistence. Several researchers have demonstrated the persistence of socioeconomic characteristics of suburban populations,[28] and one of the authors earlier demonstrated the persistence of suburban functional roles (the employing/residential character of the suburb).[29] We therefore argue that crime rates are also a persistent characteristic of urban subareas and that suburbs will exhibit persistent crime patterns.

In earlier research we isolated several determinants of change in

Table 3

Persistence of Suburban Violent and
Property Crime Rates, 1960–1980;
Standardized (Beta) and Unstandardized (B)
Regression Coefficients and Multiple R's

	1970 Violent Crime		1980 Violent Crime	
	Beta	B	Beta	B
1960 violent crime	70*	2.722*	–	–
1970 violent crime	–	–	.63	1.005*
Income	–.06	–16.675	–.14*	–59.414*
E/R ratio	.07	.521	.10*	1.067*
Intercept	–	72.026	–	379.191
R^2	.55	–	.51	–
	1970 Property Crime		1980 Property Crime	
	Beta	B	Beta	B
1960 property crime	.58*	.707*	–	–
1970 property crime	–	–	.43*	.808*
Income	–.08	–102.541	–.04	–75.752
E/R ratio	.08	2.638	.13*	8.048*
Intercept	–	1626.555	–	3213.265
R^2	.38	–	.24	–

*Statistically significant at the .05 level of probability.
a Operationalizations of the variables are included in Table 2 footnotes.

violent crime rates.[30] Specifically, suburban income and employment specialization were found to be significantly related to crime rate change. Suburbs that are employment centers are expected to exhibit the greatest increases in crime rates, whereas suburbs with high status populations are expected to exhibit the smallest increases in crime.

The four equations to be analyzed are: (1) 1970 violent crime rates related to 1960 violent crime rates, 1960 income, and 1958 employment specialization; (2) 1980 violent crime rates related to 1970 violent crime rates, 1970 income, and 1967 employment specialization; (3) 1970 property crime rates related to 1960 property crime rates, 1960 income, and 1958 employment specialization; and (4) 1980 property crime rates related to 1970 property crime rates, 1970 income, and 1967 employment specialization. The effects of 1960 variables on 1970 crime rates and the effects of 1970 variables on 1980 crime rates (controlling for 1960 and 1970 crime rates, respectively) can be interpreted as determinants of change in crime rates.[31]

Table 3 reflects the persistence of both violent and property crime rates. With respect to violent crime, the beta for the 1960 to 1970 equation is .70 (B=2.722), and it is .63 (B=1.005) for the 1970 to 1980 equation. Violent crime rates are highly persistent during both decades. However, there is some evidence to suggest that violent crime rates are becoming less persistent. The smaller B and beta for the 1970–1980 equation indicates that less of the variance in 1980 violent crime rates can be accounted for by earlier crime rates than was the case for the 1960 to 1970 equation. Additionally, the roles of both suburban population income and employment specialization have increased in importance in the last decade. For the 1960–1970 equation neither income (beta=−.06; B=−16.675) nor employment specialization (beta=.07; B=.521) was a statistically significant determinant of change. However, both doubled in size and became statistically significant in the 1970–1980 equation.

Several interesting differences exist between property crime rates and violent crime rates. First, property crime rates are not as persistent as are violent crime rates. The beta for the 1960–1970 equation is .58 (B=.707), while the beta for the 1970–1980 equation is .43 (B= .808). Both sets of coefficients are statistically significant, but both are considerably smaller than their corresponding coefficients in the violent crime rate equations. Second, the impact of income on change in property crime rates has diminished, while it has increased substantially for violent crime rates. This finding may be attributable to a bimodal trend in crimes of theft. According to a recent report by the Bureau of Justice Statistics, the highest rates of theft victimization in the United States are for those earning less than $3,000 per year (a victimization rate of 106 per 100,000) and those earning more than $25,000 per year (104 per 100,000).[32]

The analysis of change in property crime rates may best be summarized by underscoring the similarity between the two equations. The level of persistence between 1960–1970 and 1970–1980 has not changed appreciably. In making comparisons across equations (samples), the unstandardized coefficient is the appropriate basis for comparison, and the unstandardized coefficients in these equations are very similar (.707 and .808), despite an apparent difference in the standardized coefficients (.58 and .43). Finally, employment specialization has emerged as a significant predictor of change in property crime rates. The analysis here suggests that suburbs that function as employment centers have more rapidly increasing property crime rates than do other suburbs. Income, on the other hand, is not significantly related to changes in property crime rates.

THEORETICAL AND POLICY-RELEVANT IMPLICATIONS

Perhaps the most striking finding to emerge from this study is the similarity in empirical results across time for each of the three analyses. Both crime rates and their determinants exhibited substantial stability across time. Some of this stability may be attributed to the fact that no new suburbs were included at any stage of our analysis. However, we believe that most of the stability in results is attributable to the persistent nature of suburban populations and their characteristics.

Suburbs are persistent in both population and functional characteristics, and it appears that a suburb's crime rate is also a relatively unchanging property of the area. We believe that a suburb, in its earlier stages of settlement, develops a characteristic profile (including relative crime rates), which tends to persist over time. A suburb's housing stock and employment specialization determines to a large extent what types of people are attracted to it. For example, if a suburb develops in response to an industry employing a substantial number of blue collar workers, it will develop housing in accordance with blue collar demand. This "ecological niche" of a suburb attracts an initial population mix with characteristics that will either be conducive or non-conducive to criminal activity; thus, once a suburb's population is established, a level of "acceptable" criminal activity also is established. This level of crime in suburban social structure persists because a suburb's population composition affects both the formal and the informal social control mechanisms within the community. As long as a suburb's population mix persists, so will the established level of crime.

There appear to be many self-perpetuating aspects involved in the dynamics of suburban crime persistence. A recent study analyzing residential mobility in Dallas County, Texas, is instructive in this regard.[33] The researcher isolated the effects of property crime from other neighborhood characteristics, especially social composition and accessibility to the workplace. In testing his causal model he found that crime deters potential new residents (both whites and blacks), especially those with children and those who are relatively affluent. Crime did not increase the likelihood that resident families would move away, but it deterred new families from moving into the neighborhood. Given such dynamics, it is hardly surprising that crime rates persist. As indicated in a recent discussion of crime control and the quality of life, the symbolic evidence of crime (property destruction, for example) signifies to all that a neighborhood is in decline, is deteriorating.[34] This affects the residents' perceptions of the quality of life and their chances of being victimized. Further, if property is not replaced and renovation is not undertaken, such areas actually tend to attract fewer fiscal resources, even though they need such resources more than do other areas.

The results in Table 2 support our argument inasmuch as "ecological niche" characteristics such as density, region, and employment specialization remain significant determinants of both violent and property crime rates across time. The population characteristics vary somewhat, but percent black population is a persistent determinant of both violent and property crime rates. Suburbs that are denser and more employment-oriented tend to attract people who are less concerned with the social control of behavior within the community; this lack of social control is, in turn, associated with higher rates of crime. If the people who are attracted to denser, employing suburbs are also black, even higher crime rates may be expected. This is not to say (nor could it reasonably be argued) that black population composition is a direct cause of higher crime rates; rather, the presence of a large black population in a racially mixed community creates a situation of subcultural conflict wherein community social control mechanisms are further broken down because of the racial boundaries and conflicts that exist in our society.

If we are correct in our analysis of suburban crime rates, and if these crime rates tend to persist, what reasonable strategies can be suggested for crime rate reduction (crime prevention)? First, it is important to emphasize the distinction drawn between those variables that have explanatory, theoretical power and those that are policy-relevant (both manipulable and efficacious). For example, we know that the great majority of crime in the nation is committed by males. Theoretically, then, the inclusion of a sex variable in crime theories makes perfect sense. However, since we are not prepared to kill all newborn males or in any other way eliminate the attribute of "maleness" in society, that factor is not particularly policy relevant because it is not manipulable.

The data in Table 3 offer some basis for developing a strategy, inasmuch as several determinants of crime rate change are isolated. However, neither of these variables (income and employment specialization) are easily manipulable. Also, these two variables have offsetting effects on crime rates. For example, increasing local employment has the effect of increasing crime rates, whereas higher status populations are associated with lower crime rates.

One alternative (though perhaps not very pragmatic) that may affect crime rates is to distribute more evenly employment and social class groups across suburbs. For example, if jobs, blacks, and low income populations could be more evenly distributed across the suburbs of a metropolitan area, some overall reduction in crime rates could result, assuming that the basic social control mechanisms of the low crime suburbs were able to persist. One way to accomplish this goal is to make suburban housing available to all status and racial groups and to disperse employment opportunities more evenly throughout the suburban fringe.

More equal distribution of employment opportunities has been an important public policy issue in the United States for the past two decades. However, the specific problem of youth unemployment has received far less attention. Since 1958, we have never had fewer than one million unemployed 16–24 year olds in any year. Growth in jobs in the United States during the 1960s benefited adults more than young people.[35] While the aggregate unemployment rate has often declined, the relative position of teenagers has deteriorated since 1963 (in that year alone, the number of unemployed 16–19 year olds increased by one-fourth).[36] American cities have been unable to cope effectively with this problem. It appears that suburbs (especially those with large populations of minority youth) are now facing a similar challenge. If the experience of the cities is any indicator of the scope of this problem, we believe that the infrastructure and social institutions of these suburbs will continue to have a very difficult time responding to these demands.

Since a disproportionate amount (50%) of property crime in the United States is committed by offenders less than 20 years old (property crime arrests peak at age 16),[37] it seems advisable to include this subpopulation in metropolitan crime prevention planning. While we cannot simply apply aggregate national data to the crime problems of the suburbs, more equal distribution of employment opportunities, minority subpopulations, and low income groups could have at least three significant effects: (1) It would help weaken the criminogenic influences that exist in high crime neighborhoods by providing more legitimate opportunities; (2) It would benefit the entire metropolitan area, rather than one specific jurisdiction; and (3) It would avoid the crime displacement effects that often accompany crime prevention efforts focused on only one area of the metropolis.

Effective crime prevention in the suburbs must be predicated on the recognition that the suburbs and the central city together comprise a functionally integrated network. Each political jurisdiction in that network must be understood to represent an important "partner" if crime prevention planning is to be effective. We cannot afford to continue the inefficiency and failure of isolated crime control efforts. It is time to treat crime and delinquency as metropolitan problems and to develop, through integrated crime prevention planning, local crime control policies for the entire metropolitan area.

Notes

1. C.R. Shaw, *Delinquency Areas* (Chicago: University of Chicago Press, 1929); N.S. Hayner, "Delinquency Areas in the Puget Sound Region," *American Journal of Sociology* 39 (1933):314–328; C.R. Shaw and H.D. McKay, *Juvenile Delinquency and Urban Areas*, rev. ed. (Chicago: University of Chicago Press, 1969); C.F. Schmid, "Urban Crime Areas: Part I," *American Sociological Review* 25 (1960):527-542; F.H. McClintock, *Crimes of Violence* (London: MacMillan and Company, 1963); J.R. Lambert, *Crime, Police, and Race Relations: A Study in Birmingham* (London: Oxford University Press, 1970).

2. H.A. Scarr, *Patterns of Burglary* (Washington, D.C.: U.S. Government Printing Office, 1972).

3. A. Todoravich, "The Application of Ecological Models to the Study of Juvenile Delinquency in Belgrade," *International Review of Criminal Policy* 28 (1970):64–71.

4. R.E. Park and E.W. Burgess, *The City* (Chicago: University of Chicago Press, 1925).

5. J.M. Stahura and C.R. Huff, "The New 'Zones of Transition': Gradients of Crime in Metropolitan Areas," *Review of Public Data Use* 7 (1979):41–48.

6. Ibid.

7. Ibid.

8. J.M. Stahura, C.R. Huff, and B.L. Smith, "Crime in the Suburbs: A Structural Model," *Urban Affairs Quarterly* 15 (1980):291–316; C.R. Huff and J.M. Stahura, "Police Employment and Suburban Crime," *Criminology* 17 (1980):461–470.

9. J.M. Stahura and C.R. Huff, "Persistence of Suburban Violent Crime Rates: An Ecological Analysis," *Sociological Focus* 14 (1981):123–137.

10. U.S. Department of Justice, Federal Bureau of Investigation, *Crime in the United States, 1960: Uniform Crime Reports* (Washington, D.C.: U.S. Department of Justice, 1961); ibid., 1971; ibid., 1981.

11. Ibid., 1961.

12. Stahura and Huff, "Zones of Transition."

13. Ibid.

14. U.S. Department of Justice, Bureau of Justice Statistics, *Report to the Nation on Crime and Justice: The Data* (Washington, D.C.: U.S. Department of Justice, 1983), p. 13.

15. R.W. Beasley and G. Antunes, "The Etiology of Urban Crime: An Ecological Analysis," *Criminology* 11 (1974):439–461; K.R. Mladenka and K.Q. Hill, "A Reexamination of the Etiology of Urban Crime," *Criminology* 13 (1976):491–506; K.D. Harries, "Cities and Crime: A Geographic Model," *Criminology* 14 (1976):369–386.

16. Stahura, Huff, and Smith, "Crime in the Suburbs."

17. R. Farley, "The Changing Distribution of Negroes within Metropolitan Areas: The Emergence of Black Suburbs," *American Journal of Sociology* 75 (1970):512–529.

18. B. Berry and J. Kasarda, *Contemporary Urban Ecology* (New York: MacMillan, 1977).

19. J.M. Stahura, "Suburban Change and Development" (Ph.D. diss., Ohio State University, 1975).

20. Stahura, Huff, and Smith, "Crime in the Suburbs."

21. Beasley and Antunes, "Etiology of Urban Crime"; Mladenka and Hill, "A Reexamination of Urban Crime"; Stahura, Huff, and Smith, "Crime in the Suburbs."

22. L. Schnore, "Characteristics of American Suburbs," *Sociological Quarterly* 4 (1963):122–134; J. Logan, "Industrialization and the Stratification of Cities in Suburban Regions," *American Journal of Sociology* 82 (1976):333–348.

23. Beasley and Antunes, "Etiology of Urban Crime"; Mladenka and Hill, "A Reexamination of Urban Crime"; Stahura, Huff, and Smith, "Crime in the Suburbs."

24. T.J. Flanagan and M. McLeod, eds., *Sourcebook of Criminal Justice Statistics— 1982* (Washington, D.C.: U.S. Government Printing Office, 1983), p. 300; Bureau of Justice Statistics, *Report to the Nation*, p. 19.

25. Stahura and Huff, "Persistence of Crime Rates."

26. Ibid.

27. Ibid.

28. R. Farley, "Suburban Persistence," *American Sociological Review* 29 (1964): 38–47; A. Guest, "Suburban Social Status: Persistence or Evolution?" *American Sociological Review* 43 (1978):251–264; J.M. Stahura, "Structural Determinants of Suburban Socioeconomic Compositions," *Sociology and Social Research* 03 (1979):328–345.

29 J.M. Stahura, "The Evolution of Suburban Functional Roles," *Pacific Sociological Review* 21 (1978):432–439.

30. Stahura and Huff, "Persistence of Crime Rates."

31. G.W. Bohrnstedt, "Observations on the Measurement of Change," *Sociological Methodology*, ed. E.F. Borgatta (San Francisco: Jossey-Bass, 1969).

32. Bureau of Justice Statistics, *Report to the Nation*, p. 19.

33. M.T. Katzman, "The Contribution of Crime to Urban Decline," *Urban Studies* 17 (1981):277–286.

34. A.J. Reiss, Jr., "Crime Control and the Quality of Life," *American Behavioral Scientist* 27 (1983):43–58.

35. J.Q. Wilson, *Thinking about Crime* (New York: Random House, 1977), pp. 11–14.

36. U.S. Department of Labor, Bureau of Labor Statistics, *Youth Unemployment and the Minimum Wage*, Bulletin no. 1657 (Washington, D.C.: U.S. Government Printing Office, 1970), p. 5.

37. Bureau of Justice Statistics, *Report to the Nation*, p. 32.

Part 2

Spatial Patterns in
Criminal Behavior

Criminal Mobility and the Directional Component in Journeys to Crime*

C. Michael Costanzo,
William C. Halperin,
and Nathan Gale

In this paper we examine the directional component in journeys to crime. Using a nonparametric method for assessing the spatial autocorrelation of vector data, we test the tendency for nearby criminals to travel in similar directions to commit crime, and conversely whether nearby crimes can be attributed to suspects who have come from similar directions. The empirical evidence across seven crimes suggests an affirmative answer to the first question, but with regard to the latter, the results are less consistent.

Criminal mobility patterns have received a good deal of attention in the recent academic literature. Although descriptive studies dominated the early research in this area, the last decade has seen an intensified effort to model the underlying processes. This paper begins with a review of the modern studies, structured in such a way that the major spatial themes can be identified. We note that distance is the chief spatial variable to which most of that research is addressed. We then undertake an investigation into the influence of direction on criminal

*Partial support for this paper was provided by the National Institute of Justice, grant #82-IJ-CX-0019. The authors gratefully acknowledge the advice of Professors Lawrence Hubert and Reginald Golledge.

mobility, and in particular, we look at the spatial autocorrelation of directions traveled in the commission of criminal offenses.

CRIMINAL MOBILITY RESEARCH

In the traditional ecological approach to analyzing urban crime, emphasis rests on explaining crime patterns by relating the location of criminals to various characteristics of their area of residence, and by linking the location of criminal offenses to attributes of the area in which the crime is committed. For example, in Shaw and McKay's seminal ecological analysis of juvenile delinquency in Chicago, the authors discovered a relationship between delinquency and such variables as substandard housing, poverty, and the population of foreign-born residents.[1] This type of association was also found by Schmid, whose ecological study of Seattle uncovered "urban crime areas" characterized by low socioeconomic status, physical deterioration, high rates of population mobility, and various other factors.[2]

A fundamental problem associated with most ecological analyses is that they assume criminal residence locations and crime sites to be spatially identical.[3] Obviously, this would indicate that occurrence rates may be explained by the same factors that account for the prevalence of criminals in that area; however, it has been suggested that criminal residence patterns and crime occurrence distributions reflect different types of components, such as criminogenic factors that influence individuals in the former case, and target opportunity structure and criminal perception in the latter.[4] Moreover, while many crimes are committed within close proximity to a criminal's residence, it has not been conclusively demonstrated that an assumption of spatial concurrence between crime and criminal, at any level of aggregation, is indeed valid.

This relationship between criminal residence and crime occurrence locations has received considerable attention from environmental criminologists over the past decade. Most of the research has focused on analyzing criminal mobility or, more specifically, the actual journey to crime. One of the earliest studies to examine explicitly the connection between the residences of offenders and the place of their offenses, and one that anticipated the current interest in criminal mobility, was carried out by Lind.[5] He suggested that group crime patterns in Honolulu resulted from a combination of local criminal acts (the "neighborhood triangle of delinquency," or the slum areas in which delinquents

reside) and offenses committed outside the criminal's home neighborhood (the "mobility triangle of delinquency," in which offenders reside
in stable neighborhoods and travel to other areas to commit crime).
Lind attempted to explain these patterns through the notion of neighborhood social control: If a neighborhood is characterized by efficacious
social control, delinquency is curbed and offenders are forced to go outside the neighborhood to commit crime.

Another classic analysis was undertaken by White,[6] who investigated the journey to crime in Indianapolis by plotting the distance
from the center of an offender's home census tract to the center of the
tract where the crime occurred. He was among the first researchers to
indicate that criminals travel farther for property crimes than for
crimes against persons, a pattern that has been substantiated in a
number of later studies.[7] Some researchers have also found that the
longer journeys traveled for property offenses tend to yield a greater
"return" than do short trips.[8] Furthermore, Rengert[9] points out that
many journey to crime studies emphasize orientation with respect to
some area of the city, whether it be the Central Business District (CBD)
as in DeFleur,[10] high income residential areas as in Pyle,[11] or more local,
neighborhood areas, such as home/non-home, indoor/outdoor types of
crime occurrences.[12]

In an economic context, criminal mobility can be seen as a component of a criminal production process in which mobile offenders
search among areas or jurisdictions for those locations that yield the
highest net expected returns to criminal activity.[13] In analyzing the
journey to crime from this economic perspective, Hellman posited the
use of a simultaneous equation model to measure the impact of criminal spatial mobility.[14] She also discussed the notion of crime spillover
in economic terms as a negative externality—the criminal moving
from a "home" jurisdiction to another jurisdiction to commit a crime
—and addressed a number of policy implications of criminal mobility.

Another approach to examining criminal mobility, and one that
is associated with a more social psychological perspective, attempts to
relate objective crime patterns to criminals' cognitions of the urban environment. This analytical framework incorporates a number of concepts associated with more general research on environmental perception and cognition: the criminal's "mental map" (or cognitive repre-
sentation), defined as an abstraction reflecting a cross section at one
point in time of the environment as the criminal believes it to be[15]; the
criminal's action space, or the collection of all destinations about
which the offender has information, along with the subjective utility

assigned to those places; and the criminal's activity space, defined as the subset of all urban locations directly contacted by the criminal in his daily activity schedule. One of the first environmental criminological studies to utilize this approach was undertaken by Capone and Nichols.[16] In analyzing the distance biases of robbery offenders in Miami, the authors found a strong relationship between urban structure and criminal mobility. More specifically, they suggested that the distance traveled for robbery is a function of the distribution of opportunities—a subset of the complete urban structure—and their different levels of attractiveness to offenders. A similar study that more directly examined criminals' cognitions was carried out by Carter and Hill, who measured different criminals' evaluations of the same area in Oklahoma City, and how those assessments were related to their locational choice for committing crime.[17] They uncovered strong connections among journeys to crime, criminals' cognitions, and the victimization of targets.

Two articles by Phillips and by Rhodes and Conly relate the distance of the criminal commute to a number of demographic, ethnic, and spatial variables.[18] In Phillips' paper, the distance decay pattern in the length of journey to crime was further substantiated. He also found that mean journey lengths varied according to offense category, age, sex, and race, but that race and the distance of the criminals' residence from the CBD were not important determinants in that variation in the actual distance traveled to commit crime. Rhodes and Conly also examined the correlation between the length of the criminal commute and characteristics of the offender, and expanded their analysis to explore the relationship between journey length and attributes of the victim, the area of criminal residence, and the area where the crime was committed. They further differentiated between two aspects of location attractiveness for criminals, "target attractiveness" and "spatial attractiveness." The former refers to locations with potentially high gain for the offender, and the latter to locations that are generally more familiar to potential offenders. They suggested that criminals travel beyond the least attractive areas (in their study, residential neighborhoods) and search for targets a substantial distance from home. In relating this finding to criminals' cognitions of the urban environment, the authors pointed out that the private nature of residential areas may retard the development of offenders' mental maps, and are thus low on the spatial attractiveness scale.

The concept of attractiveness was also examined by Brantingham and Brantingham.[19] Using a formal deductive modeling procedure, the authors integrated the concepts of motivation and opportunity with notions of mobility and perception, and suggested that crime occurrence is mediated by "perceived opportunity"; this, in turn, is influenced by the objective distribution of opportunities, the structure of the urban environment, and the mobility of the offender. More specifically, their findings imply that potential locations for crime vary with respect to both target and spatial attractiveness. Rengert also investigated the relative attractiveness of an area by considering the accessibility of desirable physical features to potential offenders.[20] He developed an "opportunity structure model" based on gravity and potential formulations, and extended the model to account for spatial choice among alternative target locations. He concluded by emphasizing the need for redefining empirical measures of criminal opportunity structures, and by stressing that these structures should be measured probabilistically along the continuum from inaccessible opportunities (yielding zero probabilities) to extremely accessible opportunities (yielding probabilities close to one).

ACCESSIBILITY AND SPATIAL AUTOCORRELATION

The accessibility of potential offenders relative to target locations can be assessed using a variety of analytical techniques. One such method, multiple regression, has been used to determine the significance of distance from the Chicago CBD to its suburbs with respect to suburban crime patterns.[21] Regression techniques were also employed by Hakim in his investigation of journeys to suburban crime by central city residents.[22] He suggested that property crimes are "exported" from the central city to wealthy, easily accessible communities located near or adjacent to the central city. Although these studies have indicated a definite pattern of criminal movement from the CBD to suburbia, there have been very few attempts to incorporate variables related to inter-suburban criminal mobility.[23]

A number of other researchers have applied various potential models in which the "supply" of criminals at any one point in space is assumed to be a weighted sum of the number of criminals with accessibility to that point. For example, Katzman used a potential model to assess the relationship between crime rates and "potential" variables (associated with total population, teenage population, and poor families) using distance exponents of one, two and three.[24] By analyzing poverty potential, neighborhood wealth, and the local proportion of poor in a multiple regression analysis, the author determined that variations in crime rates, whether related to crimes against property or violent crimes, are very sensitive to variations in poverty potential. Katzman concluded by indicating that externalities, or criminal spill-over, may extend great distances beyond neighborhood boundaries; thus, a higher status neighborhood's crime rate may increase as a result of lower status families settling in a neighborhood several miles away.

One methodology that has received relatively little attention from environmental criminologists is spatial autocorrelation analysis.[25] Spatial autocorrelation is evaluated by assessing the degree to which the observed measurement of a phenomena, e.g., crime rates, in one area corresponds to the observed measurement of that phenomena in neighboring areas. The general evaluation strategy thus involves comparing the structure in some data defined for a set of places with the structure defined by the spatial configuration of those places, and deriving a statistic to assess the correlation between the data structure and the geographic structure.[26]

In his study of municipal crime rates in Los Angeles, Costanzo[27] used a matrix comparison strategy to test for spatial autocorrelation of murders, robberies, and aggravated assaults.[28] The procedure involves comparing a proximity matrix that characterizes the geographical contiguity of places i and j with a proximity matrix that measures the difference between the crime rates of places i and j. The results indicated that there was no significant spatial autocorrelation of crime rates at that level of aggregation.

A somewhat different approach to identifying spatial autocorrelation was developed in Brown's study of suburban crime in Chicago.[29] She integrated traditional spatial autocorrelation measures, specifically Moran's I statistic and Geary's c coefficient, with a spatial autocorrelation analysis of regression residuals. The residual analysis is carried out in two major stages. The first step involves regressing crime rates against independent variables representing the locations of criminals and potential crime sites; the second step involves testing the regression residuals for spatial autocorrelation. If autocorrelation is indicated, the influence of this factor is then removed from the original equation using spatial autoregressive methods. Brown employed this methodology to examine the spatial autocorrelation of both violent and property crime rates for 126 of Chicago's suburbs. The results revealed that although positive spatial autocorrelation exists in the distribution of violent crime—suburbs' violent crime rates were positively correlated with adjacent suburbs' crime rates—it is not a significant factor in the distribution of property crime. She suggested that the nonrandom distribution of violent crime reflects the nonrandom patterning of offender rates, thereby indicating little interjurisdictional spillover of violent crime. Moreover, consistent with other findings on violent crime patterns, the offenses tend to occur in the offender's home suburb.

With regard to property crime distributions, the regression analysis yielded no significant relationship with distance to Chicago. Brown maintained that the absence of spatial patterning for property crime rates would seem to indicate that property crime is interjurisdictional, which is consistent with the notion that criminals generally travel farther for property crimes than for crimes against persons. Brown concluded by relating her results to two probable causes of the increase in suburban crime rates in recent years: first, the migration of minority and low income populations into the suburbs, which tends to cause high offender rates; and second, the suburbanization of manufacturing and retailing activities, which tends to generate higher property crime rates.

DISAGGREGATE ANALYSIS
AND THE DIRECTIONAL COMPONENT

Most analyses of the journey to crime have been carried out at an intermediate level of aggregation. This scale ranges from large subunits, such as municipalities within a city, to smaller subareas, such as neighborhoods or individual city blocks. With respect to criminal mobility, the majority of research has focused on relating criminal residences to crime sites using census tracts, suburbs, or neighborhoods as the lowest level of aggregation. The major problem associated with analysis at this level of aggregation is the familiar notion of the ecological fallacy —the conditions shown to be important at the areal level may not apply at the individual level.[30] Indeed, it has been shown that the degree of spatial autocorrelation of violent crime rates varies with the level of aggregation.[31] It may also be the case that journeys to commit property crime, while not autocorrelated at the areal (or suburban) level, may reflect autocorrelation at a completely disaggregate level.

Another critical problem associated with most journey to crime studies is that they concentrate primarily upon distance as the fundamental behavioral component. It should be emphasized, however, that direction, as well as distance, is implicit in all spatial relationships.[32] One of the only studies that attempts to account for direction of criminal movement was undertaken by Nichols, who used premise selection as a surrogate for direction of robbery trips in Miami.[33] He suggested that the type of premise selected is a good measure of direction because criminals "plot" locations of target sites on premises on a cognitive map in relation to some known point. Nevertheless, Nichols made no attempt to analyze the vector measurement of direction—the actual direction traveled for the journey to crime.

Criminal mobility studies have therefore been constrained by the scale at which the analyses have been carried out, and also by the singular emphasis on distance as an objective measure of criminal spatial behavior. There is a need, therefore, to analyze the journey to crime at an individual level, and to ascertain the significance of direction in criminal movement patterns. One could examine, for example, whether direction varies by offense category, race, sex, age, and so on. In terms of spatial autocorrelation, one could analyze whether nearby criminals travel in similar directions to commit crime or, conversely, whether nearby crimes can be attributed to suspects who have come from similar directions. In the remainder of the paper we will concentrate on these questions of spatial autocorrelation in the directions of journeys to crime.

SPATIAL AUTOCORRELATION
IN THE JOURNEY TO CRIME: AN EXAMPLE

Data and Methodology

To illustrate how the directional component in journeys to crime can be evaluated for spatial autocorrelation, we consider a data set obtained from a study carried out in Minneapolis.[34] Only a small subset of the original data will be used here since our concern is with only those crimes for which both the offense site and the residence of the offender could be identified. Moreover, because our interest is specifically limited to the directions traveled to commit a crime, all of the cases where the offense site and the residence were identical were discarded. Table 1 lists the crimes studied and the number of observations available for each. The criminal mobility patterns for the seven crimes are illustrated in Figures 1–7; the direction of travel in each case is towards the lower left corner of the star.

Table 1

Size of Samples by Crime Type

Crime Type	Total Sample Size[a]	Analysis Sample Size[b]
Street Robbery	78	78
Commercial Burglary	211	100
Assault	194	100
Rape	11	11
Commercial Robbery	54	54
Vandalism	66	66
Residential Burglary	125	100

[a]This is the total number of observations for which both the offense site and the site of the suspect's residence could be identified. Figures 1–7 visually portray these data.
[b]Within the categories of commercial burglary, assault, and residential burglary, samples of size 100 were randomly chosen for the analysis because of software constraints.

To assess the degree of spatial autocorrelation in directions of criminal travel, we utilize a nonparametric procedure.[35] This method depends on a measure of the proximity between two directional observations, represented by d_i and d_j, that we assume has the following form:

$$(1) \qquad C_{ij} = cos \, (d_i - d_j)$$

Thus, the index C_{ij} takes on values in the range from -1 to $+1$, corresponding with opposite directions to identical directions, respectively. It is functionally equivalent to a correlation coefficient and, in fact, if the two observations are denoted by unit length column vectors, $\{x_i\}$ and $\{x_j\}$, then

$$C_{ij} = \{x_i\}^t\{x_j\},$$

where t indicates a matrix transpose. The index may be extended to multiple dimensions by the use of unit length vectors having m components, but since m=2 in the present case, it may be simpler to conceptualize the problem in terms of the proximity measure as defined in (1).

The statistic can appropriately be used within the general quadratic assignment framework for testing spatial autocorrelation

Street Robbery

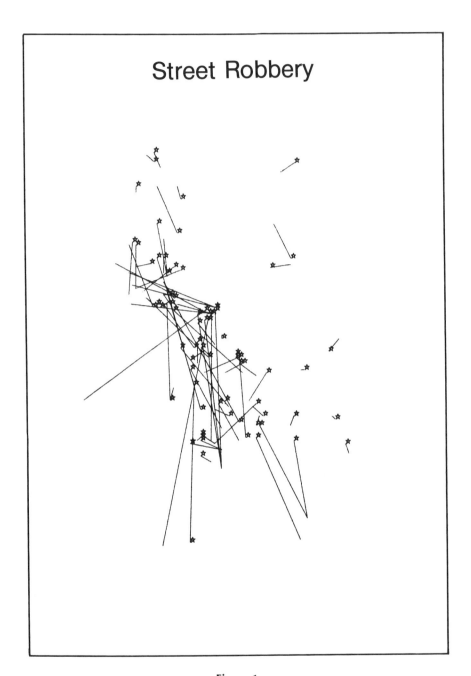

Figure 1

Commercial Burglary

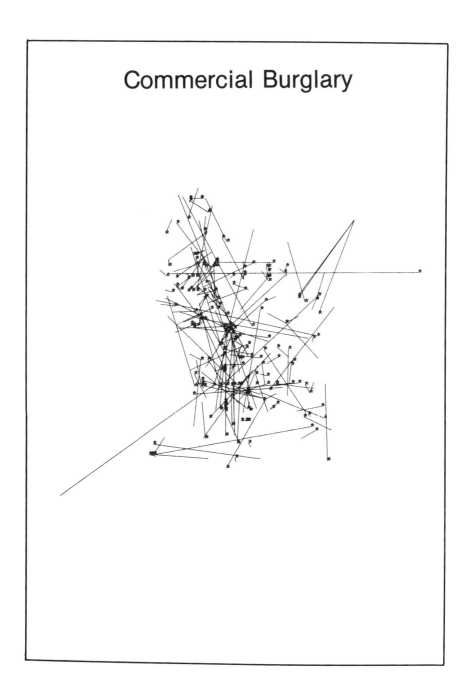

Figure 2

Assault

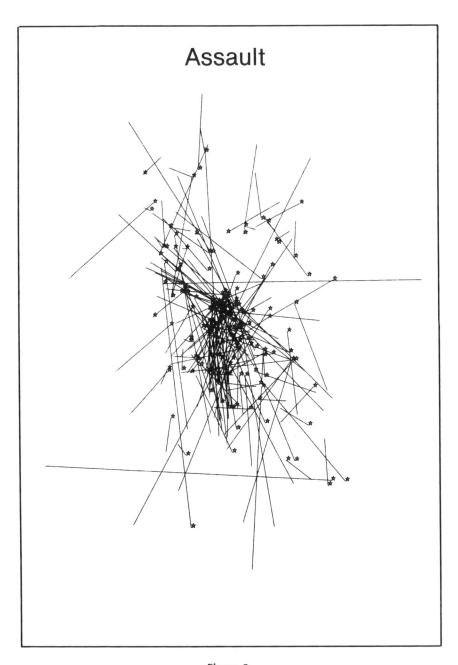

Figure 3

Rape

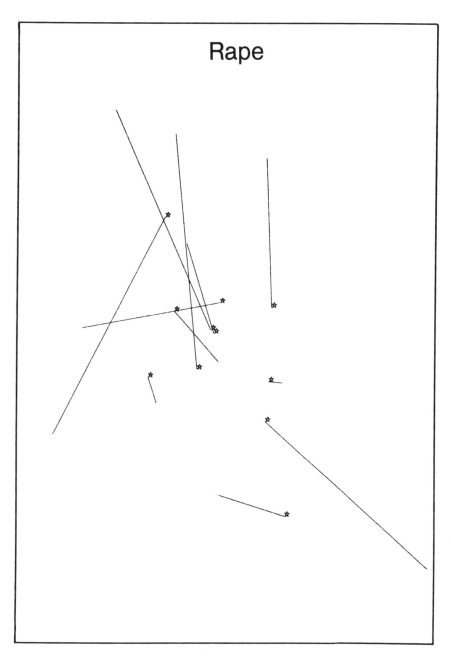

Figure 4

Commercial Robbery

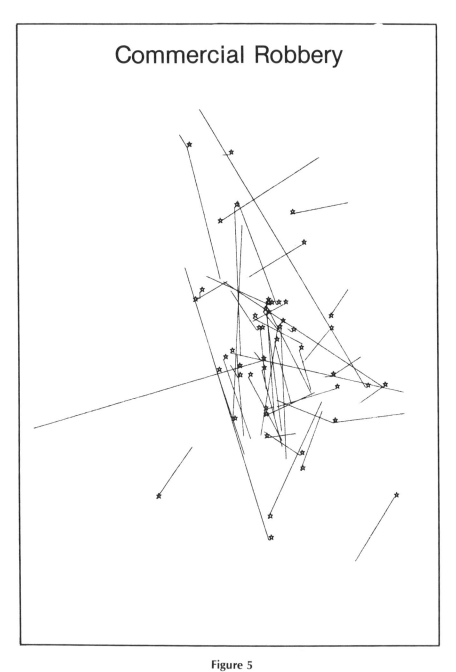

Figure 5

Vandalism

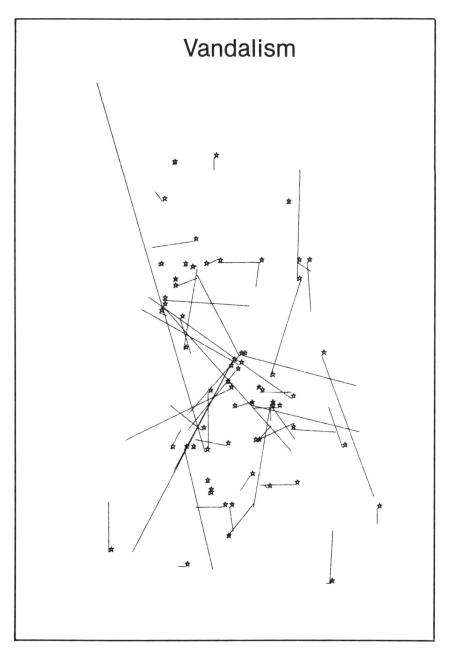

Figure 6

Residential Burglary

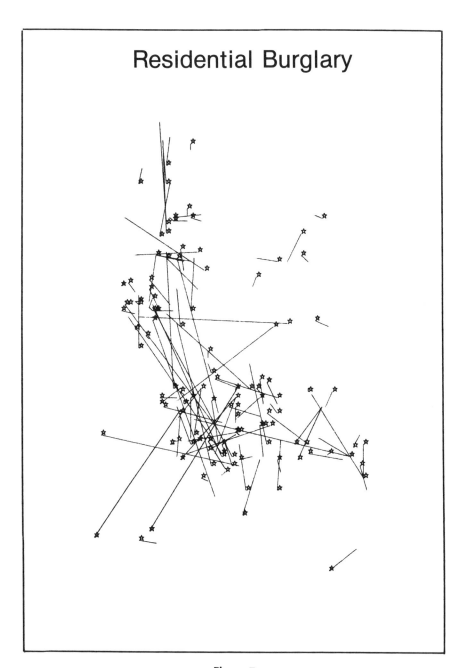

Figure 7

provided by Hubert, Golledge, and Costanzo.[36] Therefore, we calculate C_{ij} for all i and j to form the matrix $\underset{\sim}{C}$, whose entries indicate how alike each pair of directional observations are. Next, a matrix $\underset{\sim}{W}$ is calculated where W_{ij} is some measure of the spatial separation of observations i and j. The amount of structural correspondence between the two matrices reflects the degree to which nearby observations are similar. To formally test the correspondence, we calculate

$$\Gamma = \Sigma\Sigma\ C_{ij}W_{ij}$$

and compare this observed measure to what can be expected under a null conjecture that the rows and columns of $\underset{\sim}{C}$ have been matched at random with those of $\underset{\sim}{W}$.

Formulae are available for $E(\Gamma)$ and for $Var(\Gamma)$,[37] allowing us to compute a Z-statistic:

$$Z = (\Gamma - E(\Gamma))/(Var(\Gamma))$$

In the case of high *positive* spatial autocorrelation, large values of C_{ij} are matched with small values of W_{ij}, and conversely. Therefore, large *negative* Z-values indicate that nearby observations tend to be similar.

Since an assumption of asymptotic normality may be inappropriate,[38] the relative size of the Z-value is assessed in two complementary ways. First, we calculate the skewness parameter and use it to construct a significance level with a Pearson Type III approximation.[39] As a second option, a Monte Carlo approach is carried out by randomly permuting the rows and columns simultaneously of one matrix M times, while leaving the other matrix fixed, and recalculating Γ for each permutation. The Monte Carlo significance level is then given by

$$(K + 1)/(M + 1),$$

where K is the number of values of Γ obtained by random permutations that were found to be as low or lower than the initial value. Finally, as a normalized descriptive statistic, we will also report the Pearson product moment correlation (r) between the off-diagonal entries in $\underset{\sim}{C}$ and $\underset{\sim}{W}$.

Results

In examining spatial autocorrelation in the journey to crime, two basic questions are considered. The first is concerned with autocorrelation with respect to the suspects' residences, and the second with respect to the offense sites. In the former case, the question is: Do criminals who live close to each other travel in similar directions to commit a crime? In the latter case the question could be stated as follows: If crimes are committed at nearby locations, can these offenses be attributed to criminals who have come from similar directions?

To test these two notions of spatial autocorrelation, proximity matrices ($\underset{\sim}{C}$) of directions were first created for all of the crimes, with each C_{ij} entry calculated as in equation (1). Next, two types of distance matrices ($\underset{\sim}{W}$) were generated to describe geographic structure. The first contained pairwise Euclidean distances between suspects' residences; the second contained similar distance measures between crime sites. These matrices were then used to compute the spatial autocorrelation statistics reported in the tables.

Table 2 summarizes the findings of the first analysis in which the distances between suspects' residences were used as the spatial separation variable. All of the Z-values are negative and quite large; they are all significant at the 0.05 level. For the seven crimes tested, a significant tendency exists for criminals who live near each other to travel in similar directions to commit the same type of crime. To some extent,

Table 2

Spatial Autocorrelation of Journeys to Crime in Minneapolis
Case 1: Is there a tendency for nearby[a] suspects to travel
in similar directions to commit crimes?

| Crime Type | Statistics[b] | | Skewness[c] Parameter | Probability[d] | |
	r	Z		Type III	Monte Carlo[e]
Street Robbery	−.13	− 6.28	− .81	.000	.01
Commercial Burglary	−.11	− 6.77	− .64	.000	.01
Assault	−.31	−12.47	− .41	.000	.01
Rape	−.37	− 3.39	−1.19	.007	.02
Commercial Robbery	−.13	− 6.35	−1.25	.000	.01
Vandalism	−.09	− 4.24	− .92	.001	.01
Residential Burglary	−.07	− 5.29	−1.10	.000	.01

[a]Pairwise distances between suspects' homes were used as the spatial separation variable in this analysis.
[b]Negative values indicate positive spatial autocorrelation.
[c]This is a measure of distributional symmetry (all are skewed in the negative direction).
[d]This is the probability of observing values of r or Z as low or lower than those indicated.
[e]Constructed from 99 random permutations (note that the .01 level is reached when all 99 permutations yield values higher than the initial value).

this is also reflected descriptively in the size of the Pearson correlations reported in Table 2. The latter are somewhat small in absolute size, but given the uncontrolled factors that may influence directional choice in this context, it is surprising that even correlations of this magnitude are obtained.

For the second analysis, the distances between offense sites were used as the spatial separation variable; the results are listed in Table 3. In this case all of the Z-values were less extreme than those in the former analysis, producing insignificant indices for three of the seven crimes. These consistent differences are also apparent in the Pearson correlations. The evidence suggests that the spatial autocorrelation in criminal mobility patterns does not seem to be as important a factor when considered from the point of view of the offense site as opposed to the suspect site.

IMPLICATIONS FOR THE MODELING OF CRIMINAL MOBILITY

The identification of pattern is an essential aspect of the process of scientific reasoning. Few patterns of social behavior are well understood, and patterns of criminal behavior are particularly elusive. Some spatial aspects of criminal activity have been postulated, however, and have been shown to agree with observed behavior, at least in the aggregate. The role of distance as an influence on criminal activities has

Table 3

Spatial Autocorrelation of Journeys to Crime in Minneapolis
Case 2: Can nearby[a] offenses be attributed to suspects
who tend to come from similar directions?

Crime Type	Statistics		Skewness Parameter	Probability	
	r	Z		Type III	Monte Carlo
Street Robbery	−.01	−0.43	−.69	.300	.32
Commercial Burglary	−.04	−2.45	−.65	.018	.04
Assault	−.08	−2.93	−.35	.005	.02
Rape	.03	0.37	−.91	.595	.69
Commercial Robbery	−.07	−3.31	−1.01	.007	.02
Vandalism	−.04	−1.76	−.80	.056	.02
Residential Burglary	.00	0.30	−1.03	.556	.53

[a]Pairwise distances between offense sites were used as the spatial separation variable in this analysis.

received a great deal of attention, and the distance variable is now a common element in models of criminal mobility. Justification for including distance as an explanatory variable has come in the form of substantial evidence that patterns of criminal activity are related to the distances that separate potential offenders from target opportunities. The present research has identified another influence on the pattern of criminal spatial behavior: the directional bias in journeys to crime. For the city of Minneapolis during the time period covered, we found that choices of directions in which to commit crimes are autocorrelated in space.

Naturally, much more evidence will be necessary before we can safely conclude that the directional component in journeys to crime is indeed an important factor, but it can be argued that there may be little reason to believe otherwise. Consider two offenders who both reside in the same neighborhood, each of whom perceives a set of opportunities. What we know about human spatial behavior suggests that, by virtue of their relative nearness, the offenders' activity spaces should overlap and many of their sources of information are likely to be mutual. It is therefore not surprising that their choices about which direction to travel for committing crimes would coincide. With the exception of assault, all of the crimes that we have studied are ones in which the choice of location is optional. Presumably, the offenders have chosen those locations over other possible sites. Given that nearby offenders possess similar information concerning preferable locations, the results that we have observed seem to make sense. Assault is a different sort of crime in that it does not typically involve a spatial decision. Instead, an offense is likely to result from a chance encounter during the course of some other activity. However, given that nearby offenders probably move about in overlapping activity spaces, our results with respect to assault are not surprising either.

These findings may have major implications with respect to the modeling of criminal mobility. If we could more clearly delineate corridors in which criminal mobility is more predominant, then our models may be improved. For instance, spatial choice models and potential models such as those discussed by Rengert that consider opportunities as attractive forces and distance as an impeding force could be enhanced by including the directional component.[40] The result would be a model in which opportunities are weighted in accordance with their direction from potential offenders, and/or distance is weighted to account for differential mobility along certain radial axes. Alternatively, we should seek different model formulations in which neighboring offenders' movement patterns are some function of each others'. We should also study the stability of these findings over time; if they are found to be stable, then the previous patterns could be used to predict present and future patterns.

We have found conflicting results concerning the spatial auto-correlation of directions traveled with reference to offense sites. These directions were autocorrelated in some of the crimes studied, but not in others. It is possible that we are observing the effect of overlapping activity spaces again, but the activity spaces are not centered around these nodes. While there is reason to believe that nearby offenders have similar conceived opportunity sets, there is less reason to suppose that nearby offense sites are members of opportunity sets possessed by offenders living in similar directions from the sites. However, this might be the case for commercial burglary, assault, commercial robbery, and vandalism. The implications of these results are perhaps less theoretical than they are practical. Given a commission of one of these offenses, a law enforcement official might choose to search for the offender first in the general direction from which previous offenders have traveled. This particular rule of thumb, however, would probably be much less applicable if the offense were a street robbery, a rape, or a residential burglary.

In conclusion, conceptualizations of spatial patterns of criminal behavior are beginning to take shape. Most of the relevant research to date has concentrated on the distance component in these patterns; the present research has suggested the importance of the directional component as well. These are two fundamental elements of any spatial pattern, and if we expect to derive meaningful explanations of criminal mobility, we must consider them both.

Notes

1. C.R. Shaw and H.D. McKay, *Juvenile Delinquency and Urban Areas*, rev. ed. (Chicago: University of Chicago Press, 1969).

2. C.F. Schmid, "Urban Crime Areas," *American Sociological Review* 25 (1960): 527–554, 655–678.

3. P.J. Brantingham and P.L. Brantingham, "Introduction: The Dimensions of Crime," in P.J. Brantingham and P.L. Brantingham, eds., *Environmental Criminology* (Beverly Hills: Sage Publications, 1981).

4. D.C. Capone and W.W. Nichols, "Crime and Distance: An Analysis of Offender Behavior in Space," *Proceedings of the Association of American Geographers* 7 (1975).

5. A.W. Lind, "Some Ecological Patterns of Community Disorganization in Honolulu," *American Journal of Sociology* 36 (1930):206–220.

6. C.R. White, "The Relation of Felonies to Environmental Factors in Indianapolis," *Social Forces* 10 (1932):498–509.

7. P.D. Phillips, "Characteristics and Typology of the Journey to Crime," in D.E. Georges-Abeyie and K.D. Harries, eds., *Crime: A Spatial Perspective* (New York: Columbia University Press, 1980); T.S. Smith, "Inverse Distance Variations for the Flow of Crime in Urban Areas," *Social Forces*, 54 (1976):802-815; S. Turner, "Delinquency and Distance," in M.E. Wolfgang and T. Sellin, eds., *Delinquency: Selected Studies* (New York: John Wiley, 1969).

8. Capone, "Crime and Distance"; G.F. Pyle et al., *The Spatial Dynamics of Crime* (University of Chicago, Department of Geography, Research Papers 159, 1974); T.A. Reppetto, *Residential Crime* (Cambridge, MA: Ballinger, 1974).

9. G.F. Rengert, "Burglary in Philadelphia: A Critique of an Opportunity Structure Model," in P.J. Brantingham and P.L. Brantingham, eds., *Environmental Criminology* (Beverly Hills: Sage Publications, 1981).

10. L.B. DeFleur, "Ecological Variables in the Cross-Cultural Study of Delinquency," *Social Forces* 45 (1967):556-570.

11. Pyle, "Spatial Dynamics."

12. M. Amir, *Patterns in Forcible Rape* (Chicago: University of Chicago Press, 1971).

13. It has been suggested that a better understanding of criminal mobility can help local police to target more accurately their resources in the battle against crime. E.g., do the problems created by the interjurisdictional criminal require a greater resource allocation than those associated with the individual committing crimes in his or her area of residence? J.P. McIver, "Criminal Mobility: A Review of Empirical Studies," in S. Hakim and G.F. Rengert, eds., *Crime Spillover* (Beverly Hills: Sage Publications, 1981).

14. D.A. Hellman, "Criminal Mobility and Policy Recommendations," in Hakim and Rengert, *Crime Spillover.*

15. R.M. Downs and D. Stea, eds., *Image and Environment* (Chicago: Aldine Publishers, 1973).

16. D.C. Capone and W.W. Nichols, "Urban Structure and Criminal Mobility," *American Behavioral Scientist* 20 (1976):199-213.

17. R.L. Carter and K.Q. Hill, *The Criminal's Image of the City* (New York: Pergamon Press, 1979).

18. Phillips, "Journey to Crime"; W.M. Rhodes and C. Conly, "Crime and Mobility: an Empirical Study," in P.J. Brantingham and P.L. Brantingham, eds., *Environmental Criminology* (Beverly Hills: Sage Publications, 1981).

19. Brantingham and Brantingham, *Environmental Criminology.*

20. Rengert, "Burglary in Philadelphia."

21. J.P. Allison, "Economic Factors and the Rate of Crime," *Land Economics* 68 (1972):193-196.

22. S. Hakim, "The Attraction of Property Crimes to Suburban Locations: A Revised Economic Model," *Urban Studies* 17 (1980):265-276.

23. M.A. Brown, "Spatial Autocorrelation and the Journey to Crime in Suburbia," paper presented at the annual meeting of the Western Regional Science Association, Santa Barbara, California, 1982.

24. M.T. Katzman, "The Supply of Criminals: A Geo-Economic Explanation," in Hakim and Rengert, *Crime Spillover.*

25. A.D. Cliff and J.K. Ord, *Spatial Processes: Models and Applications* (London: Pion, 1981).

26. R. Geary, "The Contiguity Ratio and Statistical Mapping, *Incorporated Statistician* 5 (1954):115-145; P. Moran, "The Interpretation of Statistical Maps," *Journal of the Royal Statistical Society, Series B* 10 (1948):243-251; Cliff and Ord, *Spatial Processes.*

27. C.M. Costanzo, "A Spatial Analysis of Crime in California," paper presented at the annual meetings of the Association of American Geographers, Los Angeles, California, 1981.

28. L. Hubert, R. Golledge and C.M. Costanzo, "Generalized Procedures for Evaluating Spatial Autocorrelation," *Geographical Analysis* 13 (1981):38–50.

29. Brown, "Spatial Autocorrelation."

30. S.W.C. Winchester, "Two Suggestions for Developing the Geographical Study of Crime," *Area* 10 (1978):116–120.

31. C.M. Costanzo, "An Investigation of the Spatial Component in the Effectiveness of Gun Control Laws," unpublished M.A. Thesis, Department of Geography, University of California, Santa Barbara, 1981.

32. G.L. Gaile and J.E. Burt, *Directional Statistics, Concepts and Techniques in Modern Geography, Catmog 25* (Norwich: Geo Abstracts, University of East Anglia, 1980).

33. W.W. Nichols, "Mental Maps, Social Characteristics and Criminal Mobility," in Georges-Abeyie and Harries, *Spatial Perspective.*

34. D. Frisbie et al., *Crime in Minneapolis* (Minneapolis: Minnesota Crime Prevention Center, 1978).

35. L. Hubert, R. Golledge, C. Costanzo, N. Gale, and W. Halperin, "Nonparametric Tests for Directional Data," in G. Bahrenberg, M. Fisher, and P. Nijkamp, eds., *Recent Developments in Spatial Analysis* (Aldershot, U.K.: Gower, 1985).

36. Hubert, Golledge and Costanzo, "Evaluating Spatial Autocorrelation."

37. N. Mantel, "The Detection of Disease Clustering and a Generalized Regression Approach," *Cancer Research* 27 (1967):209–220.

38. P. Mielke, "On Asymptotic Non-normality of Null Distributions of MRPP Statistics," *Communications in Statistics—Theory and Methods* 15 (1979):1541–1550.

39. P. Mielke, K. Berry, and G. Briar, "Application of Multiple-response Permutation Procedures for Examining Seasonal Changes in Monthly Mean Sea-Level Pressure Patterns," *Monthly Weather Review* 109 (1981):120–126.

40. Rengert, "Burglary in Philadelphia."

Geographical and Temporal Changes among Robberies in Milwaukee

Ralph Lenz

Increasing urban crime during the 1970s involved a diffusion of criminal activity into areas not previously affected. The spread of crime could have been due either to neighborhood change or to altered mobility patterns by criminals. Robbery, a crime involving not only personal confrontation, but also a profit motive and some premeditation, would be particularly likely to be implicated by hypotheses of spatial change. Applications of point pattern analysis techniques to robbery patterns suggest that criminal activity fields have expanded since the 1960s.

American cities have recently experienced dramatic increases in crime. Since 1961 the rate for all serious crimes has more than doubled according to FBI data. Violent crime has increased even more sharply; robbery rates, for example, more than tripled between 1961 and 1974, despite a lull between 1970 and 1973. The stability of crime rates in the early 1970s was apparently only temporary; since 1974 the upswing began anew.

There is some evidence that increases in U.S. crime during the 1970s have been accompanied by spatial changes in the distribution of offenses. While the growth of crime has often been attributed to increasing racial tension and social disorganization in ghetto areas, crime rates in these areas have sometimes grown more slowly than rates in adjacent and suburban areas. A spread of inner city crime and even a suburbanization of crime could be partly due to neighborhood change, but it is also possible that criminal mobility patterns have altered. Federal officials have speculated about a "beltway effect," in which criminals drive to the suburbs or nearby completed interstate highways to commit crimes.[1] This paper is concerned with the possibility that there has been a distinct alteration of the mobility patterns associated with crime.

THEORIES OF INTRAURBAN CRIME VARIATION

Social theories such as anomie, differential association, and the drift hypothesis—which considers areas in the city in which criminals are likely to accumulate—actually focus on offender locations rather than crime locations.[2] If it is true that crime has been spreading, and that offender mobility has increased, the social theories will become less and less accurate indicators of crime locations. All of these social theories approach crime as a pathological response to environmental stimuli. Such stimuli include poverty, depression, privation, social disorganization, and exploitation. Environmental stimuli, however, may include physical as well as social phenomena; physical stimuli are likely to be particularly relevant in considerations of crime locations. This likelihood is recognized by a second group of theories concerned with opportunities.

Opportunity differential theories focus on targets rather than offenders. Certain areas, especially in central business districts, are characterized by high numbers of crimes, but few offenders in residence. This fact prompted Boggs to examine macroscopic variations in the availability and profitability of targets.[3] Thus, muggings may be related to pedestrian counts in an area.

While the offender's perception of profitability and ease of commission are likely to be important for property crimes, ease of access to the target is also important. Access is the spatial variable that ties opportunity theories to social theories; the distance separating offenders from potential targets can determine the probability of confrontations. The implication with social theories of crime location is that distances travelled by offenders are very limited. The effect of increased offender mobility would be to render these social theories inoperable as location predictors. Opportunity theories, on the other hand, are more flexible; increased offender mobility would simply increase opportunities in areas farther removed from zones in which large numbers of offenders reside.

Traditional criminological theory suggests that someone out to commit a property crime is not likely to do it in his own neighborhood because recognition by bystanders could be problematic.[4] But since familiarity with the area in which the crime is to occur is advantageous, and distance is an added deterrent, it is felt that the offender does not go very far, either, and never into areas where he or she might be conspicuous.[5] Suburban crimes, therefore, should largely be committed by suburbanites.

It may be that recent trends are in conflict with traditional theory. Consideration of the "journey to crime—its distance, direction, and relation to social areas," as advocated by Phillips, may lend support to this contention.[6]

HYPOTHESES AND DATA

Increases in urban crime have variously been attributed to affluence, income inequality, racial tension, social disorganization, moral laxity, and demographic factors.[7] If the increases reflect an intensification of criminal activity in already dangerous zones, traditional explanations of crime patterns need not be altered. An expansion of the criminal offender's field of activity into previously unexploited areas, on the other hand, would imply a possible decrease in the applicability of traditional social theories, especially if increased offender mobility rather than neighborhood change were implicated. Dramatic increases in offender mobility would also mean decreases in the predictability of crime locations; crime would no longer be a problem solely of certain minority groups (non-whites, the aged), but of the entire urban population.

Robbery data characteristics make them more suitable for testing offender mobility hypotheses than other crime data. Robbery is a crime against property, but it normally involves personal confrontation between offender and victim. Because it is a crime involving potential personal gain for the offender, robbery is among those crimes most likely to be affected by variables that increase access to opportunities in outlying parts of the city. At the same time, robbery is considered a serious crime; it is likely to be reported, offender apprehension rates are usually higher than for other property crimes, and, since it involves personal confrontation, it is subject to a high degree of public concern.

Even within the robbery category there are variations in crime types. Most muggings are classified as robberies, unless the victim is killed. Robbery also includes armed holdups of business establishments, for which circumstances are significantly different. Both categories will be dealt with in this paper.

The study area is Milwaukee, Wisconsin, a moderately large industrial city (Milwaukee County population in 1970 was 1,054,063), usually thought to have relatively low crime rates. The Harries crime typology of SMSAs represents Milwaukee as a city with both low violent and low general crime.[8] Robbery data were obtained from the Milwaukee County Criminal Court for two time periods, 1975 and 1965 through 1967, as representative of the 1970s and 1960s, respectively. The data represent those cases throughout the county that were brought to court; questions of political manipulation or inaccurate reporting are therefore not relevant. Although plea bargaining, which alters conviction data, can be problematic, it is less so with court case data than with conviction data. Only those crimes in which an offender has been apprehended and accused in court are included; the data by definition comprise a limited sample from the total pattern of crimes. While not a random sample, they are not a manipulated sample.

Only those cases for which addresses were listed within the county for the crime location, offender residence, and, where applicable, the location of the victim, have been included in the analysis. For 1975, the court files contained 104 business robbery cases and 75 personal robberies. For the three year time period from 1965 through 1967, the files yielded 100 business robberies and 28 personal robberies, which would indicate that robbery rates in Milwaukee have more than tripled since the 1960s. This is not improbable, since, according to national indicators, robbery is perhaps the most rapidly growing crime.

It is hypothesized that the spatial clustering of robberies in Central Milwaukee has decreased over time, that robbery patterns are expanding into outlying areas. It is further hypothesized that an expansion of crime occurrences into new locales has been accompanied by increasing offender mobility, and that increasing mobility has contributed to the diffusion of crime into previously unexploited areas.

ANALYSIS OF MACROVARIATIONS

Robbery data for which addresses are available can be expressed as point patterns on a map. The degree of clustering or evenness of an arrangement of points in a pattern can be quantified, and comparison of quantitative indices of clustering can provide evidence to support hypotheses of change in the spatial form of the pattern. Here, we test the hypothesis that crime location patterns in the 1970s exhibit less clustering in central locations than patterns for the 1960s.

An index of spatial form particularly adaptable to the analysis of change is the redundancy measure calculated for a set of polygon areas. The procedure involves the construction of Thiessen polygons around each point, such that the area closest to each point is associated with that point.[9] Individual point-areas may then be expressed as fractions of total pattern area, and these fractions may be treated like probabilities.

Arrangement in a point pattern may be taken to be representative of the spatial relationship of each point to every other point in the pattern. The polygon area describes the location of a point with respect to all adjacent points; it provides more information than a nearest neighbor distance, which only reflects the relationship between a point and the one point closest to it. Although map coordinates are not retained, the polygon area "probability" seems to be an optimum indicator of a point's relative location for a single-number index.

Theil's redundancy,

$$(1) \quad R^* = \sum_{i=1}^{N} p_i \ \ln \frac{p_i}{1/N} = H_{max} - H$$

where: $R^* =$ *Theil's redundancy index*

$H =$ *Shannon's entropy*

$p_i =$ *Proportion of total area assigned to point*

$N =$ *Number of points in the spatial pattern,*

can be calculated for any set of point-areas expressed as "probabilities."[10] The point-area R^* index is quite sensitive to variations in the arrangement of points in a pattern; its value will be zero for a completely regular pattern, and it increases dramatically with increased clustering to values as high as 2.0 or more. The average value of R^* when point locations are Poisson-generated has been found to be 0.134, regardless of variations in N; the value $^oR^*=0.2157/^{1.9}\sqrt{N}$ has also been determined empirically for Poisson-generated patterns.[11]

Milwaukee County is a somewhat elongated area located along Lake Michigan (Figure 1). Although the urbanized area extends beyond county boundaries, the county contains about 75 percent of the Milwaukee SMSA population. Most of the county is developed, and therefore capable of serving as locations for offender or crime location addresses. Lake Michigan provides a physical barrier that serves as an appropriate boundary for the polygon net; elsewhere the county line has been used as a boundary.

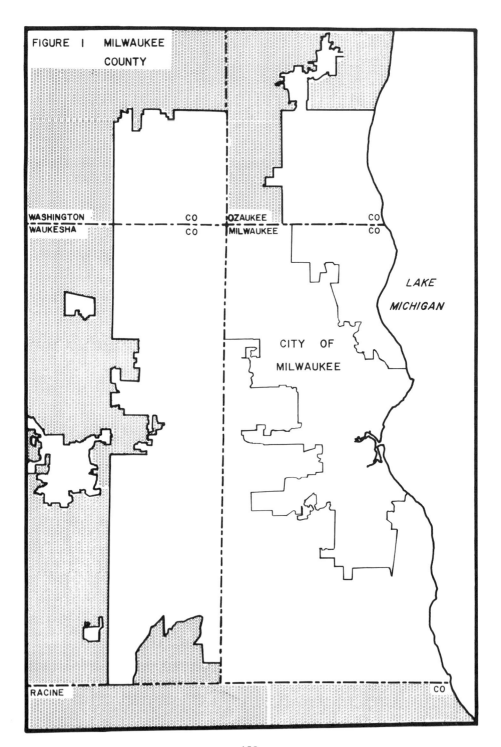

FIGURE I MILWAUKEE COUNTY

WASHINGTON CO
WAUKESHA CO

OZAUKEE CO
MILWAUKEE CO

LAKE
MICHIGAN

CITY OF
MILWAUKEE

RACINE CO

Polygons have been constructed around point patterns of offender addresses and crime locations for personal robberies in Milwaukee County during 1975 and 1965–67. Business robbery offender and crime location polygon patterns representative of the 1970s and 1960s have also been mapped. Comparisons of crime location patterns should indicate that business robbery locations are somewhat more spread out than personal robbery locations. Close visual inspection also reveals that a 1975 business robbery offender residence cluster is located further west than most of the personal robbery offender addresses, and that it has spread slightly westward since the 1960s. It also reveals that business robbery locations seem to be more spread out in 1975 than in the 1960s, but little else is visible through visual comparison of the patterns.

R^* values have been calculated for each pattern of polygon areas (Table 1). All of the patterns are highly clustered; the R^* values are much larger than the Poisson $R^*=0.134$, and the differences are statistically significant at the .001 level. Offender location patterns, however, appear to be more clustered than robbery location patterns.

Crime specific differences in R^* values are immediately apparent. Personal robbery locations in 1975 were 0.345 more clustered than business robbery locations, suggesting a difference in the patterns of these crimes. The agglomeration of 1975 business robbery offender residences is 0.169 greater than the agglomeration of personal robbery offender residences. Such a difference in R^* might justify the generation of additional spatial hypotheses about crime specific variations for social theories that deal with offender characteristics. A primary difference between personal and business robberies is the potential mobility of the personal robbery victim. R^* values for patterns of victim residences have also been calculated (Table 1). Personal robbery victim locations are less clustered than robbery locations, suggesting that some victims place themselves in jeopardy by going to locations where personal robbery is more frequent.[12]

The hypotheses require comparison of 1960s and 1970s robbery patterns. It has been hypothesized that crime has expanded recently into locales not previously bothered by crime. Lower R^* values for 1970s crime location patterns would indicate that crime not only has increased in the suburbs (as it has everywhere), but that it has also increased at a greater rate than elsewhere. The R^* values for robberies support this hypothesis (Table 1). For personal robbery locations, the R^* value decreases by 0.086 from 1965–67 to 1975, indicating a slight amount of expansion. Business robbery locations exhibit a much greater decrease of 0.510 in the value of R^*. The indication is that certain

Table 1

Comparison of Robbery Patterns
and Movement Induced Changes

	1975	1965–67	Difference
Personal Robbery			
N	75	28	
R*Values			
Offender Residences (R^*_x)	1.603	1.576	.027
Crime Locations (R^*_y)	1.437	1.523	−.086
Victim Residences	1.062	1.095	.033
$\Delta R^* = R^*_y - R^*_x$			
Offender Movements	−.165	−.052	.113
Victim Movements	.375	.428	.053
Average Distance (miles)			
Offender Movements	1.8	1.6	.2
Victim Movements	1.6	1.5	.1
Business Robbery			
N	104	100	
R* Values			
Offender Residences (R^*_x)	1.772	1.870	−.098
Crime Locations (R^*_y)	1.092	1.602	−.510
Movement Induced Change			
$\Delta R^* = R^*_y - R^*_x$	−.680	−.267	.413
Average Distance (miles)	2.5	1.8	.7
Business Locations	0.698	0.857	−.159

crimes like business robberies may have expanded much more than others, and may be largely responsible for recent reports of expanding crime.

The second hypothesis suggests that decreases in R* for crime locations between 1965–67 and 1975 will not be matched by equivalently decreased R* values for offender residence locations. Here the concern is with the cause of expanding crime: Is the expansion due to changing neighborhoods, or is it because of some kind of alteration of opportunities in the suburbs? The data indicate that R* decreases are greater for crime locations than for offender residence patterns for both personal and business robberies (Table 1). The personal robbery offender R* value has actually increased, but this phenomenon must be qualified because of the small number of points in the 1965–67 pattern. R* values for the overall pattern of both personal and business robbery offenders decrease by an amount not much different than the decrease in R* for personal robbery locations; the expansion of personal robberies may indeed be due to an expansion of offender residences into new neighborhoods.

With business robberies, the decrease in R* for crime locations (0.510) is much larger than the decrease for offender residences (0.098). The theory that neighborhood change is responsible for expanding crime is not borne out by this result. It may also be noted that the average distance of the journey to crime of the business robber increased dramatically between the 1960s and 1970s (Table 1). The second hypothesis is supported by business robbery patterns, if not by personal robbery patterns; the suggestion is that factors such as increased offender mobility have operated to alter suburban opportunities during the last decade.

Increased offender mobility appears to be responsible for expanding crime. But what is the reason for the changing mobility? Is it due primarily to shifts in criminal plans and procedures, or is it caused primarily by the diffusion of opportunities for crime? The latter possibility should provide little solace to the suburban resident, but it would mean that prediction capabilities based on opportunity patterns would not be as severely impaired.

In order to evaluate this question, random samples of 100 businesses were drawn from the 1966 and 1975 Milwaukee phone book and mapped. Each sample contained 30 bars, 20 gas stations, 20 groceries, 15 pharmacies, 8 banks, and 7 liquor stores; this distribution seemed to most closely represent the relative frequencies for the six most frequently victimized business types during the two time periods. R* values calculated for the two patterns indicate some diffusion of robbery opportunities; R* decreased from 0.857 in 1966 to 0.698 in 1975 (Table 1). But the decrease in R* for crime locations of 0.510 is over three times greater than the decrease for crime opportunities (0.159). A substantial contribution of offender mobility to the expansion of crime over and above that which is explained by diffusion of opportunities is indicated.

THE JOURNEY TO CRIME

Social theories of crime causation have associated crime occurrences with macro-level neighborhood characteristics such as socioeconomic or ethnic status, social disorganization, or crowding. An attempt has been made to divide the county into subareas which are reasonably homogeneous with respect to these variables (Figure 2). Zones one through six are city zones, although zone six also includes West Milwaukee and a small portion of West Allis, and a small part of zone one is the southern extension of Shorewood. Zones seven, eight, and

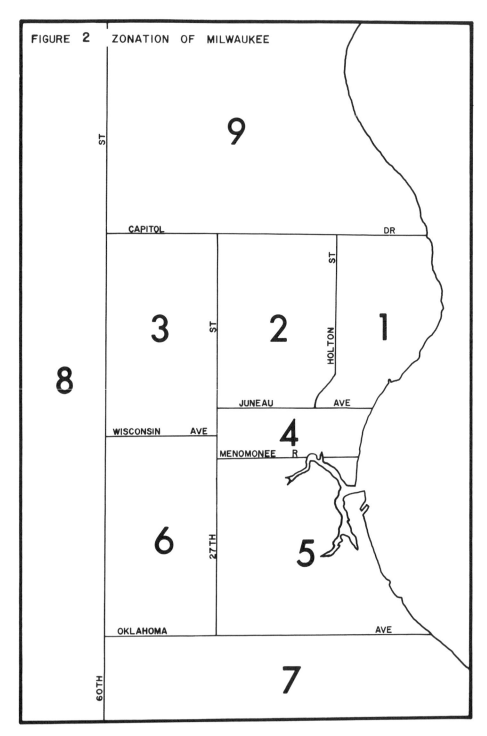

FIGURE 2   ZONATION OF MILWAUKEE

nine are more suburban in character, although each includes portions within the city limits.

Milwaukee's black population is housed in a relatively compact, well-defined area, and zone two has been defined to enclose this segregated area as defined by 1970 census tract data. Zone two is also characterized by a high degree of social disorganization, as indicated by high percentages of children in female-headed families; nearly all Milwaukee tracts with high rankings for this variable are located there. Tracts with high unemployment, low income, much renter occupied housing, and high crowding are also located there. Zone two contains the residences of over half of the accused robbery offenders in Milwaukee County.

Zones one and three lie adjacent to zone two. Zone one is a white middle-income area, although areas bordering the lake are more wealthy, and those to the south exhibit lower incomes. Zone one is characterized by high proportions of females in the labor force and high proportions of renter occupied housing. It contains lakefront parks, some industry, and the University of Wisconsin. Zone three is a white middle-class area west of 35th Street. Black neighborhood succession is occurring near zone two, and industrial zones lie in the northwest corner and along the southern border.

Zone four contains large areas of nonresidential land use, including the CBD and commercial ribbons along many of the streets aligned in an east–west direction. It is also the location of Marquette University.

Zone five is a lower middle-income white area. It is characterized by low incomes, high unemployment, and crowded areas, mostly located adjacent to the extensive industrial and transport-oriented areas to the north and east. Zone five thus might be expected to house a significant number of offenders if socioeconomic factors are responsible for crime.

Zone six, like zone three, is meant to be a buffer zone. It differs from zone three in that it contains much more non-residential land use, largely industrial in the northern part. Median incomes are also somewhat lower than in zone three.

Zones seven, eight, and nine are much larger than the city zones. Zone eight contains high-income areas in its central and southern parts, as well as a poverty locus in the north which extends into zone nine. Although adjacent to zone two, zone nine contains the wealthiest areas in Milwaukee County, located in communities adjacent to Lake Michigan.

Supportive evidence for the expanding criminal mobility hypothesis can be obtained through examination of the journey to crime. The patterns of offender trips to personal and business robberies in the 1970s and 1960s are presented in Figures 3–6. Business robbery trips

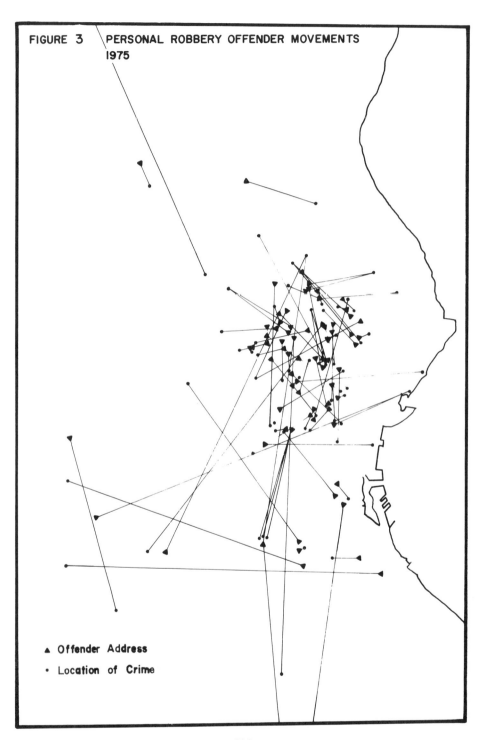

FIGURE 3   PERSONAL ROBBERY OFFENDER MOVEMENTS
1975

▲ Offender Address

• Location of Crime

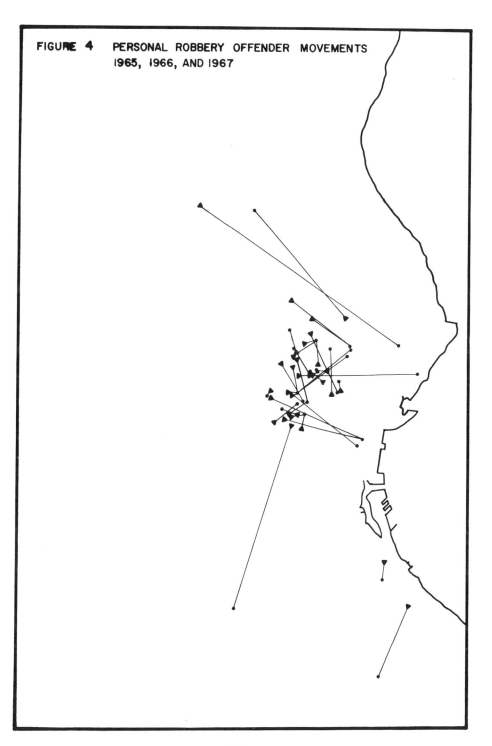

FIGURE 4   PERSONAL ROBBERY OFFENDER MOVEMENTS
              1965, 1966, AND 1967

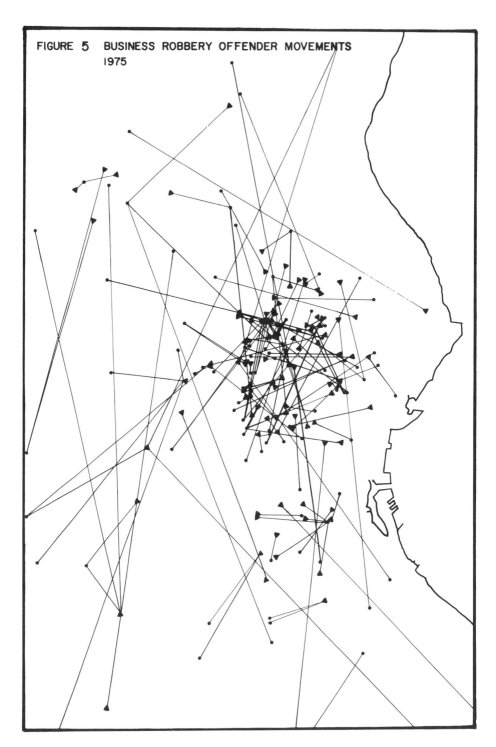

FIGURE 5   BUSINESS ROBBERY OFFENDER MOVEMENTS
           1975

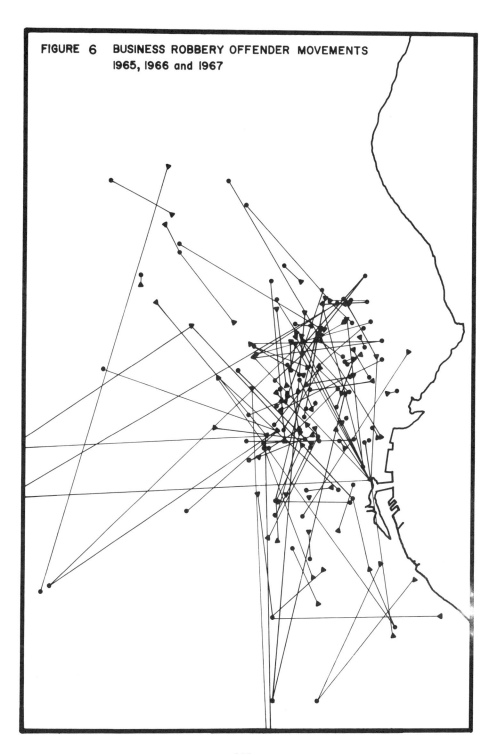

FIGURE 6   BUSINESS ROBBERY OFFENDER MOVEMENTS
1965, 1966 and 1967

in the 1970s are obviously longer, and movements perhaps appear to be more purposeful. Trip characteristics may be summarized by a regionalization of the county and subsequent construction of origin-destination tables.

Origin-destination tables for business robbery trips in the 1960s and 1970s have been depicted (Table 2). The zones are those described in Figure 2. Marginal totals for both offender zones and site zones sum to the same total if rounding errors are overlooked. This is possible because multiple offenders for the same crime have been treated as a single offender divided into fractions which then have been apportioned to the appropriate zones.

A most striking change is evident for robbers who originated in zone four, which contains the CBD. The revitalization and gentrification in this area seem to be pushing criminals' residences out of this area, and robberies have declined there as well. The spread of offender residences into zone three is also visible in Table 2; apparently zone four revitalization has resulted in an expansion of the zone two offender residence concentration into the eastern part of zone three. Similar increases of offender residences in suburban zones give some credence to the argument that the spread of crime is due to neighborhood change. But a comparison of increases in offender residences in these zones with increases in crime occurrences shows that a large proportion of increased suburban crime is not due to neighborhood change. The relative increases in movements from high offender residence zones to suburban zones visible in the origin-destination tables reinforce previous conclusions about recent changes in urban crime. The spread of crime to suburban areas in Milwaukee has been produced in part by changes in offender mobility patterns. The conclusions reached through consideration of changing R* values are not contradicted.

SUMMARY

Two hypotheses are tested in this study: (1) The spatial clustering of robberies in Central Milwaukee has decreased over time; and, (2) The cause of this decrease is increased spatial mobility of criminals as they exploit outlying opportunities. The analysis confirmed the first hypothesis; the location of robberies has spread spatially into outlying suburban areas. The cause of this spatial dispersion is less clear. Although there is support for the second hypothesis of increased spatial mobility of criminals over time, the residences of robbers are also dispersing outward from central Milwaukee. Therefore, it seems that both of these

Table 2
Origins and Destinations of Offender Movements in Business Robberies

Crime Location Zone

1965–1967		1	2	3	4	5	6	7	8	9	Total
	1	1	2.3			1.3					4.7
	2	2	31.5	3	4	2	1	1	1.5	3	49
	3	2	.3		2	.8		1.5	2	1	9.7
Origin:	4		3	3	5	2	3		1.5	1	18.5
Zone of											
Offender	5		.5			6.5	1	1.8			9.8
Residence											
	6				2		1	.3			3.3
	7				1			.3			1.3
	8		.3			.3			3		3.7
	9										0
Total		5	38	6	14	13	6	5	8	5	100

Crime Location Zone

1975		1	2	3	4	5	6	7	8	9	Total
	1	1			1				1		3
	2	3	18.5	11.3	1	2	2	1	2.3	6.5	48.7
	3		5	9.3	3	1	1	1	4	1	25.3
Origin:	4		2	.3	1			1			4.3
Zone of											
Offender	5					3.5		2			5.5
Residence											
	6					1.5		2	.3		3.8
	7							2			2
	8							1	7	1	9
	9		.5	1					.3	1.5	3.3
Total		4	26	22	6	8	3	10	15	10	104

113

factors are contributing to the increased exploitation of suburban opportunities for robberies. Given the changing offender mobility patterns, outlying jurisdictions that have little control over the socioeconomic criminogenesis factors existing in origin areas may have to concentrate on preventive strategies associated with opportunity structures existing in their neighborhoods. Ongoing micro-level analysis of target types in various sections of the city should enhance the effectiveness of preventive strategies.

Notes

1. Michael Knight, "Focus on Rising Crime Shifts to the Suburbs around New York," *New York Times*, October 8, 1974.

2. See Bernard Lander, *Towards an Understanding of Juvenile Delinquency* (New York: Columbia University Press, 1954); David J. Bordua, "Juvenile Delinquency and 'Anomie': An Attempt at Replication," *Social Problems* 6 (1958–59):230–238; Roland J. Chilton, "Continuity in Delinquency Area Research: A Comparison of Studies for Baltimore, Detroit and Indianapolis," *American Sociological Review* 29 (1964):71–83; and Robert A. Gordon, "Issues in the Ecological Study of Delinquency," *American Sociological Review* 32 (1967):927–944. Roman A. Cybriwsky has posited micro-environmental effects of anomie in "The Anomie Theory and the Geographic Study of Crime," (paper delivered at the annual meeting of the Association of American Geographers, East Lakes Division, Indiana, Pennsylvania, October, 1972).

3. Sarah L. Boggs, "Urban Crime Patterns," *American Sociological Review* 30 (1965):899–908.

4. See, for example, R. Clyde White, "The Relation of Felonies to Environmental Factors in Indianapolis," *Social Forces* 10 (1932):498–509, see especially p. 507.

5. Albert J. Reiss, "Settling the Frontiers of a Pioneer in American Criminology: Henry McKay," in *Delinquency, Crime, and Society*, James F. Short, Jr., ed. (Chicago: University of Chicago Press, 1976), p. 74; and Stanley Turner, "Delinquency and Distance," in *Delinquency: Selected Studies*, J. Thorsten Sellin and Marvin E. Wolfgang, eds. (New York: Wiley, 1969), p. 25.

6. Phillip D. Phillips, "A Prologue to the Geography of Crime," *Proceedings*, Association of American Geographers, vol. 4 (1972), pp. 86–91. Studies of the travel patterns of criminals in their movement from residence to crime site have not been very numerous. Among the prominent publications that have dealt with the journey to crime are White, "Felonies and Environmental Factors"; Turner, "Delinquency and Distance"; Menachem Amir, *Patterns in Forcible Rape* (Chicago: University of Chicago Press, 1971), pp. 87–95; Gerald F. Pyle et al., *The Spatial Dynamics of Crime* (Chicago: University of Chicago, Department of Geography Research Paper No. 159, 1974); John Baldwin and A.E. Bottoms, eds., "Crime and Distance in the City," in *The Urban Criminal* (London: Tavistock, 1976), pp. 78–98; Donald L. Capone and Woodrow W. Nichols, Jr., "Urban Structure and Criminal Mobility," *American Behavioral Scientist* 20 (1976): pp. 199–213; and Thomas Spence Smith, "Inverse Distance Variations for the Flow of Crime in Urban Areas," *Social Forces* 54 (1976): pp. 802–815. The important studies have been reviewed in Keith D. Harries, *Crime and the Environment* (Springfield, IL: Thomas, 1980), pp. 85–90.

7. Gresham M. Sykes, *Criminology* (New York: Harcourt Brace Jovanovich, 1978), pp. 143–145; Edwin H. Sutherland and Donald R. Cressey, *Criminology*, 9th ed. (Philadelphia: Lippincott, 1974), pp. 72–77; James Q. Wilson, *Thinking About Crime* (New York: Basic Books, 1975), pp. 51–53; "The Crime Wave," *Time* 105 (June 30, 1975):10–24; and Leroy C. Gould, "The Changing Structure of Property Crime in an Affluent Society," *Social Forces* 48 (1969): pp. 50–59.

8. Keith D. Harries, *The Geography of Crime and Justice* (New York: McGraw-Hill, 1974), pp. 38–60. See also Gerald F. Pyle, "Geographic Perspectives on Crime and the Impact of Anticrime Legislation," in *Urban Policymaking and Metropolitan Dynamics*, John S. Adams, ed. (Cambridge, MA: Ballinger, 1976), pp. 263–270.

9. See G.P. Chapman, "The Application of Information Theory to the Analysis of Population Distributions in Space," *Economic Geography* 46 (1970):317–331.

10. Henri Theil, *Economics and Information Theory* (Chicago: Rand McNally, 1967), p. 92.

11. Ralph Lenz, "Redundancy as an Index of Change in Point Pattern Analysis," *Geographical Analysis* 11 (1979):374–388.

12. The contribution of victim movements to the robbery process has been found to be statistically significant. See Lenz, "Redundancy as an Index of Change," p. 386.

Mobility Triangles

Alicia Rand

One of the deficiencies in criminological literature has been the practice of ignoring the spatial elements of illegal behavior. Traditional criminological research has utilized geographical locations only as proxies for the social characteristics of an area, overlooking the value of spatial variables. The omission has created a serious gap in our understanding of crime and victimization. This research focuses on the spatial context within which delinquent activities in an urban area take place. Specifically, the relationship between three spatial variables is examined: the offense location, the offender's residence, and the victim's residence. The results indicate that demographic attributes of offenders and categories of offenses mediate patterns in spatial criminal mobility. The data used are from the Philadelphia cohort study. An exhaustive review of the literature on "mobility triangles" is included.

Most research that explores criminal behavior from a spatial perspective has chosen as a focus of investigation either the distribution of offenses or the distribution of offenders. A number of authors, however, have taken both locations into account, and some have also attempted to analyze the relationship between the two.

Burgess, in his analysis of urban mobility with respect to group delinquency, defined two models according to the location of the delinquents' residences in relation to the site of the event:

1. The neighborhood triangle occurs when delinquents reside in the same neighborhood in which the offense took place.
2. The mobility triangle occurs when the delinquents do not reside in the neighborhood in which the offense took place.[1]

Burgess's triangle model was later employed by Lind in his analysis of ecological patterns of community disorganization in Honolulu.[2] Lind argued that the neighborhood triangle was an indicator of community disorganization, while the mobility triangle indicated stronger community organization. He states:

> One additional index of the effectiveness of local community standards of behavior may be found in the frequency of crime within the neighborhood of the delinquents' residence. . . . Where there are no effective gossips and self-appointed guardians of morals, one may indulge his vagrant impulses without seeking shelter in the anonymity of a strange community.[3]

Reiss compared the census tract of occurrence of the offense with the tract of residence of the offender in a study of 19,327 persons arrested in Seattle in 1965. His results show that offenders are much more likely to commit their offenses outside of their neighborhood than in the census tract of their residence.[4]

Amir, however, in his study of patterns in forcible rape in Philadelphia, found just the opposite.[5] Amir used "mobility triangle" analysis, adding to the model a third variable—the victim's residence. He analyzed the following four combinations:

1. Residential mobility triangle: offender lives in the area of the offense but not in the area of the victim's residence.

2. Crime mobility triangle: offender lives in the vicinity of the victim, but the crime is committed elsewhere.

3. Neighborhood triangle: offender lives in the vicinity of victim and offense.

4. Total mobility triangle: offender does not live in the vicinity of the victim or the offense.

In the majority of cases (82%), offenders and victims lived in the same area, while in 68 percent of cases a neighborhood triangle was observed, i.e., offenders lived in the vicinity of the victim and offense. In 26 percent of the cases, offenders lived both outside the area of the victim's residence and outside the scene of the offense. Only in three percent of the cases was the site in the area of the offender's residence but not of the victim's (residence mobility triangle). In four percent of the cases, offenders lived in the victim's vicinity, while the crime was committed outside of the area.

The remarkable fact that in over two-thirds of the cases, offense, offender, and victim were located in the same area, prompted Amir to state that,

> ... offenders ... have a tendency to cling to those areas of the city which they conceive of as their secure territory ... Offenders tend to restrict their territory to those areas where they can function inconspicuously . . . Also knowledge of the terrain assures fast and efficient escape.[6]

Amir's findings indicate that certain women have a higher chance of becoming a rape victim than others, in terms of their spatial characteristics, i.e., the area of residence and the area of routine activities.

Spatial relationship between the offense, offender, and victim in crimes of robbery was investigated by Normandeau in terms of the following five combinations:

1. Crime neighborhood triangle: the offender's residence, the victim's residence, and the offense location are all in the same census tract.

2. Offender mobility triangle: the victim's residence is in the same tract as the offense location, but the offender lives elsewhere.

3. Victim mobility triangle: the offender's residence and the offense location are in the same tract, but the victim lives elsewhere.

4. Offense mobility triangle: the offender's residence and the victim's residence are in the same tract, but the offense occurs elsewhere.

5. Total mobility triangle: the offense location, the residence of the offender, and the residence of the victim are all in different tracts.

Normandeau found that the crime neighborhood triangle occurred in 14 percent of the cases. A total mobility triangle was most frequent (38% of the cases), while the offense mobility triangle was least frequent (12%). For offender mobility the percentage was 17, and for victim mobility, it was 19 percent.[7] A comparison of Normandeau's and Amir's studies suggests that spatial patterns in robbery are quite different from those in forcible rape.

DATA AND METHODOLOGY

Studies that are limited to a single category of crime, even though they advance our understanding of spatial patterns within given crime categories, leave the overall crime structure largely unexplored. The present study covers eight categories of offenses and is therefore able to search for differences between spatial patterns displayed by different offenses. The relationship among the following three elements is examined: (1) the location of an offense, (2) the residence of an offender, and (3) the residence of a victim. The data were obtained from a larger investigation of delinquency in a birth cohort conducted by the Criminology Center at the University of Pennsylvania, and consist of records of 13,000 males and females born in 1958 who lived in Philadelphia from the ages of 10 through 17 and had at least one contact with the police by the time they attained age 18.

The offenses under investigation are: criminal homicide, forcible rape, robbery, aggravated assault, burglary, larceny, vehicle theft, and simple assault. In order to investigate spatial relationships in a systematic manner, census tracts of offenses, offenders, and victims are compared, holding the offense type constant.[8]

To investigate the possible existence of systematic spatial patterns of criminal behavior that are associated with demographic characteristics of the offenders, all tables are controlled for sex and race.

RESULTS

Table 1 presents the percentages of the offenses committed within the census tract of the offenders' residences. As the table's marginals suggest, almost one-third of the offenders (31%) find their targets in the offenders' own census tracts. Introducing race as the control variable indicates that white offenders stay in their immediate neighborhood somewhat more often than nonwhites (35% versus 30%). Sex also seems to influence the movement pattern, pointing to higher mobility of the female offenders. One-third of the male offenders, versus only 18 percent of female offenders, reside in the census tract of the offense location.

Larceny is the offense category in which the lowest percentage of offenders commit their offenses in the census tract of their residence (15%), which corresponds to 13 percent reported by Reiss.[9] There is a statistically significant association between the race and sex of the larceny offender and their spatial mobility. White larceny offenders stay more often in the census tract of their residence (23%), while for nonwhites this figure is only 13 percent. Sex is even more important in determining the mobility of a larceny offender. Nineteen percent of males as compared to only four percent of females commit larcenies in the same census tract in which they live. This finding can be attributed

Table 1

Frequency of Census Tract of Offender's Residence
Equal to Census Tract of Offense Location
by Type of Offense, Race, and Sex

Offense Type	Total (N)	Whites (N)	Nonwhites (N)	Males (N)	Females (N)
Total	30.77*	35.20*	29.71*	32.61*	18.57*
	(1446)	(320)	(1126)	(1332)	(114)
Homicide	53.13	100.00	50.00	50.00	100.00
	(17)	(2)	(15)	(15)	(2)
Rape	53.13	60.00	52.54	–	–
	(34)	(3)	(31)		
Robbery	31.87	34.00	31.73	32.41*	13.04*
	(261)	(17)	(244)	(258)	(3)
Aggr. Assault	38.60	45.45	37.24	36.76	49.15
	(154)	(30)	(124)	(125)	(29)
Burglary	42.02	40.51	42.55	41.74	51.43
	(503)	(126)	(377)	(485)	(18)
Larceny	14.77*	23.26*	12.79*	18.60*	4.35*
	(202)	(60)	(142)	(186)	(16)
Vehicle Theft	23.05	17.95	24.69	22.90	27.27
	(74)	(14)	(60)	(71)	(3)
Simple Assault	39.41	47.22*	36.34*	40.46	35.90
	(201)	(68)	(133)	(151)	(42)

*Significant at probability < .05.

to the fact that females more often than males are involved in shoplifting, which requires trips to commercial areas. On the other hand, males are more often involved in other kinds of thefts, such as bicycle thefts or thefts from vehicles, which can easily be committed within one's own neighborhood.

Of all property offenses, burglary takes place most often in the census tract of the offender's residence (42%). As many as 51 percent of female burglary offenders do not leave their census tract to commit their offenses, although these results are not statistically significant. Of robbery offenders, 32 percent committed their offenses in the census tract of their residence, a proportion almost identical to the 33 percent reported by Normandeau,[10] and very similar to the 29 percent reported by Reiss.[11]

As expected, offenses against persons tend to be committed more often in the offender's own neighborhood (53% for both homicide and rape). For aggravated assault, the percentage is 39 (49% for female offenders), and for simple assault it is 39 percent (47% for whites and 36% for nonwhites). These results can be explained by the spontaneity present in crimes against persons, which are characterized by affective motivation.

Table 2 shows five possible combinations of the offense, offender, and victim location. Confirming Reiss's and Normandeau's findings, the triangle, i.e., offender's residence, victim's residence, and offense

Table 2*

Comparison of Location of Offense and Residence
of Offender and Victim by Race and Sex: Totals

	Total (N)	Whites (N)	Nonwhites (N)	Males (N)	Females (N)
1. Offender, victim & offense in the same tract	14.16 (127)	15.48 (24)	13.88 (103)	13.32 (108)	22.09 (19)
2. Offense & victim in the same tract— offender elsewhere	19.96 (179)	22.58 (35)	19.41 (144)	20.47 (166)	15.12 (13)
3. Offender & offense in the same tract— victim elsewhere	16.16 (145)	16.13 (25)	16.17 (120)	16.03 (130)	17.44 (15)
4. Offender & victim in the same tract— offense elsewhere	4.57 (41)	5.16 (8)	4.45 (33)	4.32 (35)	6.98 (6)
5. Offender, victim & offense all in different tract	45.15 (405)	40.65 (63)	46.09 (342)	45.87 (372)	38.37 (33)
Total	100.00 (897)	100.00 (155)	100.00 (742)	100.00 (811)	100.00 (86)

*All results not significant at p < .05.

location all in different census tracts, is most prevalent, occurring in 45 percent of all cases. This pattern occurs most often among non-whites and males (46%) and less often among whites (41%) and females (38%). The neighborhood triangle, i.e., offender's residence, victim's residence, and offense location are all in the same tract, occurs only in 14 percent of the cases. It occurs most often among females (22%). The offense mobility triangle, i.e., offender and victim in the same census tract and offense location elsewhere, not surprisingly, is least frequent (5%), which was also found by Normandeau.[12]

When the offense type is held constant, as shown in Table 3, different patterns emerge for offenses against persons and offenses against property. The neighborhood triangle is most likely to occur in offenses against persons (38% of homicides and 27% of rapes). For robberies, the neighborhood triangle occurs only in 13 percent of cases, almost identical to Normandeau's 14 percent.[13] The total mobility triangle is the most prevalent pattern in robberies, occurring in 48 percent of cases. Robbery therefore follows spatial patterns of offenses against property rather than offenses against persons.

The neighborhood triangle occurs in 19 percent of aggravated assaults, while the total mobility triangle occurs in 38 percent of cases. In simple assaults, the neighborhood triangle occurs in one-quarter of the cases, while the total mobility triangle happens in 41 percent of cases. These figures indicate that in both types of assault, offender, victim, and offense site are most often located in three different census tracts.

Larceny and vehicle theft are two offense categories in which the neighborhood triangle occurs least frequently, eight percent and six percent, respectively. In cases of larceny, it happens twice as often when offenders are white (17%), indicating higher spatial mobility of nonwhite larceny offenders.

Conversely, for larceny, the total mobility pattern occurs most often of all offenses, in 56 percent of the cases, with as high as 60 percent for nonwhite offenders. For vehicle thefts, it is 44 percent, with no apparent impact of race. Almost one-third of vehicle thefts are committed in the victim's own neighborhood by an offender who comes from the outside. For white offenders, this proportion climbs to 40 percent, while for nonwhites it is 26 percent.

For robbery, the "offender mobility" and the "victim mobility" patterns are almost equally likely to occur. A robbery is committed about as often by an offender who comes from the outside to attack a victim in his own neighborhood (18%) as by an offender who, in his own neighborhood, attacks a victim who came from outside (16%). A

Table 3
Neighborhood Triangles by Race, Sex, and Offense Type

	#1		#2		#3		#4		#5	
	N	%	N	%	N	%	N	%	N	%
Homicide										
Total	6	37.5	3	18.7	3	18.7	1	6.2	3	18.7
Whites	—	—	—	—	—	—	—	—	—	—
Nonwhites	6	37.5	3	18.7	3	18.7	1	6.2	3	18.7
Males	4	28.6	3	21.4	3	21.4	1	7.1	3	21.4
Females	2	100.0	—	—	—	—	—	—	—	—
Rape										
Total	7	26.9	5	19.2	8	30.8	2	7.7	4	15.4
Whites	1	50.0	—	—	—	—	—	—	1	50.0
Nonwhites	6	25.0	5	20.8	8	33.3	2	8.3	3	12.5
Robbery										
Total	39	12.6	57	18.4	50	16.1	15	4.8	149	48.1
Whites	3	13.6	3	13.6	6	27.3	3	13.6	7	31.8
Nonwhites	36	12.5	54	18.7	44	15.3	12	4.2	142	49.3
Males*	39	13.1	51	17.1	48	16.1	15	5.0	145	48.7
Females*	—	—	6	50.0	2	16.7	—	—	4	33.0
Aggr. Assault										
Total	25	18.8	29	21.8	24	18.0	4	3.0	51	38.3
Whites	4	20.0	4	20.0	3	15.0	1	5.0	8	40.0
Nonwhites	21	18.6	25	22.1	21	18.6	3	2.6	43	38.0
Males	18	16.2	27	24.3	19	17.1	2	1.8	45	40.5
Females	7	31.8	2	9.1	5	22.7	2	9.1	6	27.3
Larceny										
Total	13	8.3	31	19.7	16	10.2	9	5.7	88	56.0
Whites	7	17.1	10	24.4	5	12.2	1	2.4	18	43.9
Nonwhites	6	5.2	21	18.1	11	9.5	8	6.9	70	60.3
Males	12	8.3	29	20.0	14	9.7	7	4.8	83	57.2
Females	1	8.3	2	16.7	2	16.7	2	16.7	5	41.7
Veh. Theft										
Total	8	6.3	38	30.2	21	16.7	3	2.4	56	44.4
Whites	1	2.5	16	40.0	4	10.0	1	2.5	18	45.0
Nonwhites	7	8.1	22	25.6	17	19.8	2	2.3	38	44.2
Males	8	6.5	38	30.9	21	17.1	3	2.4	53	43.1
Females	—	—	—	—	—	—	—	—	3	100.0
Simple Assault										
Total	29	24.8	14	12.0	19	16.2	7	6.0	48	41.0
Whites	8	32.0	2	8.0	5	20.0	2	8.0	8	32.0
Nonwhites	21	22.8	12	13.0	14	15.2	5	5.4	40	43.5
Males	20	24.4	11	13.4	13	15.8	5	6.1	33	40.2
Females	9	25.7	3	8.6	6	17.1	2	5.7	15	42.9

*Significant at p < .05.

similar pattern occurs for aggravated assaults, where 22 percent of offenders come from the outside and attack a victim in his own neighborhood, while 18 percent of offenders acting in their own neighborhood attack a victim who is an outsider. For simple assaults, however, there is more chance for an outside victim to be attacked in the offender's neighborhood (16%) than to be attacked in his own neighborhood by an outside offender (12%). Triangles for burglary cannot be computed because only two points exist: offender's residence and offense location (which is identical to victim's residence).

SUMMARY

This study examines the possibility that spatial patterns in delinquency are related to individual attributes of offenders and categories of offenses. The results of the analysis indicate that both offender and offense characteristics mediate the patterns in spatial mobility.

In almost one-half of all cases, the offender, the victim, and the offense site are each located in a different census tract, which indicates high spatial mobility.

Low spatial mobility—in which the offender, victim, and offense site are all located in the same census tract—is more likely to occur in offenses against persons than in offenses against property, thus confirming existing research findings.

The spatial patterns of delinquency are still highly speculative. Future work must employ more refined measurement and systematically test for relevant variables associated with spatial mobility of the offenders and of victims.

Notes

1. Ernest W. Burgess, "The Growth of the City," in *The City*, ed. Robert E. Park, Ernest W. Burgess, and Roderick D. McKenzie (Chicago: University of Chicago Press, 1925), pp. 47–62.

2. Andrew M. Lind, "Some Ecological Patterns of Community Disorganization in Honolulu," *American Journal of Sociology* 36 (1930):206–220.

3. Ibid., p. 218.

4. Albert J. Reiss, Jr., "Place of Residence of Arrested Persons Compared with Place Where the Offense Charged in Arrest Occurred for Part I and II Offenses," Consultant's Report, U.S. President's Commission on Law Enforcement and Administration of Justice, Mimeograph (Washington, D.C.: U.S. Government Printing Office, 1967).

5. Menachem Amir, *Patterns in Forcible Rape* (Chicago: University of Chicago Press, 1971).

6. Ibid., p. 87.

7. Andre Normandeau, "Trends and Patterns in Crimes of Robbery" (Ph.D. diss., University of Pennsylvania, 1968).

8. The ADMATCH (Address Matching System) was used in order to append census tract numbers to the addresses. U.S. Bureau of the Census, *Census Use Study: AD-MATCH Users Manual* (Washington, D.C.: U.S. Government Printing Office, 1970).

9. Reiss, "Place of Residence of Arrested Persons."

10. Normandeau, "Trends and Patterns in Robbery."

11. Reiss, "Place of Residence of Arrested Persons."

12. Normandeau, "Trends and Patterns in Robbery."

13. Ibid.

Predicting Crime Potential at Any Point on the City Map*

Marcus Felson

This paper demonstrates how the population potential concept can be used both to define crime risk at any point on the city map, and then to predict that risk from surrounding populations. The paper focuses upon points rather than areas. The results indicate that safe points are those furthest from all human populations, regardless of race. However, if one must be near other people, points surrounded by intact husband-wife couples are less risky. Prediction success is very high and calculation of certain risk for all points on the map is possible, subject to certain assumptions.

Conventional social area analysis, perhaps suitable for a non-automotive age, appears ill-suited to the study of crime in today's cities. The various actors involved in a crime—offenders, victims, and significant bystanders—have readily accessible modes of transportation, which allow them to move rapidly from one area to another, crossing census tract boundaries and spreading out over the metropolis.[1] Yet human proximity in cities still seems to have a relationship to crime distribution over space, as several studies linking crime and population density have already noted.[2]

Some of these studies have linked crime patterns to the population potential at the i-th point in space, defined below:[3]

$$P_i = \sum_{\substack{j=1 \\ j \neq i}} \frac{Q_j}{D_{ij}}$$

*The author wishes to acknowledge the advice of Daniel Nagin and Hal Winsborough in the preparation of this paper, and Leo Schuerman for the data used in this analysis.

where Q_j refers to the quantity of people at the j-th point and D_{ij} refers to the distance between i-th and j-th points. Thus, the population potential, P_j, takes all points surrounding the i-th point and sums the quantity of people at each, dividing by the distance from there to the i-th point. This measure gives extra weight to those nearby, yet allocates some weight to persons not so close. Hence, population potential would be very high in mid-Manhattan, less high in the midst of a dense college campus surrounded by fields of soybeans, and even less dense out in those fields.

One might think of the standard population potential measure as a *crude population potential*, since human distinctions are ignored. For example, past studies relating this measure to crime do not distinguish being surrounded by a gang of knife-wielding thugs or a congregation of little old ladies in tennis shoes. However, the spotty record of these studies might be overcome by disaggregating a human population into various segments differing in crime-related characteristics. For example, consider the following definition where Q_j, the quantity of persons residing at the j-th point, is disaggregated into m mutually exclusive categories:

$$Q_j = \sum_{k=1}^{m} Q_{jk}$$

where Q_{jk} refers to the quantity of persons at the j-th point within the k-th category, k=1, 2, 3, . . ., m. The segment-specific potential for the k-th category of humans at the i-th point can then be defined as follows:

$$S_{ik} = \sum_{\substack{j=1 \\ j \neq i}} \frac{Q_{ik}}{D_{ij}}.$$

It follows in this particular case that,

$$P_i = \sum_{k=1}^{m} S_{ik}.$$

The population potential concept helps us both to predict crime risk and to define it. In general, one can *predict* that crime risk at a given point will vary directly with the population potential at that point. One also should be able to improve prediction of crime risk by using as independent variables certain segment-specific potentials, taking into account those segments of the population that produce more offenders and victims and fewer guardians against crime.

We can *define* crime risk at a point in space which may never itself have been the exact scene of a crime, if we assume: (1) Surrounding incidents make a given point risky, since offenders may easily get there; and (2) people living at one point often travel to proximate points, hence exposing them to nearby risks. Hence, any point surrounded by many nearby incidents has a higher crime potential, as the following definition indicates:

$$C_i = \sum_{\substack{j=1 \\ j \neq 1}} \frac{E_j}{D_{ij}},$$

where E_j refers to the number of criminal events occurring at the j-th point in space. The crime potential can not only be interpreted like a population potential but can be calculated from the same points using the same coordinate system.

Such calculations can be made for any point on a map, from original events located at surrounding points. One might fill in a map with population potential calculations based solely upon existing crime experience. Yet the infinite number of points in space and the changes in community life might lead to another approach. Independent data about other social phenomena can yield models for predicting crime potentials. Such predictions might then be compared to observed crime potentials or used to predict or project how a certain population change would alter crime patterns over space.

Such crime potential models can be devised by incorporating census data on crime-related phenomena. Segment-specific population potentials can be interpreted as predictors of crime potentials, using regression equations to fit the model to the data and then to make predictions for other points in space. Such an approach can incorporate substantive knowledge about how population segments contribute potential offenders, victims, and significant bystanders whose presence or absence influences crime potentials. An extra advantage of such models is that they include the density of guardians against a crime, such as housewives and intact families.

DATA

Since 1970, the Community Analysis and Planning Division of Los Angeles has compiled a wealth of social indicators for Los Angeles census tracts. These include 1970 police data and census data, all assigned to census tracts whose centroids (geographic centers) were located on arbitrary x and y axis. These data were complete for most census tracts, except for the narrow isthmus of Los Angeles jutting southward to the port, an area surrounded by other municipalities. This analysis is based on the 703 remaining tracts, assigning tract data to the points located at the centroids of the tracts.

The city of Los Angeles is so large, diversified, and dispersed that it resembles in many ways a metropolis in itself. Since its growth was largely based upon the automobile, Los Angeles offers a good place to test spatial models for a motorized age. This city of 3.2 million people is nested within a larger megalopolis, ranging from San Diego to San Bernardino to Santa Barbara, spanning six Standard Metropolitan Statistical Areas, seven large counties, 41,000 square miles, and containing 11.6 million people in 1970.

The various segment-specific potentials and crime potentials are calculated at the centroids of each of the 703 census tracts using data allocated to them. For each, the surrounding 702 centroids are used to calculate measures of distance to the centroid in question based upon arbitrary but consistent map values. Although the social data are distributed over the whole census tract, they are assigned to the centroids. Since the regression analyses all involve potentials calculated from the same arbitrary map values, each metric coefficient can be interpreted as a proportional change in the crime potential resulting from a given change in the segment-specific potential.

If an error occurs anywhere in the data, its tendency to be replicated in each case renders the standard error misleading. As an alternative model test, these equations could be used to predict crime potentials for a separate set of points taken at random, and these predictions could be compared to crime potentials calculated for those points from observed crime data.

Because of multicollinearity, independent variables are limited to five: one indicator of socioeconomic status (the unemployed-male

potential), one indicator of family status (the intact-marriage potential), and three ethnicity indicators. Although most Spanish populations were coded by the census as Caucasian, some were in fact coded
Negro as well. Due to an oversight in the initial file preparation, this
nuance was ignored, yet it is not too damaging to the current analysis.
Once can obtain estimates for the majority population (that is the non-
Spanish, non-Negro population) by subtracting from each census tract's
total population both minority populations. On a few occasions, this
produced slightly negative numbers, which were then set to zero. Once
calculated for census tracts, these quantities were assigned to centroids
and the segment-specific potentials were calculated for each based
upon the surrounding 702 centroid data. The three sum to the crude
population potential, yet can be included in any regression equation as
simultaneous predictors as long as the latter is omitted.

Inclusion of the adolescent potential adds surprisingly little information beyond the crude population potential, due to an apparently
wide dispersion of adolescent population among the general population of Los Angeles.

ANALYSIS

As the correlation matrix in Table 1 indicates, various segment-specific
potentials tend to correlate positively, yet some negative or nearly zero
correlations are also observed. For example, the majority potential has
a correlation of −.212 with the Negro potential, indicating that high
concentrations of the population surrounding a given point in urban
space corresponds to low concentrations of the other population. The
majority potential has near zero correlations with the violent crime
potentials, two of these being negative. Not only are these potentials
capable of zero or even negative correlations, but they are not determined solely by distance from the geographic or population center of
Los Angeles. For example, the crude population potential correlates
−.14 and −.71 with the distance from these two centers, respectively,
with nearly half the variance unshared with the latter and most unshared with the former.

Some might argue that correlations of segment-specific potentials with crime potentials are the spurious result of their mutual correlation with the crude population potential. This can be investigated
by calculating partial correlations between each pair of segment-specific
potentials, controlling for the crude population potential. If these partial correlations were all near zero, this would suggest that all or most

Table 1

Means, Standard Deviations, Zero-Order Correlations, and Partial Correlations for Various Potentials*

	1	2	3	4	5	6	7	8	Means	Standard Deviations
0. Crude Population Potential	.956	.932	.732	.650	.543	.771	.818	.859	79,100	18,404
1. Unemployed-Male Potential	—	.797	.753	.800	.303	.909	.941	.956	5,935	1,761
2. Intact-Marriage Potential	-.882	—	.541	.418	.783	.507	.569	.616	15,158	2,930
3. Spanish Potential	.265	-.056	—	.413	.195	.690	.722	.734	14,680	6,469
4. Negro Potential	.801	-.068	-.122	—	-.212	.909	.912	.888	16,580	11,695
5. Majority Potential	-.879	.909	-.354	-.885	—	-.078	-.023	.049	47,840	11,192
6. Murder Potential	.921	-.916	.289	.842	-.928	—	.989	.983	12	17
7. Aggravated Assault Potential	.942	-.928	.314	.869	-.965	.977	—	.990	727	324
8. Robbery Potential	.925	-.995	.310	.840	-.936	.977	.972	—	417	219

*Upper triangle: zero-order correlations; lower triangle: partial correlations controlling for crude population potential.

132

of the relationship observed is spuriously due to their correlation with the crude population potential. The bottom triangle of Table 1 reveals that this is not the case. Every partial correlation (except the intact-marriage potential with the two minority group potentials) remains significantly nonzero with a meaningful sign. For example, the murder potential has a partial correlation of $-.928$ with the majority potential and .842 with the Negro potential. Clearly, there are strong relations between crime potentials and segment-specific potentials, not solely resulting from correlations with the crude population potential.[4]

Table 2 presents regression analysis taking crime potentials as dependent variables and segment-specific potentials as independent variables. These equations significantly improve upon the variance explained by the crude population potential alone. The latter explains 60 percent, 67 percent, and 72 percent, respectively, of the variance in murder, assault, and robbery potentials. The equations in Table 2 increase their explained variance from 26 percent to 37 percent above

Table 2

Regression Equations Predicting Crime Potentials
From Segment-Specific Potentials, Los Angeles, 1970

	Murder	Aggrav. Assault	Robbery
Constant	1.17	72.09	52.34
Unemployed-Male Potential	0.00175	0.11507	0.03751
Intact-Couple Potential	−0.00250	− .03730	− 0.07178
Majority Potential	0.00047	0.00333	0.01663
Negro Potential	0.00060	0.01356	0.01972
Spanish Potential	0.00040	0.01040	0.01443
R^2	0.972	0.991	0.986
r^2 with Crude Population Potential	0.601	0.669	0.722
Increase in variance explained	37.1%	32.2%	26.4%

that explained by their correlation with the crude population potential alone. Each equation explained over 97 percent of the total variance with substantively meaningful coefficients.

These analyses consistently show an interesting substantive finding—that the intact-marriage potential has a negative effect upon each violence potential net of the other variables. This indicates that certain types of population density are indeed *negatively* related (rather than positively or unrelated) to violent crime, perhaps because some population segments contribute a disproportionate share of significant bystanders whose presence helps to discourage violence. The unemployment coefficients are, not surprisingly, positive, indicating that every 1,000 units of unemployed male potential produce about 2 murders, 115 aggravated assaults, and 38 robberies.

PREDICTIONS

To test the predictive ability of these equations, 20 points were taken at random within the study area, none of these points being the centroids of census tracts. Because no data are needed to calculate the potentials of the i-th point itself, all 703 tract centroids can be used as the surrounding data points for calculating these potentials for the 20 new points. The regression equations in Table 2 can be used to predict crime potentials for these 20 points, which can then be compared to those calculated from observed data. Table 3 compares observed to expected crime potentials, which appear to be quite accurate.

SUMMARY

In predicting crime, it appears useful to disaggregate population potentials, to relate segment-specific potentials to crime potentials, to predict crime rates for any point on the city map, and to take into account how populations move about in a motorized city—still subject to the friction of space. Nonetheless, many nuances need further exploration. Distance might be put to an exponential power besides 1.0. Travel time and boundaries might be taken into account, as might subjective perceptions of the physical world. Jurisdictional spillovers of crime incidents might be considered, and crimes might be mapped more precisely when calculating crime potentials. Corrections for proximity to the edge of the city are also worth calculating. Such refinements may add to our understanding, but even this initial analysis suggests that people may find safety more at the periphery than at the metropolitan population centers, more among married couples than among others. Such information needs to be put to more use for understanding and predicting how crime patterns relate to spatial distributions of population.

This work differs in many respects from other research efforts on

Table 3

Comparisons of Observed and Forecast Crime Potentials
for 20 Test Points Within Los Angeles

Test Points***	Murder		Aggv. Asslt.		Robbery	
	Obs.	Forc.	Obs.	Forc.	Obs.	Forc.
A	3.27	3.74	264	291	125	119
B	3.90	3.92**	304	318	147	148**
C	4.01	4.28	352	354**	159	172
D	4.35	4.50	303	327	161	141*
E	4.56	4.44	423	395	189	208
F	4.66	5.06	358	359	170	164
G	4.96	4.89	467	423*	208	217
H	5.04	5.14	334	359	184	163
I	5.88	5.13	417	413	218	207
J	6.24	5.94	512	483	231	242
K	6.64	6.61	450	464	251	247
L	6.68	5.39*	491	470	239	245
M	8.16	7.92	540	553	313	302
N	9.24	8.36	606	600	368	345
O	11.34	11.31	739	743	405	421
P	11.96	11.84	751	764	418	439
Q	12.13	10.07	596	626	326	339
R	13.19	12.97	788	804	483	463
S	14.55	15.68	889	933	534	577
T	27.34	22.97	1320	1233	845	773
Root Mean Squared Error	1.1898		29.51		23.18	
Error ≤ 10%	14		19		18	
Error > 10%	6		1		2	

*Highest percent error.
**Lowest percent error.
***Selected randomly with supplementing for neglected parts of the Los Angeles map. Ordered here by observed murder potential.

this subject. No hypothesis is tested, no confidence interval is calculated, and no controls are included. Rather, the author's armchair thinking has led to a simple model that works. Alternative models should surpass the model presented here in both simplicity of theory and accuracy of prediction. Yet it appears that patterns of human aggregation set the stage for the patterns of criminal violence over space, and that this process can be understood better when one considers different segments of the population moving about quickly in a motorized city, subject yet to the friction of distance.

Notes

1. Lawrence E. Cohen and Marcus Felson, "Social Change and Crime Rate Trends: A Routine Activity Approach," *American Sociological Review* 44 (1979):588–608; Richard B. Felson, "Aggression as Impression Management," *Social Psychology* 41 (1978):205–213.

2. Harvey Choldin, "Urban Density and Pathology," *Annual Review of Sociology* 4 (1978):91–114.

3. J.Q. Stewart, "Empirical Mathematical Rules Concerning the Distribution and Equilibrium of a Population," *Geographical Review* 37 (1947):461–485.

4. One might question whether these results are the consequence of how census tracts were chosen; yet the geographic center of the 703 census tract centroids was in almost exactly the same spot on the map as the population center of gravity of the city.

Part 3

Fear of Crime and Its Effects

Perceived and Actual Crime Risks

Paul J. Brantingham,
Patricia L. Brantingham,
and Diane Butcher

Public perceptions of crime are normally studied through samples of large population aggregates such as metropolitan areas or nations, though both the research and policy implications of findings on concern with crime, fear of criminal victimization, feelings of safety, and ecological labeling generally relate to the neighborhood or community. This study explores perceptions of crime in a single high density neighborhood in Vancouver—the West End—and compares the patterns of those perceptions with objective crime patterns derived from police statistics and with the perceptual patterns derived from the U.S. National Crime Survey. The results make it clear that geographically based neighborhood level research will be a requisite of future research on perceptions of crime.

The social geography of crime is composed of two separate but related fields of study: the geography of objective crime patterns and the geography of perceptual crime patterns. The geography of objective crime maps patterns in crime occurrence. The information used in the geography of objective crime may be found in official records of reported or discovered crimes, such as those routinely collected by police, or it may be derived from victimization surveys such as those conducted by the United States Bureau of Justice Statistics or the Ministry of the Solicitor General in Canada.[1] Objective crime data are used to study the spatial and areal distributions of criminal events, of offenders, of victims and targets, and of the various social and physical elements of the environments in which crimes occur.[2] The geography of crime perception maps subjective beliefs about patterns of crime. The information used in the perceptual geography of crime is necessarily obtained through some form of survey research. Perceptual data are used to study individual estimates of crime problems at different times and places, their assessments of criminogenic environments, their feelings of safety, and the ways in which they adjust their behavior to accommodate their beliefs, concerns, and fears.[3] Study of the incongruities between objective crime patterns and perceptions of crime can provide a useful guide to understanding a community's responses to crime.

This paper is divided into sections. The first section discusses principal patterns found in the literature on perceptions of crime risk and safety. Conclusions are also drawn about the few persisting points of congruence between objective and perceptual maps of crime in North America. The second section adds to the empirical base literature on crime perceptions with a new study conducted at the neighborhood level, within a dense urban area—a type of area previously unexplored in fear of crime research.

I. CRIME PERCEPTION PATTERNS

The literature on crime perception identifies at least four different types of perception: concern with crime, fear of criminal victimization, feelings of safety, and ecological labeling. The literature also contains measures of behavioral adaptations to perceptions of crime. Studies have been conducted at five different levels of aggregation: national, multi-metropolitan aggregate, individual metropolitan area, individual municipality or governmental district, and neighborhood.[4]

CONCERN WITH CRIME AND FEAR OF VICTIMIZATION

Concern with crime and fear of victimization are two separate but interrelated study areas. Concern with crime measures how individuals rank crime as a social problem compared with other problems such as poverty, war, race relations, inflation, pollution, education, and unemployment.[5] Fear of victimization, on the other hand, measures individuals' estimates of crime trends in the nation, in the city, and in their own neighborhood, as well as the probability that they, personally, will be victimized.[6]

While frequently confused by politicians and popular writers, concern with crime and fear of victimization are entirely different concepts: People who do not fear victimization may be very concerned about crime as a social problem, while people who are more concerned about social problems other than crime may have powerful fears of victimization. Furstenberg found that concern with crime was not associated with fear of crime among the residents of metropolitan Baltimore, but that concern with crime was inversely associated with the official crime rate of the area in which a respondent lived.[7] Conklin found that residents of two municipalities in metropolitan Boston ordered both concern with crime and fear of victimization consistently with official crime rates. Thus, residents of the high crime municipality had higher levels of concern with crime and fear of victimization than residents of the low crime municipality.[8]

Perceptions of crime trends are marked by a strong tendency of respondents to hold their fear at a distance. People generally believe that crime is rising very fast in the nation as a whole, is rising somewhat less rapidly in their own city than in the rest of the country, but is not rising very rapidly at all in their own neighborhood. This tendency to hold fear at a distance is among the findings of the National Crime Survey (NCS), which conducted victimization and crime perception surveys in 26 U.S. cities in the mid-1970s.[9] Using these national survey data, Hindelang and his associates found a "crime-is-rising-at-a-distance" effect in the aggregated victimization/attitude surveys for the eight cities in the federally supported High Impact Anti-Crime Program (Atlanta, Baltimore, Cleveland, Dallas, Denver, Newark, Portland, and St. Louis).[10] The effect is also apparent in the 13 NCS reports for individual cities. To demonstrate the strength of this pattern, we will briefly discuss the research findings from one western city, San Diego; one southern city, New Orleans; and one northern city, Pittsburgh. Based on victimization surveys, San Diego is a low crime city; New Orleans is slightly above the city mean, and Pittsburgh slightly below.

The views of crime trends in the three cities were similar. In San Diego, 75 percent of respondents thought that crime in the United States was rising, but only 31 percent thought neighborhood crime was up. In Pittsburgh, 63 percent thought U.S. crime was up, but only 29 percent thought the same of neighborhood crime. In New Orleans, 86 percent thought U.S. crime was rising, but only 37 percent thought neighborhood crime was up.[11]

The tendency to hold crime at a perceptual distance is reflected in perceptions of the identity of criminal offenders. The NCS city attitude samples clearly indicate that a majority of people think that neighborhood crime is committed by outsiders rather than neighbors: In San Diego, 60 percent of respondents who thought there was neighborhood crime and expressed an opinion named outsiders; in Pittsburgh 65 percent named outsiders; and in New Orleans 79 percent named outsiders.[12]

The accuracy of citizens' fears of victimization, measured against official crime rates or victimization rates, remains an open question. Studies in Baltimore, Boston, and Minneapolis concluded that respondents' fears of victimization were directly related to the crime rates of the areas in which they lived.[13] In contrast, Thomas and Hyman found that fear of crime and crime risk perception were unrelated to actual victimization,[14] while Waller and Okihiro found no relation between the fear of burglary and the police-recorded burglary rate in Toronto.[15]

FEELINGS OF SAFETY

Feelings of safety measure another dimension in crime perceptions: whether people feel safe in specific places. The general finding is that regardless of respondents' fear of crime, the majority personally feel safe, and nearly everyone feels safer during the day than at night. In response to the question, "How safe do you feel walking alone at night in your neighborhood?" Conklin found that 86 percent of the respondents in a Boston suburb and 63 percent of the respondents in high crime "Port City" felt safe.[16] Waller and Okihiro found that 73 percent of their Toronto respondents were not worried about the prospect of burglary.[17] In San Diego, the NCS found that 73.3 percent of respondents felt safe walking alone in their neighborhood at night, and 97.6 percent felt safe walking during the day. In Pittsburgh, 56 percent felt safe at night, while 93 percent felt safe in the day. In New Orleans, 53 percent felt safe at night and 88 percent felt safe during the day.[18] It is important to note that the operative word in the questions asked in all the surveys, except in the burglary study by Waller and Okihiro, is *alone*; for example, the NCS surveys ask about perception of safety while walking alone. It is reasonable to expect that perceptions of safety might increase greatly if people were asked about walking with someone else at night.

Feelings of safety were probed in more depth by Thomas and Hyman in their study of the Norfolk-Virginia Beach area. They found some interesting anomalies. While 75 percent of their respondents felt safe walking alone in their own neighborhoods at night, and 77 percent agreed or strongly agreed with the statement, "My family and I feel reasonably safe and secure in this community," only 52 percent disagreed with the statement, "Nobody can feel safe at home anymore." Respondents felt far less safe outside their own neighborhood: 64 percent said the downtown area was not safe at night.[19] They found a strong correlation between perceptions of rising crime and declining safety: Those who perceived more crime felt less safe.[20]

People seem to place a perceptual distance between themselves and the feeling that they are not safe. Not only do they feel safer walking in their own neighborhoods than in the downtown area, most people believe that their own neighborhoods are safer than many others. In San Diego, 61 percent of residents thought their neighborhoods were safer than other parts of the metropolitan area, 33 percent thought their neighborhoods were average, and only 5 percent thought their neighborhoods were less safe than other neighborhoods. In Pittsburgh, 47 percent thought their neighborhoods were safer than others, 45 percent thought their neighborhoods were average, and 7 percent considered their neighborhoods were less safe. In New Orleans, the figures were 55 percent safer, 39 percent average, and 6 percent less safe.[21]

ECOLOGICAL LABELS

Ecological labels are expectations of particular behavioral patterns that people attach to specific places. Ecological labels are a major element of most people's cognitive maps of the world in which they live.[22] According to labeling theory, people impute reputations to specific places, treat those reputations as if they were based on factual events, and adjust their behavior in those places to accommodate the expectations drawn from the reputation. In extreme versions of labeling theory, the imputation of an ecological label eventually changes the character of a labeled place so that its factual aspects—the kind of people found and the sorts of events that occur there—come to match the content of the label.[23]

Ecological labels play an important role in criminological theory. They lie at the base of the vast literature on the spatial distribution of offender residences, exemplified by the work of Shaw and McKay,[24] from which most contemporary theories of the origins of criminal motivation derive their empirical base.[25] Ecological labels also play an important role in the perception of crime patterns. People label different places, particularly different neighborhoods in cities, as safe or dangerous, as crime ridden or crime free. These labels are known to have substantive and economic consequences. Pyle, for instance, has shown that the decline of Akron's central business district can, in part, be attributed to the propensity of that city's suburbanites to label the downtown as crime ridden and dangerous compared to suburban shopping centers.[26] Miller has shown how the imputation of a "high crime" label to a neighborhood creates a destructive positive feedback loop that sends the property values and social viability of the neighborhood into sharp decline. Several British studies have shown that growing crime rates and collapsing social order follow the wide-scale application of "criminal area" labels to specific neighborhoods.[27]

The fears and perceptions that underlie ecological labels of crime ridden or crime free, safe or dangerous, rarely reflect reality. A study of high crime/low crime patterns in a large housing complex in Tallahassee, Florida, found that respondents' perceptions of the location of high and low crime areas were inconsistent with the spatial distributions of crime obtained through an area canvass victimization survey.[28] Pyle's study of residents' perceptions of high and low crime areas in Akron found large segments of the downtown inappropriately labeled dangerous, and large segments of the suburbs, with relatively high crime rates, inappropriately labeled safe.[29]

Patterns in the location and content of "criminal area" labels vary with the characteristics of the individuals surveyed. Conklin found that residents of high crime rate "Port City" were concerned with serious offenses—the FBI index offenses, loan sharking, and narcotics—while residents of suburban "Bellville" were concerned about burglary and nuisance behavior by juveniles such as vandalism, underage drinking, loitering, and general rowdiness.[30] Smith and Patterson mapped the areas feared by a group of college students in Norman, Oklahoma. Males and females labeled distinctively different areas as dangerous; commuter and residential students also had distinctively different cognitive maps of fear.[31] A study in New Westminster, British Columbia, compared the areas labeled as high and low in crime by samples of residents, businessmen, and police. The three groups of respondents identified different sets of high and low crime areas. The reasons given for labeling areas as high in crime also differed by respondent group: residents focused on the type of nuisance behavior singled out by Conklin's Bellville respondents. Businessmen focused on areas they believed to have high theft and break-in rates—the business core of the city. Police named still different areas based on their knowledge of high official rates of serious criminal offenses in those sections.[32]

ADAPTATIONS

Individual adaptation to perceptions of crime and criminal areas can be measured in several ways: (1) through self-reports of areas avoided because they are believed to be dangerous or to have high crime rates; (2) through estimates of the behavioral changes the respondent and other individuals have made because of crime; (3) through measures of the number of people who express a desire to move or who actually do move to escape crime; and (4) through measures of the kinds and numbers of specific crime prevention activities and devices individuals report using. The studies seem uniformly to show that—contrary to labeling theory—people actually modify their behavior very little in order to accommodate their perceptions of crime.

Most people do not report avoiding specific parts of cities because those areas are perceived as having high crime rates. When asked by the NCS whether there were "some parts of this metropolitan area where you have a reason to go or would like to go . . . but are afraid to because of fear of crime,"[33] relatively low proportions of respondents reported actually avoiding certain areas because of crime. With respect to daytime, 86 percent of individuals surveyed by the NCS in San Diego, 82 percent in Pittsburgh, and 81 percent in New Orleans said that there were no areas they avoided. Even during the nighttime hours the majority said there were no areas to which they needed or wished to go that they avoided through fear of crime: 69 percent of respondents in San Diego, 64 percent in Pittsburgh, and 70 percent in New Orleans held these views. Thomas and Hyman asked people in the Norfolk-Virginia Beach area whether they avoided shopping downtown because of crime. Only 30 percent of the respondents said that they did.[34]

Most individuals surveyed by the NCS reported not changing their own personal behavior much in response to their general crime perceptions, but thought that their neighbors had changed some, and that other people, who live somewhere else, had changed a lot in response to crime.[35] In San Diego, only 28 percent reported limiting their own activities because of crime, but 32 percent thought their neighbors had, and 65 percent believed people in general had done so. In Pittsburgh, 38 percent said they had limited their own activities, but 58 percent thought their neighbors had, and 81 percent believed people in general had. In New Orleans, the comparable figures were 51 percent self-limitation, 62 percent neighbors, and 86 percent people in general.[36]

People are not prepared to move somewhere else because of their perceptions of crime. Thomas and Hyman found that 93 percent of their Virginia respondents did not want to move because of the crime problem in their area.[37] The NCS found few respondents who thought their own neighborhood was dangerous enough to make them want to move elsewhere, regardless of some degree of fear for personal safety: 85 percent said they would not move in San Diego; 81 percent in Pittsburgh; and 82 percent in New Orleans.[38] These prospective survey responses correspond strongly with the finding of urban planners that people who have in fact moved do not cite their previous neighborhood's crime problem as an important reason for having moved.[39]

More immediate crime prevention steps by individuals seem equally unaffected by crime perceptions. For instance, several studies report that people do not seem to respond to their perceptions of crime by improving the physical security of their homes or by participating in police or neighborhood crime prevention programs. Waller and Okihiro's survey of Toronto residents found that while 64 percent of respondents reported some form of insurance against burglary loss, less than half reported adding some form of lock to supplement the simple Yale-type locks on their doors. Only 30 percent reported joining some form of volunteer patrol.[40] These findings were consistent with those found in a prior study conducted in the Washington, D.C., metropolitan area.[41]

SUMMARY

Despite a belief, then, that crime rates have risen precipitously nationwide, individuals perceive their neighborhoods to be safe. Ecological labels attached to areas perceived to be high or low in crime often do not correlate with actual crime rates. And past research demonstrates that despite fear of crime, people say they do not permit their fear to limit their activities, to serve as an impetus for relocation, or to cause them to purchase home security products.

The patterns in these perceptions seem well established when data are aggregated to measure a metropolitan area or the nation as a whole. However, we felt it might be useful to conduct a fear of crime study within a specific, well-defined neighborhood, hypothesizing that the most interesting incongruities may occur at some point between the immediate home area and the more distant space represented by some larger subunit of the city. We decided to target a high density, upper middle-class neighborhood because such neighborhoods represent a major contemporary trend in North American urban development—gentrification—and because we knew of no prior study focusing on such an area.

II. WEST END, VANCOUVER STUDY

DATA AND METHODOLOGY

During the autumn of 1981 we conducted fear of crime research in an area of Vancouver called the West End. The West End is a clearly identified local area within the city. It has a special integrity as a perceptual unit, bounded on the west by English Bay, on the north by the immense, semi-wild Stanley Park, and on the south and east by the city's central business district. There are no residential areas adjacent to the West End.

The West End is the most densely settled area in the city, and one of the most densely settled areas in North America. In 1976, a census year, the West End had a population of 36,450 crowded onto 480 acres. Its population was primarily white, English speaking, and highly educated. Families were small: 78 percent had no children at home and another 16 percent had only one child at home. Some 39 percent of the West End's residents were single. The age pyramid was dominated by two groups: 38 percent were aged 20–34 and 20 percent were aged 65 and over.

The West End has an interesting history. Originally surveyed in 1855, the area was developed at the turn of the century as an exclusive residential area for executives of the Canadian Pacific Railroad, and was known at that time as "Blue Blood Alley." Population pressures during World War I led to the subdivision of many of the estates in "Blue Blood Alley" and the construction of the first apartment buildings. Successive waves of apartment construction in the 1920s, in the 1930s, in the 1950s, and in the 1970s have produced a mixture of older converted single family houses and two story apartments, middle-aged four to six story apartment buildings, and modern high rises. In 1976, the housing stock was 99 percent apartment and 94 percent rented. Over the past five years an increasing number of rental properties have been converted into owner occupied condominiums.

We studied a specific subarea within the West End. The target area was a centrally located six-by-eight block unit bounded by four commercial streets: Davie, Denman, Robson, and Thurlow. The area accommodates 450 buildings containing approximately 10,000 apartment units, and is at the core of the West End. A core area was chosen to avoid the skewed knowledge of the area that residents living on the border might have.

The study involved a comparison of objective and subjective crime maps and an analysis of the fear of crime in a local area. As an objective measure of study area and West End crime patterns, we used the addresses of all burglaries known to the Vancouver Police Department for the period January 1, 1977 through December 31, 1980. From these data we were able to calculate block and building-specific burglary rates. In addition, we gathered comparative data on a wider set of crimes known to the police in the West End and in Vancouver as a whole.[42]

PERCEPTIONS OF CRIME

Data on crime perceptions were gathered through an interview schedule adapted from a much larger questionnaire used by the Royal Canadian Mounted Police in a series of local studies of crime and criminal justice system perceptions across Canada. One set of items measured the respondent's socio-demographic characteristics. A second set measured home tenure, length of residence in the area and in the building, feelings of belonging to the neighborhood, and perceptions of neighborhood boundary. A four-item set measured fear of crime. A four-item set that included a cognitive mapping exercise using a base map determined the areas of the West End that had acquired ecological labels as high crime areas. A four-item set addressed feelings of safety. A final set measured responses to crime perceptions. The questions were designed to limit the confusion found in other fear of crime surveys, primarily the National Crime Surveys, where "neighborhood" is not defined and where questions seem to confuse different types of criminal behavior. Specific questions were asked about breaking and entry (burglary) as well as crime in general. Using mapping exercises, distinctions were also made between "local," "within the West End," and "the West End as a whole."

Our sample was based on a geographically staged random sampling procedure similar to that employed in the NCS cities surveys. A ten percent random sample of the blocks in the target area, and a ten percent random sample of buildings on each selected block, were chosen. Dwelling units in selected buildings were oversampled in order to allow for refusals. The first available adult at each selected dwelling unit was interviewed. Interviews were conducted on Sunday afternoons in the autumn, during Canadian Football League playoffs, in an effort to find people at home and to prevent a sampling bias toward unemployed females. After refusals, 91 interviews were conducted.

The characteristics of the population sample are reasonably consistent with general West End patterns, given recent trends toward gentrification. The sample was 54 percent male, and highly educated: 13 percent had completed post-graduate education; another 9 percent had graduated from college; another 25 percent had completed some college; and another 25 percent had completed high school. Twenty-three percent had incomes under $10,000; 30 percent had incomes between $10,000 and $20,000; 13 percent had incomes between $20,000 and $30,000; and 13 percent had incomes of $30,000 and over.[43] Ethnically, the sample was representative of the West End: 86 percent were white; 4 percent East Indian; 3 percent Oriental; and 7 percent from all other ethnic groups. Most respondents (87%) rented. Almost 60 percent of the respondents had lived in the area five years or less, while 26 percent had lived in the West End ten years or more. Almost three-quarters had lived in the specific building for less than five years; half for less than two years; a fifth under six months.

FEAR OF CRIME

The respondents were given a map of the West End that set the areal limits of the study. They were asked in the last year whether crime had increased, decreased, or stayed about the same in the West End as a whole and in the area[44] where they lived. The responses show that crime is perceived as a growing problem in both the West End as a whole and in the home area. For the West End as whole, 54 percent of the respondents who had an opinion thought that crime had increased, 24 percent thought that it had stayed about the same, and 33 percent thought that it had decreased. These percentages are comparable to perceptions of national crime trends found in the literature. For the specific area in which they lived, 41 percent of the respondents who had an opinion thought that crime had increased in the past year, 31 percent thought that it had stayed about the same, and 8 percent thought it had decreased. These percentages are higher than neighborhood crime trend estimates found in the literature, where only about 30 percent felt that neighborhood crime trends were up, while about 45 percent thought rates were unchanged, and between 5 and 10 percent thought crime trends were down (see Table 1).

Table 1
Perception of Crime Trends

	Vancouver Survey		National Crime Survey		
	West End	Local Area	San Diego	Pittsburgh	New Orleans
Crime up	53.8	40.7	30.6	29.2	36.9
Same	24.2	30.8	44.0	48.1	43.4
Decreased	3.3	7.7	5.1	10.4	5.6
Don't Know	18.7	20.9	20.3	12.4	14.1

Respondents were asked to compare crime in their area with crime in other parts of the city. A substantial majority thought crime was higher in their own area than in other parts of the city: 55 percent said there was more crime "in my own area" than in other parts of the city; 20 percent said the levels of crime were about the same in their area and other parts of the city; 18 percent said there was less crime in their area than other parts of the city. These findings are radically different from the response patterns found in other studies. For example, in the NCS cities surveys, about 60 percent of respondents typically felt their own neighborhoods were safer than other areas in the city, about 3 percent felt that all areas were about the same, and only about 6 percent felt that their own neighborhoods were less safe.

The respondents' perception that crime levels were higher in their own area than in other parts of the city is also striking because it is inconsistent with the objective crime pattern derived from police records. The West End had rates at or below the overall Vancouver crime rates for murder, sexual offenses, assault, robbery, commercial breaking and entry, residential breaking and entry, and motor vehicle theft. West End rates were marginally above the citywide rates for automobile thefts (see Figure 1).

Respondents were asked where they thought the offenders who committed crimes in their area resided. Forty-two percent said that area crimes were mostly committed by people from within their area. Thirty percent said that offenders came primarily from outside their area. The remainder had no opinion. This measure of fear of crime is almost the inverse of the pattern found in the literature.

Fear of crime was also measured by asking respondents how likely they thought it was that someone would try to break into their home in the coming year. Twenty-three percent thought there was no chance; 70 percent thought there was some chance; and only 3 percent felt certain that a break-in attempt would occur. The remaining 4 percent had no opinion. Estimates of the likelihood of being victimized by a break-in were not significantly associated with the sex, age, education, or income of respondents.

In summary, three of the four measures of the fear of crime show that residents of the target area fear crime more than generally reported in the literature on the fear of crime. This fear is not congruent with the objective crime patterns derived from police report data, which show West End crime to be the same or lower than the citywide average. Estimates of the risk of break-in show lower fear levels, suggesting that residential burglary is not the basis for the respondents' fear. In the next section we will examine perceptions of criminal areas as a possible basis for explaining their perceptions of crime.

Figure 1

West End and Total Vancouver Crime Rates

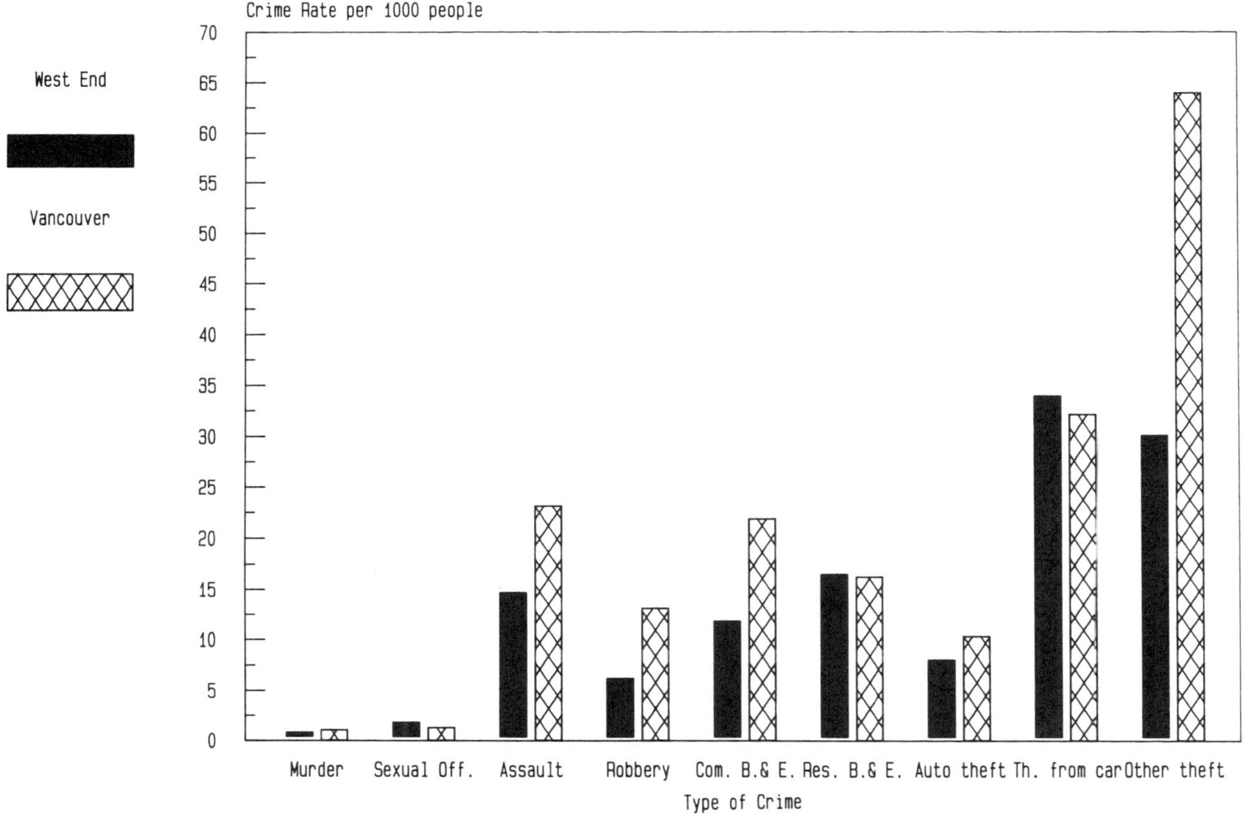

FEELINGS OF SAFETY

Feelings of safety were assessed by asking respondents if they felt safe in the building in which they were living. Twenty-five percent said they felt very safe; 57 percent said they felt reasonably safe; and only 17 percent said they felt unsafe. In this sample, feelings of safety were not significantly related to sex, age, education, or income. Larger samples might reveal such relationships.

Among our measures of fear of crime, feelings of safety were statistically associated only with estimates of the risk of victimization. Feelings of safety and estimates of risk were strongly associated; those who felt very safe tended to think that there was no chance of a break-in; those who felt unsafe tended to think that a break-in was certain during the coming year. On the other hand, respondents' feelings of safety in the buildings in which they were living were not related to the official burglary rates of the buildings.

A number of scholars have attempted to assess fear of crime as the loss of feelings of safety brought on by a breakdown of the sense of community.[45] We tested this notion among our respondents through the use of a direct question and a two-item indirect measure. First, we asked respondents whether "you feel a part of this area where you live, or do you think of this area more as just a place to live?" Sixty percent of the respondents said they felt a part of the area. Thirty-nine percent said it was just a place to live. It is fair to assume that it takes five years of living in a place before people begin to put down roots and feel they belong. Given that 57 percent of the respondents had lived in the area less than five years, and that 74 percent had lived in their current building less than five years, these figures suggest that fear of crime and feelings of safety in the West End cannot be attributed to breakdown in a direct sense of community.

Second, respondents were asked whether they thought their neighbors would notice a break-in attempt at their apartment. This question measures perceptions of community as related to mutual protection through surveillance of the sort postulated by Newman's theory of defensible space.[46] Forty-six percent of the respondents thought that there was no chance that their neighbors would notice a break-in attempt. Thirty-seven percent thought that there was only a slight chance that the neighbors would notice. Only 15 percent of the respondents thought that there was a good chance that the neighbors would notice. The remainder had no opinion. A "sense of community," using this measure, is relatively weak among West Enders. Neither estimates of the risk of victimization nor feelings of safety were significantly associated with this measure of community, however.

Respondents were asked what they thought a neighbor noticing a break-in attempt would do. Sixty-three percent said "call the cops." Twenty-three percent said "nothing." The perception that neighbors noticing a break-in would call the police was weakly associated with feelings of safety in the building, while respondents who felt unsafe tended to think that their neighbors would do nothing.

We asked those in the latter group why they thought neighbors would do nothing. Forty percent said that it was the responsibility of the building management, not fellow tenants, to protect them. One-third said neighbors would do nothing out of apathy. Fear, or lack of certainty that they were witnessing a break-in attempt, were cited by 13 percent of the respondents. This would seem to suggest an absence of any strong sense of community among these respondents. This measure, however, was not significantly associated with either estimates of the risk of victimization or feelings of safety.

In summary, most respondents felt safe. Feelings of safety were associated with low estimates of the risk of victimization. Different measures of a sense of community among respondents produced mixed results. Generally, however, feelings of safety did not seem to be related to a sense of community.

PERCEPTIONS OF CRIMINAL AREAS

Ecological labels were measured by asking respondents whether they could identify parts of the West End with "bad reputations for crime." Half of the residents identified specific places as having reputations for criminal activity. There was a clear consensus on the West End's most notorious criminal area, Davie Street, which forms one boundary of the study area. Davie Street was named by 65 percent of the respondents who identified a criminal area. Robson Street, another boundary of the study area, was named by 11 percent. Stanley Park, which forms one boundary of the West End, was named by 7 percent, while a miscellaneous collection of other places in the West End was named by another 7 percent of respondents. Places identified as criminal areas outside the West End were named by 11 percent of the respondents.

Asked why they thought the area they had named was a criminal area, 34 percent gave prostitution as the reason. The occurrence of serious crimes such as robbery, burglary, or assault was cited by 13 percent, while the presence of urban related problems such as noise, traffic congestion, and litter, was cited by another 13 percent. The presence of drug addicts was cited by 9 percent, and the presence of "transients" was cited by another 9 percent.

In other words, the ecological label of "criminal area" was appended to specific places not because they were thought to be centers of serious criminal activity, but, in 65 percent of the cases, because they were centers of nuisance behaviors like solicitation (prostitution is not a criminal act in Canada) or panhandling, were congested or messy, or had a lot of "street people" present.

Given that the areas labeled as high crime were labeled primarily for non-criminal behavior, the lack of relationship between perception of crime and official crime statistics makes more sense. When a general "Is crime going up?" question is asked, the respondent may very likely not be thinking about criminal code violations. If this is the case, then the lack of a relationship among perceptions of safety, risk of victimization, and the view that crime is increasing also makes more sense. Questions about perception of safety and risk of victimization are often framed in language that may lead the respondent to think about specific crimes, such as assault or burglary. Questions about increasing crime seem to elicit information about general urban concerns or nuisance behavior, not about perceptions of the risk of assault or burglary.

BEHAVIORAL RESPONSES TO CRIME PERCEPTIONS

When asked whether they had taken any security measures to protect their homes, 63 percent of the respondents said they had done nothing, 22 percent had installed special locks or dead bolts, and 3 percent said they had taken out insurance specifically because of crime. Taking security measures, however, was not significantly related to either estimates of the risk of being victimized by a break-in or feelings of safety in the building.

Respondents were asked whether they were participating in some crime prevention program. Four-fifths of the respondents said they were not. Twelve percent said that they were, but did not indicate what kind of program. Operation Identification was named by 3 percent. Participation in a crime prevention program was not significantly associated with either fear of break-in or feelings of safety.

Respondents were also asked whether they had seen a crime occur during the previous year, but had not reported it to the police. Seventy percent answered "no," while 26 percent said "yes." Reporting behavior was not significantly associated with either fear of a break-in or feelings of safety.

In summary, very few respondents engaged in any kind of behavior intended to cope with their perceptions of crime. Most took no steps to secure their homes. Fewer than one-fifth participated in a crime prevention program. Three-fifths did not avoid areas they had labeled "criminal." Coping behavior, therefore, was not statistically associated with either fear of crime or feelings of safety.

SUMMARY

The fear of crime literature explores perception of crime trends, perception of risk of victimization, feelings of safety, ecological labeling of crime areas, and coping behavior. Most fear of crime research has been conducted at a low level of resolution, yet results are used to describe patterns at high levels of resolution. This study represents an analysis of fear of crime at a fine level of resolution, a neighborhood level, within a dense urban area. A study at this level adds a new perspective to the fear of crime literature, while reinforcing some trends found in studies done on large areal units and conflicting with others.

Residents of the West End generally perceived greater crime problems close to home than at a distance and thought that many offenders came from their own neighborhood. Crime was perceived as more immediate in this dense urban environment than is reported in studies of whole cities with their many neighborhoods of varied density. Despite higher perceptions of the immediacy of crime in their neighborhood, residents of the West End generally felt safe and did not perceive much risk of personal burglary. They also took few security precautions and participated in few crime prevention programs. There was a high identification with the area, but generally low perception of protection coming from the neighbors. Finally, perception of risk was not related to actual reported victimizations. The general perception was that crime was a problem, but not a personal problem.

The pattern found in the West End raises several questions. From a research perspective, studies at the city level, such as the NCS city sample, appear to be masking lower level variations. National or city level surveys lead one to believe that crime is not perceived as a local or neighborhood problem. Yet, as this study shows, there are neighborhoods where crime is considered an immediate problem. Unlike most other fear of crime research samples, the West End residents acknowledged that crime was a reality in their own neighborhood. The remarkable finding is that despite this impression, residents felt little fear for their personal well-being and did not believe that they themselves would be victimized.

Our attempt to measure a sense of community among West End residents, both directly and indirectly, and to relate those measures to fear of victimization or feelings of safety, revealed no strong relationships. It seems clear that sense of community as it was measured did not relate to crime perceptions. This may be due to the type of measures that were used, or it may be due to the homogeneous ethnicity of the neighborhood, or it may be that Canadians fear "strangers" less than Americans do. We suspect, however, that fear of crime in dense, urban neighborhoods can no longer be associated with an individual sense of personal alienation and a yearning for the close community spirit of a distant rural past. Both Canada and the United States are urban nations, and have been so for several generations. We believe that research efforts should be directed to other modes of explanation.

From a policy perspective, the West End study raises the following question: How can individuals be induced to increase personal protection, watch out for their neighbors, and participate in community crime prevention programs if they have a high sense of personal safety? To gain cooperation in crime prevention on both a personal and community level, public information programs may have to be designed to "create" sufficient fear of crime so that individuals will see themselves and their neighbors as potential crime victims, and hence be motivated to take adequate steps to protect themselves and their community.

Fear of crime research is still relatively new. Most research has been conducted at the city or national level. As this study demonstrates, more research is needed at low levels of aggregation. Studies in other specific types of neighborhoods may produce different patterns, including other patterns of inconsistencies. With more neighborhood studies, we may begin to understand variations in the fear of crime and develop more effective crime control policies.

Notes

1. Such data, particularly official crime statistics, underenumerate the total set of crime occurring in any given time and place. The limited evidence that exists, however, suggests that these data sets are not spatially based. R.I. Mawby, "Police Practices and Crime Rates: A Case Study of a British City," in P.J. Brantingham and P.L. Brantingham, *Environmental Criminology* (Beverly Hills: Sage, 1981), pp. 105–147.

2. See, e.g., K.D. Harries, *The Geography of Crime and Justice* (New York: McGraw-Hill, 1974); K.D. Harries, *Crime and the Environment* (Springfield, Ill: Thomas, 1980); Brantingham and Brantingham, *Environmental Criminology*.

3. See, e.g., Brantingham and Brantingham, *Environmental Criminology*; Harries, *Crime and the Environment*; D.E. Georges-Abeyie and K.D. Harries, *Crime: A Spatial*

Perspective (New York: Columbia University Press, 1980); R.D. Carter and K.Q. Hill, *The Criminal's Image of the City* (New York: Pergamon Press, 1979).

4. *National level:* F. Clemente and M.B. Kleiman, "Fear of Crime in the United States: a Multivariate Analysis," *Social Forces* 56 (1977), pp. 516–531; *Multi-metropolitan:* M. Hindelang, M. Gottfredson, and J. Garofalo, *Victims of Personal Crime: An Empirical Foundation for a Theory of Personal Victimization* (Cambridge: Ballinger, 1978); J. Garofalo and J. Laub, "The Fear of Crime: Broadening Our Perspective," *Victimology* 3 (1978), pp. 242–253; J. Garofalo, "Victimization and the Fear of Crime," *Journal of Research in Crime and Delinquency* 16 (1979), pp. 80–97; *Metropolitan level:* F.F. Furstenberg, Jr., "Public Reaction to Crime in the Streets," *American Scholar* 40 (1971), p. 610; C.W. Thomas and J.W. Hyman, "Perceptions of Crime, Fear of Victimization, and Public Perceptions of Police Performance," *Journal of Police Science and Administration* 5 (1977); I. Waller and N. Okihiro, *Burglary: The Victim and the Public* (Toronto: University of Toronto Press, 1978); *Individual municipality:* J. Conklin, *The Impact of Crime* (New York: Macmillan, 1975); P.J. Brantingham, P.L. Brantingham, and E.R. Fister, "Patterns in Crime Perception," paper read at Academy of Criminal Justice Sciences meetings, 1979; Royal Canadian Mounted Police (RCMP), *Crime Problem Analysis of Selkirk Rural* (Ottawa: RCMP, 1981); *Neighborhood level:* S. Damer, "Wine Alley: The Sociology of a Dreadful Enclosure," *Sociological Review (N.S.)* 22 (1974), pp. 221–248; J. Baldwin, "Problem Housing Estates—Perceptions of Tenants, City Officials, and Criminologists," *Social and Economic Administration* 8 (1974), pp. 116–135; P.J. Brantingham, P.L. Brantingham, and T. Molumby, "Perceptions of Crime in a Dreadful Enclosure," *Ohio Journal of Science* 77 (1977), pp. 256–261; M. McPherson, "Realities and Perceptions of Crime at the Neighborhood Level," *Victimology* 3 (1978), pp. 319–328.

5. During the late 1960s and through much of the 1970s crime was ranked as the first concern by large segments of North American society. Furstenberg, "Public Reaction to Crime"; Conklin, *Impact of Crime*; Waller and Okihiro, *Burglary*; J. Brooks, "The Fear of Crime in the United States," *Crime and Delinquency* 20 (1974), pp. 241–244. In comparison to the 1960s and 1970s, in the 1980s concern with crime has become relatively less important, and other social issues such as inflation, unemployment, and energy have taken precedence.

6. Furstenberg, "Public Reaction to Crime."

7. Ibid., p. 604.

8. Conklin, *Impact of Crime*, p. 77.

9. Data on crime perception have been released in two ways: in several studies of aggregated data from eight cities participating in the U.S. Law Enforcement Assistance Administration's High Crime Impact Program (Atlanta, Baltimore, Cleveland, Dallas, Denver, Newark, Portland, and St. Louis); and, to date, as individual volumes for 13 of the 26 cities surveyed. These fear of crime surveys form the backbone of most fear of crime research. They were broad based and used sample sizes that individual nongovernmental researchers could never hope to obtain.

The survey instruments themselves contain some wording that causes problems in analysis. Because the National Crime Surveys are of such central importance, a few of the language problems will be briefly discussed. The major problem arises from use of the word "neighborhood" in the survey instrument. There is a vast literature that attempts to define and describe the word "neighborhood." Since the meaning of this word may vary from one block to some vast subdivision of a city, the results of the fear of crime survey can at best be read with neighborhood meaning some ambiguous area, smaller than the metropolitan area. Similarly the word "city" is used without definition. Finally, questions appear to be slanted towards specific categories of "street crimes," and they are often imprecise; consequently, responses are equally imprecise.

Nonetheless, the surveys provide the major, if fuzzy, picture of perception of crime. The results of the surveys will be reported, but the lack of precision in defining concepts must be kept in mind while interpreting the results.

10. Hindelang, Gottfredson, and Garofalo, *Victims of Personal Crime*; Garofalo and Laub, "Fear of Crime."

11. U.S. Department of Justice, *San Diego: Public Attitudes about Crime*, National Crime Survey Report No. SD-NCS-C-30, NCJ-42245 (Washington, D.C.: U.S. Government Printing Office, 1977); U.S. Department of Justice, *Pittsburgh: Public Attitudes About Crime*, National Crime Survey Report No. SD-NCS-C-29 (Washington, D.C.: U.S. Government Printing Office, 1979); U.S. Department of Justice, *New Orleans: Public Attitudes about Crime*, National Crime Survey Report No. SD-NCS-C-27, NCJ-46242 (Washington, D.C.: U.S. Government Printing Office, 1977). Hereinafter, this set of reports is cited as NCS reports. Unless otherwise indicated, reference is to pp. 4–5 in each of the volumes.

12. These percentages were calculated from NCS by adjusting for individuals who thought there was no neighborhood crime, who said they did not know origin of criminals, and for whom no data were available. This effect of naming outsiders is also found in a number of British studies probing fear of victimization and perceptions of criminal residence at the neighborhood level. See R.F. Sparks, H.G. Genn, and D.J. Dodd, *Surveying Crime: A Study of the Measurement of Criminal Victimization, Perceptions of Crime, and Attitudes to Criminal Justice* (New York: Wiley, 1977); Baldwin, "Problem Housing Estates"; Damer, "Wine Alley." A number of scholars have tried to explain this perceptual pattern in terms of a loss of the sense of community in urban areas. See J.Q. Wilson, "The Urban Unease: Community vs. City," in H.J. Schmandt and W. Bloomberg, Jr., *The Quality of Urban Life* (Beverly Hills: Sage, 1969), pp. 455–472; Conklin, *Impact of Crime*; Garofalo, "Victimization and Fear of Crime"; Garafalo and Laub, "Fear of Crime," p. 246.

13. Furstenberg, "Public Reaction to Crime"; Conklin, *Impact of Crime*; McPherson, "Realities and Perceptions of Crime."

14. Thomas and Hyman, "Perceptions of Crime."

15. Waller and Okihiro, *Burglary*, p. 80.

16. Conklin, *Impact of Crime*.

17. Waller and Okihiro, *Burglary*, p. 80.

18. NCS reports.

19. Thomas and Hyman, "Perceptions of Crime," Table 1.

20. This finding was also made by Conklin, *Impact of Crime*, p. 85, and by Garofalo, "Victims of Personal Crime, pp. 86–87.

21. NCS reports.

22. P. Gould and R. White, *Mental Maps* (Harmondsworth: Penguin, 1974).

23. L.H. Lofland, *A World of Strangers: Order and Action in Urban Public Space* (New York: Basic Books, 1973).

24. C.E. Shaw and H.D. McKay, *Juvenile Delinquency and Urban Areas*, rev. ed. (Chicago: University of Chicago Press, 1969).

25. P.J. Brantingham and C.R. Jeffery, "Afterword: Crime, Space, and Criminological Theory," in Brantingham and Brantingham, *Environmental Criminology*, pp. 227–238; D.C. Gibbons, *The Criminological Enterprise* (Englewood Cliffs: Prentice-Hall, 1979); H. Finestone, *Victims of Change: Juvenile Delinquency in American Society* (Westport, Ct.: Greenwood Press, 1977).

26. G.F. Pyle, *The Spatial Dynamics of Crime* (Chicago: Department of Geography, University of Chicago, 1974); G.F. Pyle, "Systematic Sociospatial Variation in Percep-

tions of Crime Location and Severity," in Georges-Abeyie and Harries, *Crime: A Spatial Perspective*, pp. 219-245.

27. E. Miller, "Crime's Threat to Land Values and Neighborhood Vitality," in Brantingham and Brantingham, *Environmental Criminology*, pp. 111-119; J. Baldwin and A.E. Bottoms, *The Urban Criminal* (London: Tavistock, 1976); O. Gill, *Luke Street: Housing Policy, Conflict, and the Creation of the Delinquent Area* (London: Macmillan Press, 1977); Damer, "Wine Alley."

28. Brantingham, Brantingham, and Molumby, "Perceptions of Crime."

29. Pyle, "Systematic Sociospatial Variation."

30. Conklin, *Impact of Crime*, p. 78.

31. C.E. Smith and G.E. Patterson, "Cognitive Mapping and the Subjective Geography of Crime," in Georges-Abeyie and Harries, *Crime: A Spatial Perspective*, pp. 205-218.

32. Brantingham, Brantingham, and Fister, "Patterns in Crime Perception."

33. NCS, San Diego report, attitude questionnaire, items 13a and 13b, p. 48.

34. Thomas and Hyman, "Perceptions of Crime; NCS reports.

35. The question asked in the survey was extremely vague: "In general, have you/ people in this neighborhood/people in general limited or changed your/their activities in the past few years because of crime." With such an imprecise question, changes might range from "locking the car door" to "never leaving the house." Even with such imprecision, the general pattern of more perceived behavioral change as perceptual distance from the individual increased held for the eight Impact cities, and it was apparent in the responses of the other National Crime Survey cities as well. See Garofalo and Laub, "Fear of Crime," p. 245.

36. NCS reports.

37. Thomas and Hyman, "Fear of Crime."

38. NCS reports.

39. T. Droettboom, Jr., R.J. McAllister, E.J. Kaiser, and E.W. Butler, "Urban Violence and Residential Mobility," *Journal of the American Institute of Planners* 37 (1971), pp. 319-325.

40. Waller and Okihiro, *Burglary*, pp. 83-84.

41. H. Scarr, *Patterns in Burglary*, 2d ed. (Washington, D.C. U.S. Government Printing Office, 1973).

42. These data were compiled from Vancouver Police Department files by Wendy Sokoloff with the assistance of Constable Ron Gale.

43. Twenty percent either did not know what their incomes were or refused to answer.

44. In assessing the "area where you live" residents were given a base map of the West End with a mark identifying their building and asked to draw the boundaries of their area. People generally defined a unique subset of blocks around their own home. The aggregate pattern tended to coincide with the boundaries of our study area. For more on this technique, see T. Lee, "Urban Neighborhood as a Socio-Spatial Schema," *Human Relations* 21 (1968), pp. 241-267.

45. Wilson, "Urban Unease"; Conklin, *Impact of Crime*; Garofalo, *Victims of Personal Crime*.

46. O. Newman, *Defensible Space* (New York: Macmillan, 1972).

Crime, Community Organization, and Causes of Neighborhood Decline*

D. Garth Taylor,
Richard P. Taub,
and Bruce L. Peterson

Dissatisfaction with the level of safety in a neighborhood is a result of how residents evaluate the strength of community organization and the amenities of the neighborhood and not a result of victimization or crime rates per se. *This paper, and our earlier work on which this paper is based, shows that perception of community organization and neighborhood amenities must be considered in measuring the relationship between crime and urban change. Our study, unlike most studies of the effects of crime, is based on individual-level samples of residents within neighborhoods as well as an aggregate-level sample of neighborhoods. By comparing the results from these different samples, and by using state-of-the-art statistical techniques, we arrive at a markedly different estimate of the role of victimization in neighborhood change than is suggested by "common knowledge."*

The fears that motivate economic decay and demographic flight from central cities are fears about the ability to maintain a high quality of

---

*This paper was written by D. Garth Taylor. The findings are based on a multiple-year study. In a project of such complexity, the research products belong to all who contributed to them.

life in urban neighborhoods. Crime affects the quality of life in a neighborhood but it is not the single, determinative factor. Some neighborhoods possess the political, organizational, or economic resources to respond effectively to crime and thus provide some insurance against a decline in the quality of life. These neighborhoods maintain a high quality of life whatever their level of victimization. A neighborhood's housing stock as well as its location can also help maintain a high quality of life in spite of high victimization rates. But some neighborhoods do not possess the amenities or the social organization to solve the crime problem. For residents of these resource-poor neighborhoods, victimization is interpreted as a sign that crime is a serious problem in the community, that the area is in decline, and that one is better off moving to some other location.

We have documented in a previous work that the experience of victimization and even knowledge of crime rates in the immediate area do not have as powerful an influence on how people respond to crime as common knowledge might lead us to believe.[1] Our previous research shows that personal victimization does not account for an individual's decision to move from a neighborhood, experiences of victimization do not result in a reduced willingness to upgrade or maintain one's property, nor does victimization affect a person's expectations of racial change or perceptions of weakness in the local housing market.[2]

The purpose of this paper is to analyze further the relationship between victimization, fear of crime, and other characteristics of urban neighborhoods. We examine the extent to which an individual's assessment of neighborhood security is related to: (1) personal or household experiences of victimization; (2) the crime rate in the neighborhood; and (3) neighborhood features other than crime rates. In addition, we examine the effectiveness of defensive action—installing security devices, owning guard dogs, avoiding unsafe areas of the neighborhood—in reducing one's chance of criminal victimization and in enhancing a sense of neighborhood security.

THE DATA

Eight neighborhoods in the Chicago central city area were selected to be surveyed and studied observationally. The neighborhoods were not randomly chosen. Rather, a systematic procedure was used to achieve a balanced sample of different neighborhood environments. Half of the neighborhoods are above the city's average crime rate, half below. Half of the neighborhoods have "strong" housing markets, with appreciation levels above inflation, half do not. Half of the neighborhoods are racially stable, half are experiencing turnover.[3]

Approximately 400 telephone interviews were conducted in each of the eight neighborhoods. The telephone interview collected a great deal of information on recent personal and household victimization experiences, fear of crime, and whether the respondent or household had taken protective steps against victimization.

In addition to the telephone survey data, certain neighborhood and census tract statistics were made available by the Chicago Police Department. We calculated the rate of personal victimization and the rate of property crime in the census tract for each respondent in the survey. Each neighborhood in our study contains about ten census tracts. The average tract rate of police-reported personal crime for the approximately 400 respondents in each neighborhood is shown in Table 1. The second column of Table 1 is the standard deviation of the tract victimization rate in each neighborhood. This is reported to show that there is a fair amount of heterogeneity among census tracts within each neighborhood. The average of the neighborhood average tract rates, shown at the bottom of Table 1, is not meant to be representative of the city of Chicago. The figure, as calculated here, is weighted by the proportion of the total sample in each neighborhood. This figure is provided solely for comparative purposes to show which neighborhoods are the comparatively high crime areas and which neighborhoods are the comparatively low crime areas in our sample. The third column of Table 1 shows the average tract rate for property crime in a neighborhood and the fourth column shows the standard deviation for this variable within each neighborhood.

The last two columns of Table 1 show a different type of personal and property crime rate. These rates were estimated using the individual-level telephone survey data. Several questions were asked about types of victimization suffered by the respondent in the neighborhood in the last year. The combined answers to several measures of personal and property crime are indexed in the last two columns of Table 1.

As frequently occurs in community studies of victimization, the survey estimates show the experience of crime to be more widespread than do the estimates based on police records. Part of the reason for this is that people are not completely accurate in their recollection of when crimes occur and tend to report as happening "within the last year" something that took place longer ago. This is the "telescoping" phenomenon.[4] But not all of the difference between survey-estimated and police-recorded crime can be attributed to telescoping. Some crimes

Table 1

Neighborhood Differences in Victimization

	Tract Rates				Survey-Based Measures	
	Personal Crime		Property Crime		Personal Crime	Property Crime
Neighborhood	Mean	Std Dev	Mean	Std Dev	Mean	Mean
Portage Park	.009	.09	.043	.08	.048	.190
Lincoln Park	.023	.12	.098	.11	.086	.264
Austin Park	.034	.12	.090	.13	.157	.258
Back of the Yards	.033	.15	.069	.15	.132	.254
Beverly	.025	.15	.052	.14	.075	.180
Hyde Park-Kenwood	.020	.08	.105	.09	.099	.236
South Shore	.028	.10	.090	.10	.105	.252
East Side	.007	.07	.032	.07	.044	.202
Total	.023	.11	.07	.12	.093	.23

are not reported to the police but are reported to survey interviewers, suggesting an undercount in the police records.[5] Of course, the undercounting of crime may not be as extensive as suggested by the comparison of police and survey statistics in Table 1. A number of the survey reports would most likely be considered unfounded by the standards of normal police practice.

AGGREGATE RELATIONSHIPS BETWEEN VICTIMIZATION AND FEAR

Measures of Fear of Crime

A number of different measures of fear of crime are analyzed in this chapter. To allow comparison with other studies, the questions about fear of crime were asked, in the interview, before the battery of questions on victimization. Respondents were first asked: "How much crime would you say there is in your own immediate neighborhood—"a lot, some, or only a little?" Following this was the question "Would you say that the likelihood you will be a victim of crime in your neighborhood during the coming year is high, moderate or low?" A series of questions were then asked about sources of information regarding the level of crime in the community. Questions were also presented on whether the respondent had ever taken defensive measures against crime. Finally, there followed another short battery of questions on worries about crime. In this part of the interview respondents were asked whether the following statements are mostly true or mostly false: "I'm often a little worried that I will be the victim of a crime in my neighborhood," and "When I have to be away from home for a long time, I worry that someone might try to break in." These four measures of fear of crime were factor analyzed using polychoric correlations along with other measures of fear and worry for our survey. They are a consistent set of measures, with strong face validity, that scale well with and in some cases are identical to measures of fear of crime used in other landmark studies.[6]

The neighborhood differences in our multiple measures of fear are shown in Table 2. If we rank the neighborhoods on the four victimization measures in Table 1, and rank the neighborhoods on the four measures of fear and worry in Table 2, the aggregate-level correlation is nearly perfect. Neighborhoods with relatively higher levels of victimization also have relatively higher levels of fear and worry about crime. In the type of research design where only aggregate-level data are used, the size of this rank order correlation would be interpreted as evidence that victimization is the cause of fear and worry about crime in the neighborhood.

Table 2
Neighborhood Differences in Fear and Worry About Crime

	Perceived Quantity of Crime	Perceived Risk of Being Victimized	Worry About Being Victimized	Worry About Being Burglarized
Neighborhood	Mean	Mean	Mean	Mean
Portage Park	2.40	1.24	0.22	0.38
Lincoln Park	2.71	1.46	0.24	0.43
Austin	2.68	1.68	0.45	0.57
Back of the Yards	2.56	1.50	0.39	0.51
Beverly	2.33	1.18	0.15	0.24
Hyde Park-Kenwood	2.66	1.49	0.37	0.35
South Shore	2.71	1.58	0.36	0.42
East Side	2.42	1.25	0.19	0.38
Total	2.56	1.42	0.30	0.41

The analysis later in this paper shows, however, that the aggregate-level correlation between victimization and fear may give a misleading impression of the way people react to crime and form opinions about the level of safety in their neighborhoods. The conclusion that victimization causes fear, which is suggested by the aggregate correlation between victimization and fear is, in fact, an "ecological fallacy." It is an example of an individual-level relationship that is incorrectly surmised from an aggregate-level finding.[7]

Measures of Defensive Action

One part of the statistical model analyzed in this paper for reactions to crime shows the extent to which defensive action reduces one's risk of victimization, and the fear and worry one has about the likelihood of victimization. A number of measures of defensive action were asked in the survey including the three shown in Table 3. Respondents were asked: "In order to avoid crime have you ever avoided using public transportation?" "Have you ever arranged to go out with someone so you wouldn't have to be alone when going somewhere in the neighborhood?" "Have you ever taken other security measures such as using timers on your lights, putting bars on your windows, or adding new locks?"

The neighborhood differences in our multiple indicators of defensive action are shown in Table 3. At the aggregate level, the degree of

Table 3
Neighborhood Differences in Defensive Action

Neighborhood	Avoid Public Transportation Mean	Walk in Groups in Neighborhood Mean	Install Home Security Devices Mean
Portage Park	.21	.31	.57
Lincoln Park	.38	.37	.55
Austin	.27	.41	.60
Back of the Yards	.29	.44	.48
Beverly	.32	.24	.56
Hyde Park-Kenwood	.40	.45	.58
South Shore	.36	.45	.66
East Side	.29	.25	.54
Total	.32	.37	.57

neighborhood defensive action is not as strongly related to victimization as is the level of neighborhood fear. The smaller aggregate correlation between defensive action and fear may show the effect of community organization or other attempts to fight crime. In some communities the level of victimization would apparently be higher were it not for the level of community crime preventive action.

INDIVIDUAL REACTIONS TO CRIME

A statistical model is used to analyze neighborhood differences in fear and worry about crime. This model measures the extent to which these differences are due to victimization. By calculating the individual-level relationship between victimization and fear, we find that fear of and worry about crime do not result directly from victimization, but rather from an evaluation of the seriousness of the crime problem in the neighborhood. Those who are not fearful of crime are those who have a sense that something positive and effective can be done about crime, and that it is worthwhile to stay in the neighborhood while community crime prevention programs are implemented.

Special attention is given, whenever possible, to the problems that might arise because of error and unreliability in the measurement of each of our important concepts. The survey measures of individual victimization are constructed using a scale of questions designed for this survey that took suggestions from all previous studies on the best way to ask questions about crime.[8] In our model fear of crime and defensive action are handled using a multiple-indicator approach that estimates and corrects for errors in measurement and unreliability that might otherwise impede the analysis.[9] Although there is literature on the reliability and validity of police-reported crime rates,[10] we have no means within the framework of our own analysis to assess the accuracy of the police indices. The two measures of police-reported crime used here, separate rates for personal and property crime, correlate at .95 within neighborhoods in our sample. Because of the high correlation, a multiple-indicator approach to the measurement of police-reported crime would not add much to our ability to interpret the data. Therefore in using the victimization data from the survey and from the police reports, the decision was made to specify a model relating crime to fear and estimate the model twice, once using tract and individual measures of property victimization and once using tract and individual measures of personal victimization.

Two-Way Relationships Involving Defensive Actions

We expect that defensive actions, if effective, will reduce the chances of victimization and reduce the level of fear and worry about victimization. Such a finding would suggest that self-protection programs can provide a key to halting some of the aspects of urban decay that would otherwise result from people's direct experiences with victimization.

But it is also possible that people take defensive actions because they are afraid of crime or because they have already been victimized. In other words, it is quite likely that there are two-way causal relationships between taking defensive action and fear of the neighborhood or experience with victimization. Defensive action may reduce fear, but one of the reasons people take such action might be that they are afraid. Defensive action may reduce the chance of being victimized, but one of the reasons people take such actions may be that they have already been victimized.

The bi-directional relationships involving defensive action, fear of crime, and victimization will be disentangled using a statistical technique known as "instrumental variables regression."[11] We know of no other survey study of crime and its impact where attempts have been made to deal directly with the problem of two-way causal relationships among key variables. One purpose of this chapter is to provide an example of the use of this methodology.

The Model

The model presented in this chapter is a four-equation system showing the relationships among the key variables in the analysis—police-reported crime rates, survey-reported victimization, fear and worry about crime, defensive actions, and a set of what are known as "dummy" variables showing the impact of neighborhood context on each of the variables controlling for the others. Two of the variables, fear and defensive action, are measured using multiple-indicator methodology. The slopes in the system of equations are estimated, with the appropriate steps taken to allow estimation of each part of the two-way relationships involving defensive action, fear, and victimization.[12]

At this point we will describe, in general terms, the substantive importance of each equation. The most important part of the model is the equation showing the effect of victimization (tract rates and individual experience), neighborhood context, and defensive action on fear of and worry about crime. Equation 1 can be represented as follows:

(1)   Fear = f [Tract Victimization, Individual Victimization,
Defensive Action, Neighborhood Context]

Intuition tells us that the slopes relating victimization and fear should be positive. Living in a tract with a relatively high rate of victimization or actually experiencing victimization ought to increase one's level of fear and worry about crime. This is the relationship strongly suggested by the ecological analysis conducted earlier in this paper. Similarly, for reasons discussed earlier, the slope showing the effect of defensive action on victimization should be negative, since effective defensive actions should make one less fearful, even if the reason for originally engaging in such actions was fear of crime.

The effect of neighborhood context on fear is shown by the slopes for the dummy variables measuring neighborhood differences in fear, controlling for victimization and defensive action. These slopes are "residual" differences, and show how fear and worry about crime are affected by neighborhood factors not explicitly related to crime, such as the level of neighborhood organization, the amenities of the neighborhood, the feeling that crime can be controlled so as not to adversely affect one's self-interest in the neighborhood, and the feeling that it is worthwhile to continue to live in the neighborhood. It seems, again on the basis of intuition, that the residual effects of neighborhood context on fear and worry about crime should be small, at least relative to the effect of the victimization variables.

The residual effects of neighborhood context on fear and worry about crime are important for evaluating studies of the effect of crime that do not take into account non-victimization aspects of neighborhood life. To the extent that these residual neighborhood differences, controlling for victimization, explain fear and worry about crime, aggregate-level models or any other kinds of models that rely only on victimization as the variable explaining patterns of economic and demographic change in the metropolis are misleading. They yield a faulty picture of the process of urban change and faulty predictions about the effects of anti-crime programs that address the causes of neighborhood fear related solely to victimization.

For reasons relating to what statisticians call "collinearity" and "identifiability," the effects of tract victimization rates and survey measures of victimization cannot be estimated simultaneously.[13] Different versions of equation 1 were estimated, using in some cases tract rates and in other cases survey reports, to determine the effect of victimization. The results are similar either way.

The remaining parts of the model are three equations analyzing defensive action, individual victimization, and tract victimization rates. The equation for the causes of defensive action can be represented as follows:

(2)   *Defensive Action = f[Individual Victimization, Fear]*

This specification assumes that neighborhood differences in defensive action, as shown in Table 3, are mediated by proximal, individual-level causes of defensive action, such as fear and recent prior victimization experience. The results show strong support for this assumption.

The equation for the causes of victimization can be presented as follows:

(3)   *Individual = f[Tract Victimization, Neighborhood*
         Victimization Context, Defensive Action]

The chances of victimization are assumed to vary greatly by context and by whether or not one takes defensive action. The tract level of victimization is a measure of the amount of crime in one's immediate geographic context. We also assume additional neighborhood effects on victimization over and above tract differences in environmental threat. The neighborhood differences are contextual differences of a broader geographic scope. Thus, one can live in a particularly safe tract that is in a particularly unsafe general area (i.e., neighborhood) of the city.

Finally, to complete the model, the average tract rate of victimization is assumed to vary by neighborhood (as shown in Table 1), but to be otherwise unaffected by the other variables in the model. The fourth equation is represented as follows:

(4)   *Tract Victimization = f[Neighborhood Context]*

The two-way causal relationships in the full model are represented by the fact that the effect of defensive action on fear is estimated in equation 1 and the impact of fear on defensive action in equation 2. The effect of defensive action on victimization is estimated in equation 3 and the impact of victimization on defensive action in equation 2.

INDIVIDUAL-LEVEL RELATIONSHIPS
BETWEEN VICTIMIZATION AND FEAR

Figure 1 shows the empirical estimates for most of the regression slopes for one solution of our four equation model of individual reactions to crime. Figure 1 is similar to a path diagram. Each variable in the analysis is shown cased in a square box. The arrows connecting the square

Figure 1

Causal Model Relating Individual Reactions of Fear and Defensive Behavior to Property Crime Victimization

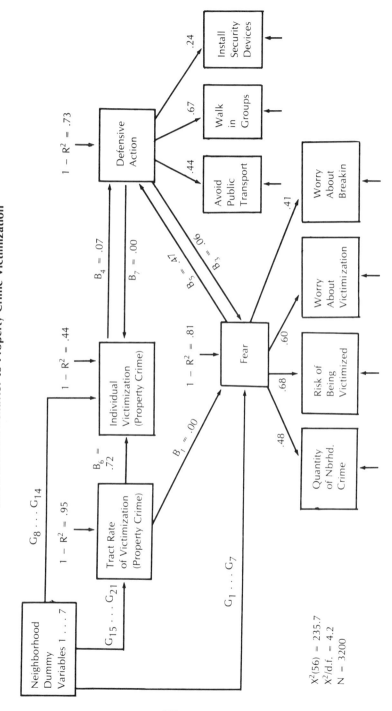

171

Table 4

Neighborhood Effects on Tract Victimization,
Individual Victimization and Fear,
(Estimates From Model 1 Shown in Figure 1)

Neighborhood Dummy Variable (Beverly Excluded)	Standardized Slope From Neighborhood To . . .		
	Tract Rate	Victimization	Fear
Portage Park	−.03	.05	.08
Lincoln Park	.13	.13	.21
Austin	.11	.13	.37
Back of the Yards	.05	.16	.28
Hyde Park-Kenwood	.15	.04	.25
South Shore	.11	.12	.29
East Side	−.06	.10	.07

boxes, labeled b1 to b7, show the causal linkages between the variables. The numbers just above the arrows show the standardized regression slopes that are our estimates for the parameters in equations 1-4. Seven dummy variables were used to estimate the neighborhood effects. To keep the diagram legible, the standardized effects of the dummy variables are not written in but rather symbolized with the notation G1 . . . G7 (neighborhood effects on fear), G8 . . . G14 (neighborhood effects on individual victimization, and G15 . . . G21 (neighborhood differences on average tract victimization rate). The numerical estimates for these slopes are shown in Table 4.

As noted earlier, a number of different solutions for the four equation model were tried. In one case tract rates and individual reports of property were used as the victimization variables, and in another case personal crime measures were used. Figure 1 and Table 4 show the results for the model using property crime estimates of victimization experience. Figure 2 shows the results using personal crime. As any comparison between Figure 1 and Figure 2 shows, the substantive results are similar regardless of which measure of victimization is used, so the discussion here will refer to the effects of "crime" without specifically referring to the findings in one or the other particular analysis.

The rounded boxes below "Fear" and "Defensive Action" show results for the multiple-indicator model used to correct for errors of measurement and unreliability in these variables. The paths between

Figure 2

**Causal Model Relating Individual Reactions of Fear
and Defensive Behavior to Personal Crime Victimization**

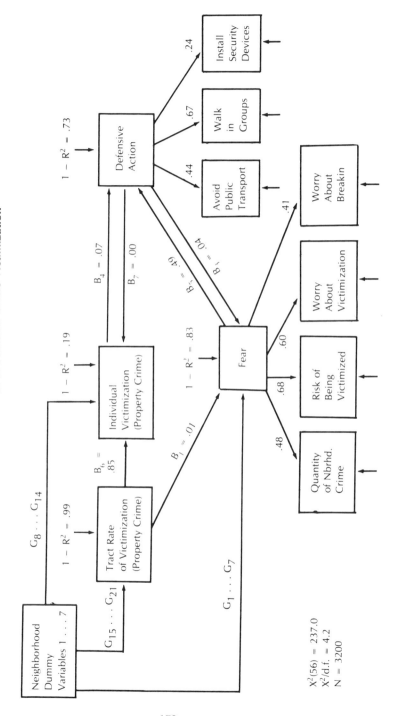

$X^2(56) = 237.0$
$X^2/d.f. = 4.2$
$N = 3200$

173

the rounded boxes and the square boxes show an acceptably high level of validity for each survey question as a measure of the general concept it is designed to represent.[14] Also shown in Figures 1 and 2 is a chi square statistic indicating an extremely good fit for our model, given the large sample size—about 3,200 cases.[15]

We noted earlier that, at the aggregate level, there is a strong relationship between victimization and fear. When the data are disaggregated and the relationship examined at the individual level, however, the correlation is not at all significant. The path relating tract-level victimization rates to fear of crime is estimated to be zero in Figure 1 and not significantly different from zero in Figure 2. Only the path from tract rate to fear is shown in these figures because of the statistical limitations noted earlier on our ability to estimate the effect of both victimization variables simultaneously on fear. When we draw the arrow from personal victimization to fear, however, the result does not change. At the individual level the relationship between victimization and fear is nil whether we examine personal or property crime and whether we use tract rates or personal experience as the measure of individual exposure to crime.

There is no evidence that individual levels of fear or worry about the neighborhood are increased because of experience with or awareness of victimization. On the other hand, there is a great deal of evidence that features of the neighborhood that are not explicitly tied to the direct experience of victimization have a very significant impact on how people react to the problem of crime in the city. Figure 1 shows that 19 percent of the variation in the measure of fear is explained in our system of equations and that almost all of this is due to the "residual" neighborhood effect. The pattern is nearly the same in Figure 2, where 17 percent of the variation in fear is explained. Paths G1 . . . G7 (shown in the third column of Table 4) are far from zero and, taken as a group, highly significant. In other words, fear of crime varies substantially by neighborhood but for reasons not directly measured by neighborhood differences in victimization.

The neighborhood qualities that stimulate a fearful evaluation of the crime problem have been suggested earlier in this paper and in our earlier research.[16] How secure one feels depends on whether one believes there are neighborhood resources available to fight the crime problem, whether these resources can be deployed effectively, and whether the amenities of the neighborhood make it worthwhile to remain in the area.

There are a number of intervening steps between the experience of victimization and the way individuals in a community react to crime.

Statistical models, at the individual level or at the aggregate level, that estimate only the relationship between victimization and dissatisfaction, disinvestment, and demographic flight, are misspecified. When individual reactions to crime are studied, community characteristics, and not the experience of victimization *per se*, are the most significant forces in shaping reactions to crime.

Defensive Action

According to the statistical analysis, the causes of defensive action are about as predicted. Twenty-seven percent of the variation in defensive action is explained by our model in Figures 1 and 2. The primary cause of such action is fear ($b5 = .47$ in Figure 1, $b5 = .49$ in Figure 2). Those who are more fearful are more likely to avoid public transportation, walk in groups, and install security devices than those who are not. There is also a small, but significant effect of victimization on defensive action ($b4 = .07$ in Figures 1 and 2). People are also somewhat more likely to take defensive action if they have been victimized.

The causes of defensive action are in the predicted direction. This does not apply to the effects of defensive action, however. At the individual level there is no tendency for defensive action to produce victimization ($b7 = .00$ in Figures 1 and 2). Figure 1 also shows that those who engage in defensive actions are also more likely to have increasing, rather than decreasing fear ($b3 = .06$ in Figure 1, $b3 = .04$ in Figure 2). People who take defensive action are apparently reminding themselves of the need for such action and are, on balance, slightly more fearful for having made this investment of time or money.

The failure to find that defensive actions reduce individual levels of fear and victimization relative to the others in a community does not mean that defensive actions are useless or counterproductive. Increasing the level of defensive action in a community can reduce the crime rate and lower the level of fear if the defensive actions are taken as part of an effort to mobilize all community resources against crime, and if people identify with this effort.

Figures 1 and 2 show, however, that defensive actions do not alter the difference between one's probability of victimization and that of the neighbors. Secondly, in any community, those who engage in defensive actions are slightly more fearful than their neighbors who do not engage in such actions. A community-wide program of defense against crime will benefit the community, but the system of causal relationships works in such a way that within the community those who take the defensive actions are more afraid than those who do not, and the two groups experience the same change in the probability of victimization.[17]

SUMMARY

Any theory linking crime, population redistribution, and urban decay rests ultimately on a causal link between victimization and devaluing one's neighborhood. The findings here and in our other works suggest that fear of crime is primarily a judgment that the government and the social structure will not be able to provide the collective good of safety, given the level of threat posed by the crime problem. Fear of crime results from the expectation that there are not enough neighborhood resources available to fight the crime problem, the belief that these resources cannot be deployed effectively, and the belief that "it is not possible to do something about crime in this community."

Our studies show that people's reactions of fear are more likely to be keyed to their perceptions of these qualities of neighborhoods than to the prevailing rates of victimization or even their own victimization. Perhaps the most important implication of this finding is that public policy programs designed to change the level of victimization in a community must also take into account how a neighborhood is perceived by its residents, and whether a strong enough sense of community exists to support crime control efforts.

Notes

1. Richard Taub, D. Garth Taylor, and Jan Dunham, *Paths of Neighborhood Change* (Chicago: University of Chicago Press, 1984).

2. Ibid.

3. The procedure for choosing the neighborhoods, the historical background of each neighborhood, the survey methodology, and the question wordings are analyzed in detail in Taub, Taylor, and Dunham, *Paths of Neighborhood Change*. In addition to this work, there are several other books that provide further information about the neighborhoods in this study. See Carole Goodwin, *The Oak Park Strategy* (Chicago: University of Chicago Press, 1979); Harvey Molotch, *Managed Integration* (Berkeley: University of California Press, 1972); W. Kornblum, *Blue Collar Community* (Chicago: University of Chicago Press, 1974); H. Zorbaugh, *The Gold Coast and the Slum* (Chicago: University of Chicago Press, 1929); Andrew Greeley, *Neighborhood* (New York: Seabury, 1977); Peter Rossi and Robert Dentler, *The Politics of Urban Renewal* (Glencoe, Ill.: Free Press, 1961); B. Berry, *The Open Housing Question* (Cambridge: Ballinger, 1979); B. Berry, C. Goodwin, and K. Smith, "Attitudes Toward Integration: The Role of Status in Community Response to Racial Change," in B. Schwarz (ed.), *The Changing Face of the Suburbs* (Chicago: University of Chicago Press, 1976).

4. National Research Council, *Surveying Crime* (Washington, D.C.: National Academy of Sciences, 1976).

5. Richard Sparks, Hazel Genn, and David Dodd, *Surveying Victims* (New York: Wiley, 1977).

6. See Wesley Skogan, *Sample Surveys of the Victims of Crime* (Cambridge: Ballinger, 1976); Sparks, Genn, and Dodd, *Surveying Victims*.

7. W.S. Robinson, "Ecological Correlations and the Behavior of Individuals," *American Sociological Review* 15 (1950):351-357. In later sections of this paper a model is presented that explains at the individual level the relationship between victimization and fear of crime. This model addresses the problem of the ecological fallacy and points the way to variables that should receive more attention in studies of the relationship between victimization, fear of crime, and neighborhood change.

8. See, for example, Skogan, *Sample Surveys*.

9. See K. Joreskog, "A General Linear Method for Estimating a Linear Structural Equation System," in A. Goldberger and O. Duncan (eds.), *Structural Equation Models in the Social Sciences* (New York: Academic Press, 1972); J. Sullivan and S. Feldman, *Multiple Indicators: An Introduction* (Beverly Hills: Sage, 1979); L. Carmines and R. Zeller, *Reliability and Validity Assessment* (Beverly Hills: Sage, 1979).

10. Sparks, Genn, and Dodd, *Surveying Victims*.

11. Joreskog, "A General Linear Method."

12. Ibid.

13. See E. Hanushek and J. Jackson, *Statistical Methods for Social Scientists* (New York: Academic Press, 1977), chs. 8 and 9.

14. See Carmines and Zeller, *Reliability and Validity Assessment*; P. Converse and G. Markus, "Plus Change . . . The New CPS Election Panel Study," *American Political Science Review* 73 (1979):32-49.

15. Joreskog, "A General Linear Method"; B. Wheaton, "Assessing Reliability and Validity in Panel Models," in D. Heise (ed.), *Sociological Methodology 1977* (San Francisco: Jossey-Bass, 1977).

16. Taub, Taylor, and Dunham, *Neighborhood Change*.

17. This highlights one of the collective benefits of crime prevention. If everyone participates, the aggregate rate of crime goes down. All during the time of the decrease in the crime rate, however, those whose life style or living circumstances predispose them to a higher probability of victimization, compared to their neighbor, are more likely to be victimized.

Part 4

Metropolitan Policing Expenditures

City–Suburban Variations in Police Expenditures*

Roy Bahl and Greg Lewis

The objective in this paper is to describe and explain city-suburban disparities in expenditures for police protection. The question is whether cities have higher police expenditures than suburbs because they face different conditions or because they respond differently to those conditions. A model for the determination of police compensation and employment levels is specified and tested on 1979 data for 66 SMSA's with central city populations in excess of 100,000. The results of this analysis show that city-suburban disparities in per capita expenditures for police services are both pronounced and variable by region. In part the disparities are due to the greater need for police services in cities—crime rate and population size exert important pressures on police spending in cities, but not in suburbs. In part, however, the disparities are due to institutional arrangements and policy choices—unionization and local government structure.

The study of city-suburb fiscal disparities is not new to those interested in local public finance. The courts have asked in deciding school finance cases whether the higher level of central city spending is necessary or discretionary. The federal government has asked whether higher levels of need justify increased aid to central cities. Bond rating agencies have asked whether central cities are inherently poorer credit risks than their surrounding suburbs. So far, there have been no clear

---

*The authors are indebted to Professors Janet Johnson and Jan Ondrich for a number of helpful comments regarding the preparation of this paper.

answers. Such ambiguities, together with the prospects of another new federalism, which shifts more fiscal responsibility to state and local governments, underline the need to gain a better understanding of intra-metropolitan fiscal disparities.

The objective in this paper is to describe and explain the city/suburban disparity in expenditures for one locally provided service, police protection. The question is whether cities have higher police expenditures than suburbs because they face different conditions or because they respond differently to those conditions. A model for the determination of police compensation and employment levels is specified and tested on 1979 data for 66 Standard Metropolitan Statistical Areas (SMSA) in the U.S. with central city populations in excess of 100,000.

The unit of analysis is overlapping governments within SMSAs. "Central city" refers to all city governments overlying the central city area (as defined by the census), i.e., multiple central cities like Los Angeles-Long Beach are treated as one city. "Suburb" refers to all governments except the "central city." Note that comparisons based on these definitions will understate disparities between cities and suburbs, because county and special district police employment and expenditures are attributed wholly to suburbs. This bias should be minimal because police protection is primarily the responsibility of municipalities.

VARIATIONS IN POLICE SERVICES

Both criminal activity and police expenditures vary substantially between cities and suburbs as well as among regions (Table 1). In all regions, crime rates, police employment, salaries, and expenditures are higher in central cities than in suburbs. Suburban crime rates average only 57 percent of their respective city rates. On average, suburban governments hire only 61 percent as many uniformed officers per 10,000 population, but each officer has to deal with only 89 percent as many reported crimes. The suburbs pay their officers from 10 to 20 percent less and have a much lower level of per capita expenditures (45 percent less) than do cities.

Regional variations are not so consistent. Northern cities have the lowest crime rates but hire the most police. The West differs in many respects. Western cities suffer the most crime, hire the fewest police, and pay them the highest salaries, but have relatively low per capita expenditures. Western cities hire only 63 percent as many police officers as do northern cities, despite a crime rate that is 16 percent higher. Among suburbs, those in the West have the highest crime rates, the highest police compensation, and the lowest police employment levels, but, unlike western cities, they also have the highest per capita expenditures. In general, the West also displays the least disparity between cities and suburbs. Suburban crime rates are over 70 percent as high as city crime rates in the West, but only 50 percent as high as the urban rates in the rest of the nation. Although the greatest pay differentials are in the West, western suburbs hire 72 percent as many police as their cities, while other suburbs hire only about 60 percent as many. They spend 66 percent as much as their central cities overall, while suburbs in other regions spend only 50 to 56 percent as much as their cities.

The result of these regional differences is that per capita expenditures in SMSAs are highest in the West, where salaries are the highest and employment levels the lowest, and in the North, where employment levels are the highest and salaries are low.*

THE DETERMINANTS OF POLICE EXPENDITURES

Most recent work on police expenditure determinants relies on a straightforward constrained maximization model from microeconomic theory. A set of community preferences for government and private goods is assumed, and the community is assumed to maximize its satisfaction given a set of prices for public and private goods and an income constraint. This process and another heroic assumption or two lead to the estimation of a demand function in which police output is a function of the price of a unit of police services, the price of all other goods, personal income, and various indicators of tastes, needs, or preferences.[1]

The major difficulty with this approach is how to finesse the problem of measuring a unit of police service or its price. Two schools of thought have emerged. One, the expenditure approach, uses per capita expenditures as the proxy for output and assumes a constant labor share in total output,[2] and the other assumes that police output is proportional to police employment and that a fixed amount of nonlabor input is required for each employment unit.[3]

The primary weakness of the expenditure approach is that price

---

*Although there is no statistically significant simple correlation between average police compensation and police employment, per capita police expenditure is highly and positively correlated with both: for the 66 SMSAs, the correlation is .71 with employment and .54 with compensation.

Table 1

Variations in Components of Police Expenditures and Activities: Means and Coefficients of Variation[a,b]

	Total	North	Central	South	West
Number of SMSAs	66	17	15	22	12
Per Capita Expenditures					
SMSA	$49.42 (27.6)	$51.36 (32.9)	$47.46 (25.8)	$47.84 (29.4)	$52.04 (18.4)
city	69.83 (44.9)	74.37 (36.0)	70.14 (36.8)	67.19 (65.4)	67.81 (19.7)
suburb	38.95 (32.5)	41.36 (35.9)	34.74 (24.2)	36.81 (36.3)	44.72 (24.4)
city/suburb	1.87 (38.5)	1.91 (32.8)	2.03 (28.7)	1.87 (49.6)	1.61 (34.7)
Police Employment per 10,000 population					
SMSA	19.2 (28.2)	23.0 (32.7)	18.5 (25.4)	18.6 (16.9)	15.9 (18.7)
city	25.6 (38.9)	31.2 (29.8)	25.4 (38.2)	24.8 (44.0)	19.6 (26.7)
suburb	15.8 (28.2)	18.8 (35.2)	14.7 (18.9)	15.1 (18.5)	14.2 (20.8)
city/suburb	1.66 (34.8)	1.76 (29.7)	1.71 (26.0)	1.68 (44.2)	1.43 (31.1)
Average Compensation[c] Per Police Officer					
SMSA	$17,738 (16.5)	$17,145 (8.4)	$17,563 (11.1)	$16,205 (16.9)	$21,608 (12.2)
city	19,204 (21.4)	18,128 (10.7)	18,763 (11.0)	17,490 (18.5)	24,423 (22.9)
suburb	16,375 (17.7)	16,337 (10.0)	16,429 (13.1)	14,648 (20.1)	19,524 (13.0)
city/suburb	1.18 (18.5)	1.11 (12.6)	1.15 (8.0)	1.21 (13.0)	1.27 (32.8)

Table 1 (Continued)

Variations in Components of Police Expenditures and Activities: Means and Coefficients of Variation[a,b]

	Total	North	Central	South	West
Crimes per 10,000 population					
SMSA	632.9 (21.2)	538.5 (22.8)	575.8 (14.1)	675.0 (18.5)	760.6 (10.7)
city	865.8 (23.9)	816.8 (29.9)	831.4 (25.6)	884.4 (22.8)	943.9 (14.4)
suburb	500.7 (30.3)	404.0 (21.9)	445.6 (19.8)	518.2 (32.9)	674.5 (12.2)
city/suburb	1.82 (27.2)	2.04 (23.8)	1.93 (28.8)	1.80 (24.9)	1.41 (17.0)
Crimes per Police Officer					
SMSA	35.0 (31.9)	24.6 (24.4)	32.7 (25.1)	37.0 (21.8)	49.0 (17.6)
city	37.5 (34.7)	27.9 (35.8)	35.4 (30.4)	39.3 (30.5)	50.2 (19.9)
suburb	33.5 (37.3)	22.8 (25.7)	31.6 (32.5)	34.4 (29.2)	49.1 (20.3)
city/suburb	1.20 (38.6)	1.28 (42.2)	1.18 (30.1)	1.25 (44.9)	1.04 (21.3)

[a]Coefficients of variation shown in parentheses.
[b]Unweighted means.
[c]Average October earnings multiplied by twelve.

Sources: U.S. Department of Commerce, Bureau of Census, *Local Government Finances in Selected Metropolitan Areas and Large Counties: 1978-79* (Washington, D.C.: U.S. Government Printing Office, 1980) pp. 104–145; *Local Government Employment in Selected Metropolitan Areas and Large Counties: 1979* (Washington, D.C.: U.S. Government Printing Office, 1980) pp. 80–116; U.S. Department of Justice, FBI Uniform Crime Reports, *Crime in the United States 1979* (Washington, D.C.: U.S. Government Printing Office, 1980) pp. 60–86.

and quantity variations are collapsed into one measure. This suggests the underlying assumption that either (a) both higher prices and higher service levels increase community satisfaction, or (b) all governments pay the same price for a unit of police services. By ignoring relative prices, these studies mask the process of resource allocation and make little headway in separating the factors that affect demand for public goods from those that affect supply.

The public employment approach treats per capita police employment as the output proxy and then estimates supply and demand equations for police employees. This approach is plausible if the quantity and quality of police protection are dependent on the number of police officers. On the other hand, such non-labor inputs as patrol cars, dispatching systems, and police computers also affect the quality of service. The employment approach assumes a fixed-factor production function. If there is a trade-off between police manpower and non-labor inputs, the employment approach cannot capture it. Nonetheless, the view here is that the decided advantage of being able to separate price and quantity effects makes employment the superior proxy.

MODEL SPECIFICATION

The approach taken here is to specify a behavioral model of police spending, to estimate its parameters, and to use these observed relationships to better understand central city-suburban variations in police expenditures. The model used is an adaptation of one developed by Bahl, Johnson and Wasylenko and benefits from other police expenditure determinants studies, which are summarized in Appendix Table A.[4] It requires estimation of compensation and employment equations to represent supply and demand effects, respectively. A third equation to allow for the simultaneous determination of crime rates and police employment, which has been used with success in various studies of city crime and police,[5] is rejected here because of the weak interaction between police employment and crime rates at the metropolitan area level. Variable sources, definitions, and mean values are listed in Appendix Table B.

The Compensation Equation

The average salary (SALARY) of uniformed police officers is specified as a function of the level of unionization of police employees (UNION), the opportunity wage in the private sector (MFGWAGE), per capita personal income (INCOME), central city dominance of the police labor market (PCTCITY), the number of officers employed (OFFICERS), and region (WEST, SOUTH, NORTH).

UNION. Many researchers have found that strong unions mean higher police salaries. Police unions have been reputed to have not only the economic power of private sector unions but to benefit from (a) political power over relevant politicians, (b) the sympathy of local citizens, and (c) an inelastic demand for police services. Though some research on union power in comparable public and private occupations finds no significant advantage for public sector unions, most studies have found that unions have small but statistically significant positive effects on police and firefighter salaries.[6] Union strength is measured here as the percentage of central city police officers who are union members.

MFGWAGE. Theory leads us to expect that public sector wage rates will rise with the opportunity wage. For a service-intensive, multiple goal public good such as police protection, measurement of output is so difficult that setting salaries equal to marginal productivity would present an impossible task. Instead, the expectations of both public employers and employees are that governments will pay the "going rate" for employees—based on some notion of comparability. In past determinants studies, that rate has generally been specified as a fixed proportion of average manufacturing wages in the SMSA. The same practice is followed here.

INCOME. Per capita income or some other measure of community prosperity has been introduced as an explanatory variable in most studies and found to have a positive and significant coefficient. Generally, it has been taken as a measure of ability to pay, but a case can also be made for using income as a proxy for the opportunity wage. As employment shifts increasingly from manufacturing to the service sector, police officers have far more job alternatives than factory work. Per capita income may offer a better proxy for what workers in general are earning in an SMSA than do manufacturing wages.

PCTCITY. Researchers have found evidence of monopsony power in the determination of teacher salaries,[7] but the one study of monopsony power in police hiring found that the greater the share of SMSA population residing in the central city, the higher the police salaries.[8] This study rejected the monopsony hypothesis, but the potential for the dominant employer to exert market power remains. Most SMSAs are dominated by one central city government, which hires the bulk of the police. The larger the city relative to the SMSA, the greater should be its market power and, accordingly, the lower should be average salaries.

OFFICERS. Monopsony power is effective only if demand is restricted. In any type of market, as the quantity of police officers demanded rises, the price should also rise. Schmenner, Victor, Wasylenko, and Bahl et al.[9] have demonstrated a positive effect of employment levels on salaries, but there is little agreement on whether the response is elastic or inelastic.

REGION. As discussed earlier, variations in salaries across regions are substantial, with compensation being particularly high in the West and particularly low in the South. To account for these variations, dummy variables were entered with the expectation of a positive coefficient for WEST and negative ones for SOUTH and NORTH.

The Employment Equation

The demand for police officers (OFFICERS) is specified as a function of the price of a uniformed officer (SALARY), the price of other goods and services (COST), the crime rate (CRIME), the size of the population to be served (POP), the degree of metropolitan fragmentation (PCGOVT), and the form of city government (MGR).

SALARY. A higher cost for a police officer should discourage the hiring of police. Ehrenberg performed two-stage least squares regression to adjust for the simultaneous determination of salaries and employment.[10] Both found inelastic demands for police employees. Ehrenberg estimated the own-price elasticity at -0.281, while Bahl et al., estimated -0.320.

COST. Where prices of other goods and services are higher, the hiring of police will appear cheaper in comparison, and accordingly, the quantity of police demanded should be greater. The intermediate budget for a family of four, computed by the U.S. Bureau of Labor Statistics, is used as a proxy for those prices.

CRIME. The effect of crime rates on police expenditures is not as strong as one might expect. Most researchers using two-stage least squares have found crime rates to have a statistically significant, though not necessarily large effect on police employment and expenditures. Hakim, for instance, argues that police expenditures are determined primarily by resource availability and only secondarily by crime rates.[11] On the other hand, Jones examined 12 one-year changes for 155 cities and found that year-to-year changes in expenditures and employment had virtually no relationship to year-to-year changes in crime rates.[12] Carr-Hill and Stern, using two-stage least squares and police employment, also found that knowledge of crime rates added nothing significant to their employment equation.[13] In fact, the crime coefficient was negative.

POP. While Hirsch's study of St. Louis found no significant correlation between population and per capita police expenditures once other factors were held constant,[14] most studies have found per capita expenditures rising with population. The conclusion that positive correlations measure diseconomies of scale is only one of several possible interpretations of the data, however. The reported results may also mean that,

(a) while population grows arithmetically, externalities grow geometrically;[15]

(b) economies of scale exist but are hidden by factors such as population density, which are associated with large populations; or

(c) larger cities provide higher quality services (and more services to non-residents) than do smaller cities.

Kasarda presents an interesting perspective with a path analysis that finds central city police expenditures more highly correlated with suburban than with central city population growth.[16] He argues that this could be expected because cities must provide "free" services to suburban commuters.

PCGOVT. Several researchers suggest that political fragmentation of the metropolitan area leads to lower police expenditures. Adams entered the number of jurisdictions per county as a variable "under the premise that balkanization of a county area leads to an undervaluation of social benefits by each political unit due to benefit spillovers, and thus to an underallocation of resources."[17] Others have found evidence to support a negative correlation between number of jurisdictions and per capita public expenditures, but do not all agree with Adams on the normative implications. Braswell in particular implies that the same quality of public services is provided at lower cost in fragmented metropolitan areas due to efficiency gains.[18] If we accept the findings of Mehay and Hakim,[19] among others, that increased police effectiveness in one jurisdiction drives crime to neighboring jurisdictions, the "balkanization" of metropolitan areas should more likely lead to over- rather than underallocation of police services.

MGR. The form of city government may also affect the delivery of services. The literature on city reform has argued that professional management leads to more efficient and lower cost service provision.

Lineberry and Fowler have also found that reformed cities tend to be less responsive to citizen demands than unreformed cities.[20] Either theory would suggest lower police expenditures in city manager cities, either from pure efficiency improvements or from failure to respond to public pressure for unproductive police deployment. A dummy variable is used in this model to indicate the presence of a council-manager form of government.*

The Model Restated

A set of equations is proposed to account for the simultaneous determination of police compensation and employment levels. The equations to be estimated are:

(1) $SALARY = f(UNION, MFGWAGE, INCOME, PCTCITY,$
$OFFICERS, NORTH, WEST, SOUTH)$

(2) $OFFICERS = f(SALARY, COST, CRIME, POP, PCGOVT,$
$MGR)$

In the compensation equation, all coefficients are expected to be positive except those for PCTCITY, NORTH, and SOUTH. In the employment equation, the coefficients should be positive for COST, CRIME, and POP and negative for the others.

This approach ignores private alternatives to public police protection, despite work by Clotfelter and Vehorn suggesting significant cross-price elasticities between public and private protection methods.[21] The difficulty of obtaining prices for such goods as padlocks, firearms, and private detective agencies is the weak justification for their omission.

STATISTICAL RESULTS

The employment and compensation models are estimated using two-stage least squares with OFFICERS and SALARY as endogenous variables. Separate equations have been estimated for central cities and suburbs. The prime objective here is to derive a reduced form equation for explaining city-suburb variations in per capita police expenditures. Results are presented in Table 2.

---

*In most cases of multiple central cities, all cities had the same form of government. In the six cases where forms differed, the dummy variable was coded to represent the form of the largest government.

Table 2
Regression Coefficients and T-Statistics for Compensation
and Employment Equations: SMSAs, Central Cities, and Suburbs[a]

Salary Equations

	SMSA	City	Suburb
UNION	27.4	32.7	20.7
	(2.82)	(2.01)	(2.07)
MFGWAGE	− 11.2	− 15.4	− 9.3
	(1.61)	(1.35)	(1.28)
INCOME	0.90	0.93	0.84
	(2.84)	(1.90)	(2.47)
PCTCITY	− 27.6	− 18.5	− 44.1
	(1.64)	(0.62)	(2.60)
OFFICERS	169	106	262
	(2.08)	(1.40)	(2.29)
NORTH	− 2390	− 2740	− 2220
	(2.75)	(1.96)	(2.42)
WEST	3220	4830	2050
	(3.55)	(3.18)	(2.30)
SOUTH	− 1370	− 1460	− 1780
	(1.73)	(1.11)	(2.19)
Constant	9000	11000	8200
R^2	.64	.50	.61
Standard Error	$1940	$3200	$2000

Employment Equations

	SMSA	City	Suburb
SALARY	− 0.0012	− 0.0012	− 0.0006
	(3.85)	(3.06)	(1.40)
COST	0.0015	0.0015	0.0014
	(4.89)	(2.69)	(3.48)
CRIME	0.0035	0.0081	0.0028
	(0.67)	(1.67)	(0.54)
POP	0.0020	0.0034	0.0008
	(5.45)	(4.55)	(1.18)
PCGOVT	− 0.157	—	− 0.197
	(2.67)	—	(3.63)
MGR	—	− 3.9	—
	—	(1.77)	—
Constant	5.96	6.89	2.81
R^2	.54	.44	.34
Standard Error	3.86	7.75	3.85

Compensation Equation

All coefficients in the salary equation, except the manufacturing wage, have the correct sign. The effects of unionization and per capita income are positive and significant. A strong union in the central city increases police salaries not only in the city but also in the surrounding suburbs. A point estimate of the effects of total unionization (100%) versus no unionization is a salary difference of $3,262 among central cities (16.9%) and $2,072 (12.2%) among suburbs. This is within the 6–16 percent range estimated by Ashenfelter[22] and the 2–18 percent range estimated by Ehrenberg[23] for firefighters' wages, and similar to the 17.5 percent estimated by Bahl et al.[24] for police salaries. Higher per capita income is associated with higher police salaries: a one-dollar higher per capita income is associated with an 85¢ to $1 higher level of police salaries.

There is some support for the monopsony hypothesis in the suburban equation. The average salary is about $44 lower for each 1 percent greater share of the metropolitan population living in the central city. No such effect is evident in the central city. The surprising implication is a monopsony effect from which the non-monopsonists benefit.

The troubling result in the salary equations is the negative coefficients on the manufacturing wage variable. This suggests that police salaries rise when the opportunity wage falls, and vice versa. This may be an artifact resulting from the depressed state of the manufacturing sector in the late 1970s, making manufacturing earnings a poor proxy for opportunity wage. In any case, our results contradict those in Ehrenberg[25] and Bahl et al.[26]

Even controlling for all of these effects, regional variations are important. Treating the Midwest region as the base, we find that western salaries are substantially higher, by $2,000 in the suburbs, and nearly $5,000 in the cities. Northern and southern salaries are lower than those in the Midwest—from $2,100 to $2,700 lower in the North and from $1,400 to $1,800 lower in the South.

Employment Equation

The coefficients of the SMSA employment equation all have the hypothesized sign and, except for the crime variable, are significant at the .01 level. The estimated own-price elasticity for police employment is −1.03, which is considerably more elastic than the −0.281 reported by Ehrenberg[27] and the −0.320 found by Bahl et al.[28] The number of officers hired rises with the cost-of-living, with a cross-price elasticity of

1.61. As the relative price of goods in general becomes higher, hiring more police looks like a bargain.

Police employment per 10,000 population rises with SMSA population, suggesting that large populations present adverse conditions for supplying police services. It may also imply diseconomies of scale, since employment is lower where there are more governments per 100,000 population. These results are consistent with the hypothesis that more fragmented SMSAs hire too few police because small governments ignore external effects of their police expenditures. Research on the exportation of crime, however, suggests that the primary externalities of increased police effectiveness experienced by neighboring jurisdictions are negative. Lower police employment levels in "fragmented" metropolitan areas imply either that these smaller governments are able to provide services more cheaply or that they are responding to less public demand for police services.

The employment equations do not fit so well for the separate city and suburban samples. City police employment is positively correlated with crime rates, the cost-of-living, and SMSA population. The results also suggest substantially lower employment levels (four fewer officers for every 10,000 population) in council-manager cities. This coefficient, significant at the .05 level for a one-tailed test, indicates either greater efficiency or less responsiveness to demands for greater police expenditures.

The suburban employment equation shows lower coefficients and significance levels for salary levels, crime rates, cost-of-living, and population size than does the city employment equation. Only the cost-of-living and fragmentation coefficients are clearly significant. If a metropolitan area had ten more local governments per 100,000 population, we would expect it to have approximately two fewer officers per 10,000 residents.

Pooled Results

To test whether suburban governments respond to the same socioeconomic factors differently from city governments, the data were pooled and a dummy interaction variable was introduced for each independent variable (cities were coded zero). Where these interaction dummy variables are statistically significant, suburban responses may be interpreted to be different from those of cities.* The results are presented in Table 3.

---

*The "interaction" variables are the product of the one-zero dummy variable and each independent variable.

Table 3
Pooled City and Suburban Regression Equations

Salary Equations

	Estimate For Cities	Differential For Suburbs
UNION	31.6 (2.48)	− 16.2 (.71)
MFGWAGE	− 16.2 (1.92)	8.5 (.82)
INCOME	1.21 (3.50)	− 0.81 (2.01)
PCTCITY	− 21.1 (.94)	− 26.0 (.91)
OFFICERS	68.4 (1.22)	305.1 (2.59)
NORTH	− 2600 (3.09)	
WEST	3670 (4.17)	
SOUTH	− 1770 (2.28)	
Constant	10100	
R²	.55	
Standard Error	$2693	

Employment Equations

	Estimate For Cities	Differential For Suburbs
SALARY	− 0.0014 (3.56)	0.0008 (1.34)
CRIME	0.080 (2.03)	− 0.057 (.73)
COST	0.0020 (4.96)	− 0.00079 (1.83)
POP	0.0033 (5.11)	− 0.0028 (3.42)
PCGOVT	− 0.093 (1.08)	− 0.095 (.77)
MGR	− 3.77 (2.01)	
Constant	1.65	
R²	.58	
Standard Error	6.18	

The suburban police salary response to central city unionization is not significantly different from the city response, though the coefficients reported in Table 3 are quite different. However, suburban salary levels are significantly less responsive to variations in metropolitan area per capita income. We are unable to reject a null hypothesis that city and suburban salaries react equally to differences in city population shares, again suggesting suburban benefits from an oligopsony market. Finally, the suburban salary response to variations in employment levels is substantially and significantly higher than the city's response. One additional officer in the city, holding all else constant, is associated with a salary increase of approximately $70. In the suburbs, the salary increase is $300 greater.

In the employment equation, variations in police salaries, crime rates, and the cost-of-living seem to have somewhat less impact in the suburbs than in the cities, but we are unable to reject the null hypothesis that cities and suburbs respond similarly to these variations. Population size has significantly less impact on suburban than on city employment levels. This is consistent with either the diseconomies of scale or the city-services-for-suburban-commuters argument.

The Expenditure Equation

These structural employment and compensation equations may be combined to get at the issue in question in this paper: the determinants of city-suburb disparities in police spending. The equation for per capita expenditures is calculated from the estimated employment and compensation equations. We begin with the identity,

$$(3) \qquad\qquad EXP = LC + NLC,$$

where,

$$EXP = police\ expenditures;$$
$$LC = labor\ costs;\ and$$
$$NLC = non\text{-}labor\ costs.$$

Now if we assume a fixed factor production function and assume a constant non-labor cost per employee, i.e.,

$$(4) \qquad\qquad \beta = \frac{NLC}{OFFICER}$$

then, dividing by population,

$$EXP = [SALARY][OFFICER] + [\beta]OFFICER = $$
$$[SALARY + \beta]\ OFFICER.$$

By substituting the estimated equations for OFFICER and SALARY (as reported in Table 2), a reduced form can be obtained that expresses the marginal expenditure impact of each exogenous variable in terms of its effects on compensation and employment.

Table 4

Elasticities of Per Capita Police Expenditures
with Respect to Selected Variables:
All Variables Taken at Mean Values

Variable	SMSA	City	Suburb
Unionization	− .035	− .016	.007
Per Capita Income	− .170	− .065	.042
City Share of SMSA Population	.019	.006	− .009
Crime Rate	.098	.297	.079
Population Size	.162	.215	.049
Number of governments per 100,000 Population	− .118		.188
Cost of Living	1.55	1.16	1.86
Number of Officers per 10,000 Population	1.12	1.12	1.17
Average Compensation	− .378	− .158	.096

One approach to studying central city-suburban disparities is to calculate and compare the per capita expenditure elasticities of each independent variable. The results, shown in Table 4, must be interpreted as showing *magnitudes* of response and not statistical significance. The clearest difference between cities and suburbs derives from the more elastic demand for police officers in cities. Thus, elasticities for average salaries and the variables that drive them up (unionization and per capita income) are negative for cities and positive in the suburbs. The effect of a larger city share of SMSA population is the opposite, as it drives down salaries. In each case, however, the response is quite inelastic.

The number of officers has a much stronger impact on per capita expenditures, with a 1 percent increase in employment associated with a 1.12 percent increase in city expenditures and a 1.17 percent increase in suburban expenditures. Elasticities of response to crime rates and population size are higher in cities than in suburbs, though still quite inelastic. City elasticities are 0.30 for crime and 0.22 for population, whereas suburban elasticities are only 0.08 and 0.05, respectively. Only variations in the cost of living elicit elastic response in expenditures. Increases in the cost of living drive up suburban expenditures more rapidly, with a suburban elasticity of 1.86 versus only 1.16 in the cities.

SUMMARY

City-suburban disparities in per capita expenditures for police services are pronounced and vary by region. The underlying causes of this variation, however, are more complex than has been indicated in most previous research. In part, the disparities are due to the greater needs faced in cities, but they are also due to institutional arrangements and policy choices.

Unionization of city employees not only increases city police salaries, but has a clear rollout effect on suburban salaries as well. The smaller the suburban share of SMSA population, the lower are suburban police salaries. Yet suburban salaries rise much more rapidly with increased police employment than city salaries.

The higher crime rates in central cities explain part of the higher level of police employment in cities, but do not have a significant effect in suburbs. Higher police salaries in cities dampen the level of police employment more than in suburbs, perhaps a result of greater budget constraints. Police spending is also affected by governmental structure. For instance, police employment levels are lower in council-manager cities and "fragmented" suburbs. This suggests greater efficiency in more professional and smaller governments.

The reduced form expenditure equations give some interesting insights into the magnitude of various effects on city and suburban police spending. Crime rate and population size exert important pressures on police spending in cities but not in suburbs. Unionization dampens city spending for police services, but has relatively little effect on suburban expenditures. This would seem to provide some support for the municipal overburden argument that has so interested the courts. Cities appear to spend more for police because they have to, rather than because they choose to.

Another interesting policy implication emerges from the suburban equations. Suburban expenditures tend to be lower where there is more governmental fragmentation. Perhaps this is due to more competition among suburban governments in keeping the tax price low, or perhaps it is because there is increased use of private substitutes. In either case, no support is found for the argument that governmental consolidation will lead to lower per capita expenditures.

These are important policy implications, and they require a more thorough statistical analysis than has been possible here. Despite the great amount of work that has been done in this area, further studies are required.

Notes

1. Robert Inman, "The Fiscal Performance of Local Governments: An Interpretive Review," in *Current Issues in Urban Economics*, ed. Peter Mieszkowski and Mahlon Straszheim (Baltimore: Johns Hopkins Press, 1979).

2. Thomas E. Borcherding and Robert T. Deacon, "The Demand for Services of Non-Federal Governments," *American Economic Review* 62 (1972):891–901.

3. Roy W. Bahl, Richard D. Gustely, and Michael S. Wasylenko, "The Determinants of Local Government Police Expenditures: A Public Employment Approach," *National Tax Journal* 31 (1978):67–79.

4. Roy Bahl, Marvin Johnson, and Michael S. Wasylenko, "State and Local Government Expenditure Determinants: The Traditional View and a New Approach," and "A Public Employment Model," in *Public Employment and State and Local Government Finance*, Roy Bahl, Jesse Burkhead, and Bernard Jump, Jr. (Cambridge, MA: Ballinger, 1980), pp. 65–154.

5. Bahl, Gustely, and Wasylenko, "Determinants of Local Police Expenditures."

6. Daniel S. Hammermesh, "The Effects of Government Ownership on Union Wages," in: *Labor in the Public and Non-Profit Sectors*, ed. Daniel S. Hammermesh (Princeton: Princeton University Press, 1975).

7. Marvin Johnson, "The Effect of Monopsony Power on Teachers' Salaries," *State and Local Government Review* 10 (1978):56–61.

8. Roger Schmenner, "The Determination of Municipal Employee Wages," *Review of Economics and Statistics* 55 (1973):83–90.

9. Ibid.; Bahl, Gustely, and Wasylenko, "Determinants of Local Police Expenditures"; Richard B. Victor, "The Effects of Unionism on the Wage and Employment Levels of Police and Firefighters," *Rand* Paper No. P-5924 (Santa Monica: Rand Corporation, 1977); Michael S. Wasylenko, "Some Evidence of the Elasticity of Supply of Policemen and Firefighters," *Urban Affairs Quarterly* 12 (1977):356–379.

10. Ronald G. Ehrenberg, "The Demand for State and Local Government Employees," *American Economic Review* 63 (1973):366–379.

11. Simon Hakim, "Interjurisdictional Spillover of Crime and Police Expenditures," *Land Economics* 55 (1979):200–212.

12. E. Terrence and E. Jones, "Evaluating Everyday Policies: Police Activity and Crime Incidence," *Urban Affairs Quarterly* 8 (1973):267–279.

13. R.A. Carr-Hill and N.H. Stern, "An Econometric Model of the Supply and Control of Recorded Offenses in England and Wales," *Journal of Public Economics* 2 (1973): 289–318.

14. Werner Z. Hirsch, "Expenditure Implications of Metropolitan Growth and Consolidation," *Review of Economics and Statistics* 41 (1959):232–241.

15. William Baumol, "Macroeconomics of Unbalanced Growth: The Anatomy of Urban Crisis," *American Economic Review* 57 (1967):415–425.

16. John D. Kasarda, "The Impact of Suburban Population Growth on Central City Service Functions," *American Journal of Sociology* 77 (1972):1111–1124.

17. Robert Adams, "On the Variation in the Consumption of Public Services," *Review of Economics and Statistics* 47 (1965):400–405.

18. Ronald C. Braswell, "An Empirical Test of the Effect of Political Fragmentation Upon Municipal Expenditures," *Akron Business and Economic Review* 8 (1977):25-30.

19. Hakim, "Spillover of Crime and Police Expenditures"; Simon Hakim, "The Attraction of Property Crimes to Suburban Localities: A Revised Economic Model," *Urban Studies* 17 (1980):265-276; S.L. Mehay, "Interjurisdictional Spillover of Urban Police Services," *Southern Economic Journal* 43 (1977):1352-1359.

20. Robert L. Lineberry and Edmund P. Fowler, "Reformism and Public Policies in American Cities," *American Political Science Review* 61 (1967):701-716.

21. Charles T. Clotfelter, "Public Services, Private Substitutes, and the Demand for Protection Against Crime," *American Economic Review* 67 (1977):867-877; Charles L. Vehorn, "Market Interaction Between Public and Private Goods: The Demand for Fire Protection," *National Tax Journal* 32 (1979):29-39.

22. Orley Ashenfelter, "The Effect of Unionization on Wages in the Public Sector: The Case of Firefighters," *Industrial and Labor Relations Review* 24 (1971):191-202.

23. Ronald G. Ehrenberg, "Municipal Government Structure, Unionization, and the Wages of Firefighters," *Industrial and Labor Relations Review* 27 (1973):36-48.

24. Bahl, Gustely, and Wasylenko, "Determinants of Local Police Expenditures."

25. Ehrenberg, "Government Structure, Unionization, and Wages of Firefighters."

26. Bahl, Gustely, and Wasylenko, "Determinants of Local Police Expenditures."

27. Ehrenberg, "Government Structure, Unionization and Wages of Firefighters."

28. Bahl, Gustely, and Wasylenko, "Determinants of Local Police Expenditures"; Bahl, Johnson, and Wasylenko, "A Public Employment Model."

Appendix Table A

Police Expenditure Determinants Studies

Authors	Dependent Variable	Unit of Analysis	Data Year	Statistical Method[1]	Effect of Independent Variables[2]										
					Wealth/Income	Unionization	Employment Level	Opportunity Wage	City Pop. Share	Salary	Population	Crime Rate	% Nonwhite	Fragmentation	City Manager
Ashenfelter[3]	wages of firefighters	cities 25,000 – 100,000 pop.	1961 – 1966	MR	–	P	–	–	–	–	–	–	–	–	–
Schmenner[4]	wages of police & firefighters	11 large cities	1962 – 1970	MR	P	P	P	P	–	–	–	–	–	–	–
Ehrenberg[5]	wages of firefighters	cities	1969	MR	P	M/P	P	P	–	–	–	–	–	–	M
Wasylenko[6]	wages of police & firefighters	175 cities over 50,000 pop.	1968	MR	–	I	P	P	–	–	–	–	–	–	–
Bartel & Lewin[7]	police wages	215 cities over 25,000 population	1973	MR	P	P	–	P	–	–	P	–	–	–	P

Appendix Table A (Continued)

Police Expenditure Determinants Studies

Authors	Dependent Variable	Unit of Analysis	Data Year	Statistical Method[1]	Effect of Independent Variables[2]										
					Wealth/Income	Unionization	Employment Level	Opportunity Wage	City Pop. Share	Salary	Population	Crime Rate	% Nonwhite	Fragmentation	City Manager
Victor[8]	police salaries &	cities over 50,000	1975	MR	P	P	N	P	—	—	—	—	—	—	—
	police employment				P	P	—	P	—	I	P	—	—	—	—
Bahl, Gustely, Wasylenko[9]	police salaries	79 cities	1972	MR	—	I	P	P	—	—	—	—	—	—	—
	police employment				P	—	P	P	—	N	P	P	P	—	—
Ehrenberg[10]	police employment	50 states	1958 – 1969	MR	P	—	—	—	—	N	P	P	P	—	—
Morris & Tweeten[11]	police employment	754 cities over 25,000 population	1967 – 1968	MR	—	—	—	—	—	—	—	P	—	—	—
Carr-Hill & Stern[12]	police employment	police districts in England & Wales	1961 & 1966	MR	N	—	—	—	—	—	—	I	—	—	—

Appendix Table A (*Continued*)

Police Expenditure Determinants Studies

Authors	Dependent Variable	Unit of Analysis	Data Year	Statistical Method[1]	Effect of Independent Variables[2]										
					Wealth/Income	Unionization	Employment Level	Opportunity Wage	City Pop. Share	Salary	Population	Crime Rate	% Nonwhite	Fragmentation	City Manager
Jones[13]	police employment & expenditures	155 cities	1958 – 1970	MR	—	—	—	—	—	—	—	—	—	—	—
Weicher[14]	police manpower allocation	38 Chicago police districts	1959	MR	N	—	—	—	—	—	N	—	—	—	—
Bahl[15]	police expenditures	198 cities	1960	MR	P	—	P	—	—	—	—	—	P	—	—
Sunley[16]	police expenditures	4 SMSAs	1962	MR	P	—	—	—	—	—	—	—	—	—	—
Kasarda[17]	police expenditures	168 SMSAs	1950, 1960 & 1970	PA	—	—	—	—	—	—	P	—	—	—	—
Greenwood & Wadycki[18]	police expenditures	199 SMSAs	1962	MR	P	—	—	—	—	—	—	N	—	—	—

Appendix Table A *(Continued)*

Police Expenditure Determinants Studies

Authors	*Dependent Variable*	*Unit of Analysis*	*Data Year*	*Statistical Method*[1]	Effect of Independent Variables[2]										
					Wealth/Income	*Unionization*	*Employment Level*	*Opportunity Wage*	*City Pop. Share*	*Salary*	*Population*	*Crime Rate*	*% Nonwhite*	*Fragmentation*	*City Manager*
Beaton[19]	police expenditures	562 New Jersey cities	1970	MR	P	—	—	—	—	—	P	P	—	—	—
McPheters & Stronge[20]	police expenditures	43 cities	1970	PC	P	—	—	—	—	—	—	P	—	—	—
Isserman[21]	police expenditures	21 New Jersey cities	1970	MR	P	—	—	—	—	—	—	—	—	N	—
Lyons & Morgan[22]	public safety expenditures	242 cities over 50,000	1950–1970	MR	P	—	—	—	—	—	P	—	P	—	I
Hakim[23]	police expenditures	94 New Jersey communities	1970	MR	P	—	—	—	—	—	—	P	P	—	—
Hutcheson & Prather[24]	city employment	all cities over 25,000 population	1970	MR	—	—	—	—	—	—	P	—	—	—	—
Gustely[25]	local expenditures	25 cities in Florida SMSAs	1952 & 1972	MR	—	—	—	—	—	—	—	—	—	N	—

203

Appendix Table A *(Continued)*

Police Expenditure Determinants Studies

Note: All studies of expenditures and employment standardize them for population, i.e., most are on a per capita basis.

[1]MR = multiple regression; PA = path analysis;

[2]P = principle components.

P = positive relationship; N = negative; M = mixed;

I = insignificant; — = variable not tested.

[3]Orley Ashenhelter, "The Effect of Unionization on Wages in the Public Sector: The Case of Firefighter," *Industrial and Labor Relations Review* 24 (1971).

[4]Roger Schmenner, "The Determination of Municipal Employee Wages," *Review of Economics and Statistics* 55 (1973).

[5]Ronald G. Ehrenberg, "Municipal Government Structure, Unionization and the Wages of Firefighters," *Industrial and Labor Relations Review* 27 (1973).

[6]Michael S. Wasylenko, "Some Evidence of the Elasticity of Supply of Policemen and Firefighters," *Urban Affairs Quarterly* 12 (1977).

[7]Ann Bartel and David Lewin, "Wages and Unionism in the Public Sector: The Case of Police," in Peter Mieszkowski and George E. Peterson (ed.), *Public Sector Labor Markets, COUPE Papers on Public Economics* 4 (Washington, D.C.: The Urban Institute Press, 1981).

[8]Richard B. Victor, "The Effects of Unionism on the Wage and Employment Levels of Police and Firefighters, Rand Paper No. P-5924 (Santa Monica: Rand Corporation, 1977.

[9]Roy Bahl, Richard D. Gustely, and Michael S. Wayslenko, "The Determinants of Local Government Police Expenditures: A Public Employment Approach," *National Tax Journal* 31 (1978).

[10]Ronald G. Ehrenberg, "The Demand for State and Local Government Employees, *American Economic Review* 63 (1973).

[11]Douglas Morris and Luther Tweeten, "The Cost of Controlling Crime: A Study in Economies of City Life," *The Annals of Regional Science* 5 (1971.

[12]R.A. Carr-Hill and N.H. Stern, "An Economic Model of the Supply and Control of Recorded Offenses in England and Wales," *Journal of Public Economics* 2 (1973).

[13]Terence E. Jones, "Evaluating Everyday Policies: Police Activity and Crime Incidence," *Urban Affairs Quarterly* 8 (1973).

[14]John C. Weicher, "The Allocation of Police Protection by Income Class," *Urban Studies* 8 (1971).

[15]Roy W. Bahl, *Metropolitan City Expenditures* (Lexington: University of Kentucky Press, 1969).

[16]Emil M. Sunley, Jr., "Some Determinants of Government Expenditures Within Metropolitan Areas," *American Journal of Economics and Statistics* 30 (1971).

[17]John D. Kasada, "The Impact of Suburban Population Growth on Central City Service Functions," *American Journal of Sociology* 77 (1972).

[18]Michael J. Greenwood and Walter J. Wadycki, "Crime Rates and Public Expenditures for Police Protection: Their Interaction," *Review of Social Economy* 31 (1973).

[19]W. Patrick Beaton, "The Determinants of Police Protection Expenditures," *National Tax Journal* 27 (1974).

[20]L.R. McPheters and W.B. Stronge, "Law Enforcement and Expenditures and Urban Crime," *National Tax Journal* 27 (1974).

[21]Andrew M. Isserman, "Interjurisdictional Spillovers, Political Fragmentation and the Level of Local Public Services: Reexamination," *Urban Studies* 13 (1976).

[22]William Lyons and David R. Morgan, "The Impact of Intergovernmental Revenues on City Expenditures: An Analysis Over Time," *Journal of Politics* 39 (1977).

[23]Simon Hakim, "The Attraction of Property Crimes to Suburban Localities: A Revised Economic Model," *Urban Studies* 17 (1980).

[24]John D. Hutcheson, Jr. and James E. Prather, "Economy of Scale or Bureaucratic Entropy? Implications for Metropolitan Government Reorganization," *Urban Affairs Quarterly* 15 (1979).

[25]Richard D. Gustely, "The Allocational and Distributional Impacts of Governmental Consolidation: The Dade County Experience," *Urban Affairs Quarterly* 12 (1977).

Appendix Table B

Variable Names, Definitions, Sources, and Mean Values

Variable Name	Definition	Mean Value
SALARY	Average monthly salary of full-time uniformed officers in October, 1979, multiplied by twelve (U.S. Bureau of Census, Local Government Employment in Selected Metropolitan Areas and Large Counties: 1979, pp. 80–116)	$17,738 (SMSA) 19,205 (CITY) 16,375 (SUBURB)
UNION	Percentage of central city police employees belonging to union in 1980 (unpublished U.S. Bureau of Census data).	68.2 percent
INCOME	Per capita income in SMSA in 1979 (U.S. Bureau of Economic Analysis, Survey of Current Business, April 1981, pp. 43–45).	$ 9,264
MFGWAGE	Average weekly earnings in the manufacturing sector in 1979 (U.S. Bureau of Labor Statistics, Employment and Earnings, May 1981, pp. 132–6).	$ 281.
PCTCITY	City Share of SMSA population in 1980, expressed as a percentage (U.S. Bureau of Census, Census of Population: Advance Reports, 1980, PHC80-V).	38.9 percent
NORTH	Northern region	.18
WEST	Western region	.26
SOUTH	Southern region	.33
OFFICERS	Uniformed officers per 10,000 population in 1980 (Local Government Employment in Selected Metropolitan Areas and Large Counties: 1979, pp. 80–116).	19.2 (SMSA) 25.6 (CITY) 15.8 (SUBURB)
CRIME	FBI crime index for 1979, expressed as crimes per 10,000 population (U.S. Department of Justice, Crime in the United States – 1979).	632.8 (SMSA) 865.8 (CITY) 500.7 (SUBURB)
COST	Intermediate budget for family of four in 1979 (U.S. Bureau of Labor Statistics, Handbook of Labor Statistics, 1979, p. 387[1])	$20,348
POP	SMSA population in 1980, expressed in thousands (Census of Population: Advance Reports, 1980).	1,656.9

Appendix Table B (Continued)

Variable Names, Definitions, Sources, and Mean Values

Variable Name	Definition	Mean Value
PCGOVT	Governments per 100,000 population in 1979 (*Local Government Employment in Selected Metropolitan Areas and Large Counties, 1978–1979*).	14.6
MGR	City has council-manager form of government (International City Managers Association, *The Municipal Yearbook: 1981*, pp. 10–45).	.33
EXP	Per capital expenditures on police services (U.S. Bureau of Census, *Local Government Finances in Selected Metropolitan Areas and Large Counties: 1978–79*, pp. 104–145)	$ 49.43 (SMSA) 69.83 (CITY) 38.95 (SUBURB)

[1] For those SMSAs for which the BLS does not compute an intermediate budget, COST was estimated from the following regression equation:

$$COST = \$10952 + \$0.9881\ INCOME - \$2325\ NORTH - \$1127\ SOUTH.$$
$$R^2 = .45$$

This equation was derived from data for the 26 SMSAs where the BLS does estimate COST.